westland ltd
THUNDERGOD

Before setting out on a writing career, Rajiv G Menon was an actor, occasional screenwriter, traveller and beach bum. A voracious reader since childhood, he was fascinated by stories and characters from Indian, Greek and Norse mythology. *Thundergod* was born as a result of that fascination.

THUNDERGOD

The Ascendance of Indra

Rajiv G Menon

Westland Ltd

westland ltd
Venkat Towers, 165, P.H. Road, Maduravoyal, Chennai 600 095
No. 38/10 (New No.5), Raghava Nagar, New Timber Yard Layout, Bangalore 560 026
Survey No. A-9, II Floor, Moula Ali Industrial Area, Moula Ali, Hyderabad 500 040
23/181, Anand Nagar, Nehru Road, Santacruz East, Mumbai 400 055
4322/3, Ansari Road, Daryaganj, New Delhi 110 002

First published in India by westland ltd 2012

ISBN: 978-93-81626-97-9

Typeset in 10.5/13 pts. Goudy Old Style by SÜRYA, New Delhi
Printed at Thomson Press (India) Ltd.

Cover Illustration by Aditya Chari chariaditya.blogspot.in

To my grandmother Sowdamini Menon,
for introducing me to the fascinating world of mythology

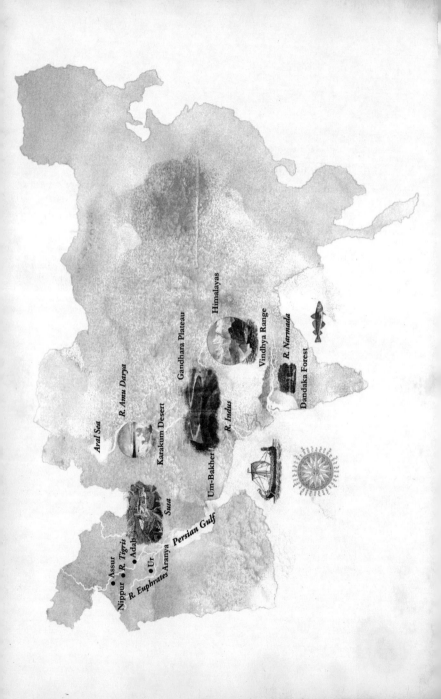

ACKNOWLEDGEMENTS

Nirmala Gopalakrishnan, my mother, for her unwavering trust and support in allowing me to pursue my passion.

My father, K.P. Gopalakrishnan, for inculcating in me my reading habit, a gift whose true value I have finally come to realise now.

Dimple, my wife and rock, without whose strength and support I would never be able to do what I do.

My son Vir, for asking the right questions; I hope someday he'll read this and agree that Indra is 'cooler' than Hercules.

Paul and Deepthi at Westland, for giving direction to my flight of fancy.

Sameer 'Daddy' Malhotra for, well . . . just being himself.

My friends and family—I cannot thank you'll enough for being there for me through the years. Lots of love and gratitude to you all.

1

It was a full moon night. Mount Meru stood out amidst the glistening summits of the mighty Himalayas, a colossal dark rock surrounded by snow-capped peaks. At the top of the mountain a man sat in deep meditation. The heat generated from his tapas had melted the snow off the peak. Around him a blizzard raged, the thick snowflakes struck his naked chest and melted away, sizzling. His face was calm, devoid of any emotion. He was completely oblivious to the fury of the elements around him.

In spite of the rigours of his intense meditation, his body was in extremely good physical condition. The thick muscles and the scars on his chest and arms revealed a martial past. His long, white hair and beard thrashed about in the stiff breeze. Suddenly something seemed to have disturbed him and a furrow appeared on his brow.

Deep in his subconscious mind, a vision had come to him.

It was a bright summer's day on a cliff face of red sandstone. On a tiny ledge a few metres from the top, a young peregrine took its first steps out of its nest. It balanced carefully at the edge of the precipice for a few seconds as it felt the breeze ruffle the feathers of its crest. Then with a screech of excitement, it launched itself into the void.

From the ledge, the father watched the little bird as it vigorously flapped its wings trying to slow its downward descent, then the panic settled and instinct took over. Its tiny wings soon found a rhythm and the little falcon began to fly. Before long it found a thermal column and began to soar upwards along with the rising air. The father watched proudly from his perch on the cliff face. He had lost his mate to a hunter's arrow a few days ago, and this had made him wary. Suddenly a glint of something shiny on the ground caught his attention. With a screech he swooped down into the trees.

On the ground below, a group of hunters drew their bowstrings, all attention on the young falcon. In a land where game was scarce, another hunter meant more competition for the limited resources. From the corner of his eyes, one of the hunters saw a shadow flit across the sky. He looked up and saw the adult bird drop like a giant arrow towards them. He shouted a warning to the others.

The falcon felt the trees come up rapidly around him as he brought his talons to bear. The hunters turned their attention towards the bigger bird and a volley of arrows crashed into it.

The falcon's body, wings still spread, crashed into the hunters and knocked a couple of them off their feet. Its talons caught one of them in the face and gouged one of his eyeballs out. The hunter screamed in agony, rattling the nerves of his comrades. The leader recovered quickly and shouted at the others to prepare for another chance at the young falcon. Suddenly, a giant eagle appeared. It placed itself directly in the path of their arrows as it swooped down on them. The hunters hesitated for one brief second, in shock. An older falcon protecting its young was natural, but in this harsh environment where prey was scant, they had never seen one species of predator rush to protect another. That split second was all that the eagle needed; it broke off its attack and disappeared above the canopy.

The young falcon now soared high, far removed from any threat from below. Even as it flew, it started to grow bigger and bigger. Its dark brown plumage started to change into bright gold. From below, the old male eagle watched in amazement as the young falcon grew and grew till it slowly began to eclipse the sun.

On the mountain, the man's head rocked back, his eyes opened wide, amazed at the clarity of the vision. Slowly, the man called Mitra gathered his belongings while he pondered over its meaning and made his way down the steep mountain slope.

Lit by the full moon and a million stars, the magnificent city-state of Susa shone like a jewel among the barren plains of Central Asia. Within its giant walls of sandstone lived twenty thousand souls, the greatest congregation of humanity in the world. The city was a marvel of its age, with its own water supply, sewage system, tree-lined avenues paved with cobblestones and beautiful gardens. These were interspersed with rows of stone houses in which the citizens lay fast asleep, completely oblivious to the omen that had shown up in the night sky above them.

In the middle of the city stood a gigantic structure that outstripped even the beautiful royal palace of Susa in its splendour. It was a magnificent ziggurat that reached out high into the heavens, a temple erected to honour Ishtar, the living goddess of Susa.

That night, Ishtar, daughter of the moon, stood atop her temple and stared out into the distance towards the northeast. One particular star caught her attention; it shone a little brighter than all the rest. Even as she watched, a tiny black hole appeared in its centre. Her beautiful face now wore a troubled expression as she saw the hole rapidly increase in size, till it engulfed the star and swallowed it whole. Ishtar opened her arms wide; her pale green eyes had a wild, vacant expression as she began to chant fervently. A glow started to appear in the middle of her chest, just below her beautiful breasts. Slowly it spread through her exquisitely-shaped naked body till it shone with an incandescence that could be seen for miles across the barren plains. It cast a warm protective glow over her adopted city.

A thousand miles away, in the direction of her gaze lay the Karakum Desert, one of the most desolate places on earth. A man and woman lay beside each other on a sand dune and stared up into the million stars that lit up the desert sky. The man brushed his long, blond hair off his face as he gazed up at the heavens. His features were sharp, almost perfect, as if chiselled from sandstone by a brilliant sculptor. Yet, closer examination revealed something in the deep recesses of those bright blue eyes, a certain wildness that made his countenance more fearful than attractive. His heavily-muscled torso, covered with numerous scars inflicted by shaft and blade, gleamed with a light sheen of perspiration.

Raja Daeyus, chief of the Deva clan, turned to the woman who lay next to him. Her beautiful face was tilted up to the starlit sky; her hair cascaded around her shoulders in a thick, dark cloud. She looked straight ahead, hugged her knees to her chest and rocked gently on her back. Her bronzed body, bathed in starlight, shone against the white desert sand.

Daeyus lay back on the sand and shut his eyes. He was glad to be alive. The last six months had been taxing to say the least. Yet they had more than accomplished their seemingly impossible mission and managed to put down most of the Scythian rebellion. Only one tribe, the Saka, still offered any semblance of resistance. Till about five days ago, the Deva campaign against them had been fairly successful. They had drawn the Saka away to the northwest and cut them off from their regular supply lines. Just when it had seemed that victory was finally theirs for the taking, their luck ran out. Daeyus and his men were caught in a violent desert storm.

For three days and nights the Devas waited. Crouched behind their horses, they prayed for nature's fury to abate. The sand was everywhere, in their eyes, their noses and their lungs. When they had just about reached the end of their tether, on the third night, just as suddenly as it had appeared, the sandstorm was gone. The desert was still again.

At dawn, Daeyus, along with his two commanders Vasu and Krupa, surveyed the situation. It was critical to say the least; their water reserves were long gone. In addition to this, the sand dunes had shifted, completely changing the topography of the land. They had no idea where they were or in which direction they should go to find water. Only of one thing they were certain: somewhere in the vast dunes, the Saka, the last and most feared of the Scythian tribes, lay in wait for them.

The Deva chief turned to the east, shut his eyes, and said a quick prayer to Surya, the Sun God. Just as he opened his eyes, he saw her, astride a huge black stallion, silhouetted against the rising sun. Her long, black hair and robes flowed in the morning breeze as she reined in her steed and indicated for them to follow her.

A captivated Daeyus threw caution to the winds and rode off behind the woman. For two days and nights the Devas rode behind their raja and the mystery woman. Although consumed by doubt, they did not once question his judgment or decision. They simply called upon their last reserves of strength and braved the scorching sun and sands. At long last, on the third morning, sunrise revealed the tall palms of the Oasis of Illum. Daeyus looked around for the woman, but she was gone.

The raja chose his campsite well within the tree line, so there would be no indication to anyone who arrived from the desert that the oasis was inhabited. The exhausted men watered and fed the horses and spent the hottest part of the day asleep in the shade of the trees.

It was almost dark when Daeyus awoke with a start. He wondered what it was that had so suddenly woken him. In the air, there lingered a strange, alluring perfume. The place was deathly quiet except for the occasional snoring of one of his men. He walked round the perimeter of the camp and inspected the defences. The sentries he had posted were all fast asleep.

Daeyus drew his sword and looked around, all his senses on alert. His men never slept on duty. He suspected this to be some kind of Scythian sorcery. He slowly made his way towards the edge of the tree line. As he stepped into the desert, he saw her. She stared at him, her dark eyes filled with longing. The wind swept her robe aside and Daeyus caught a glimpse of her bronzed, voluptuous body. It took his breath away; he dropped his sword and started to run.

Gaia watched as this beautiful man came towards her, then she rushed forward to meet his embrace and together they fell on the dune. Their hands worked feverishly as they tore at each other's clothing. No words were exchanged between them as their lips found each other; none were necessary. Their coupling was swift, savage and intense. Gaia moved her hips and matched him thrust for thrust as she drove him wild with desire.

Daeyus had been totally unprepared for the pleasure he now experienced. His previous amorous escapades had been with either scared, eager to please slave girls, or with the grieving widows of his vanquished enemies. This was incredible; not only did this woman treat him as an equal she now challenged him to match her in intensity. The weariness of the last few days was gone as the raja thrust with the ferocity of a bull. Then, suddenly, she threw her head back, ground her hips into his pelvis and screamed at the top of her lungs.

Wave after wave of pleasure crashed into her body and threatened to completely overwhelm her. She heard a growl escape his throat as she felt the heat of his seed deep within her. She smiled as his body stiffened and he collapsed in a heap on top of her. She cupped his hard buttocks in her hands and pulled him closer. She held on for a few moments and then her grip relaxed.

Gaia opened her eyes; the intense joy she had felt was gone now, replaced by a hint of anxiety. Slowly she came to terms with what had just happened. She gently pushed him off her and did not look in his direction or say a word. There would be consequences for her actions; of this she was certain. Gaia was an Elemental who drew her powers from the earth. It was forbidden for her kind to consort with humans or any other earthly beings. She wondered why, when she could have had her pick of the gods, it was this beautiful savage that had drawn her attention. But it had been worth it; every glorious moment had been a memory she could treasure. He had made love to her with the passion of one who did not know if he would live to see another day. Something she could never expect from a god.

She had watched him for months as he battled the insurmountable odds that a resilient enemy and the uncompromising desert had thrown at him. Through it all there had been an unwavering, god-like strength to his spirit that had reached out across the ether and drawn her to him.

Now Gaia, Earth Goddess, knew there was nothing she could do but await the judgment of the Elders. She smiled as she felt a pleasant sensation in her womb; it was the warmth of his seed. She turned to her lover as he slept, gently placed her head on his chest, and closed her eyes as she listened to the beating of his heart.

On the ziggurat at Susa, Ishtar dropped her arms and shut her eyes. Her light dimmed as her body took on its normal form. She looked down at the sprawling city that lay beneath her, lost in thought about the events she had just witnessed.

In keeping with the laws of the Cosmos, every great act of destruction preceded an equally powerful act of creation. This night she had witnessed both, and she was troubled. The death of the star could only mean one thing; the forbidden sexual act that she had witnessed just after would produce a life force so powerful that, if left unchecked, it could destroy the prevalent order in the world and create a new one. And, as an integral part of the current order, she would have to do everything in her power to ensure that such an event did not come to pass. She had recognised both participants of the unholy union she had just witnessed. While she knew she had no power over the woman, the man's fate was very much under her control.

Braega, high priest of Susa, stood behind the goddess. He kept his gaze down, trying not to stare at her lovely body. Her unblemished skin was the colour of pale ivory. He tried to keep his trembling hands steady as he stepped forward and draped a blue robe over those exquisitely-shaped shoulders.

Ishtar turned to him, her beauty now had a cold edge to it and a dark shadow lurked behind her pale green eyes. Braega hurriedly averted his gaze. His discomfort did not go unnoticed by the goddess; she took her time to draw the robe across her bare breasts. She liked the effect her naked body had on men; it completely disarmed them and robbed them of their wits.

'What news do you have of this Deva, the one who is called Daeyus?'

Braega had no love for the Devas and their savage ways. He replied with all the dignity he could muster.

'The king has sent the barbarian to quell the Scythian rebellion in the Karakum Desert.'

Ishtar allowed herself a smile.

'A clever ploy, I must admit. Shalla conserves the strength of his own army by hiring these barbarians to do his dirty work. Do you think this man will be successful in his mission?'

Braega's reply was scornful. He could not fathom the interest his goddess had in Daeyus and his boorish band of thugs.

'It is unlikely that they will return from this task. The Scythians and their horses are born and raised in that hellish desert; they will slowly but surely wipe out these barbarians.'

Ishtar probed further.

'Shalla knew this and yet he sent them out to die.'

The high priest chuckled. 'It was a political masterstroke on the part of the king. In one move, he has taken care of his enemies and removed a potential threat. These barbarians will weaken the Scythian tribes considerably before they perish. There will be no Scythian raid on our lands for some time to come.'

Ishtar was thoughtful; the overconfidence of the Elamites would be their undoing. But she could not allow that to happen as long as it was within her power.

'How can you be so sure of the outcome? The bravery and military prowess of the Devas are already legendary. It has come to my attention that they have many admirers even within these walls.'

Braega allowed himself another little chuckle.

'Divine excellency! The sands of the Karakum are littered with the bones of countless such brave men. Let me assure you, even if the Devas do return, they will be in no position to challenge the might of Elam.'

Ishtar knew the high priest echoed the sentiments of his sovereign, Shalla, king of Susa. She now trod carefully; she did not want to reveal the true reason behind her interest just yet.

'Perhaps you are right. But humour me this once, my dear Braega. I want you to bring me a regular report on all further activities of this Daeyus. I also need you to send a messenger to Sumer and find a man for me. He is known in those parts as, "The Marksman".'

Braega bowed low as he conveyed both his understanding and will to obey her orders. Shalla had a supremely efficient espionage system to monitor the activities in the lands outside the walls of Susa. As high priest, Braega had access to this intelligence. It would not be difficult for him to keep an eye on the Deva chief.

The goddess' second request, however, piqued his curiosity; he hadn't the faintest idea who this man was that she wanted him to find.

'How will we find this man you seek in the vast expanse of Sumer?'

'Instruct your messenger to ask around in the right places. The Marksman will find him.'

She dismissed him with a wave of her hand. Braega bowed low and left.

Daeyus woke up and looked around. There was absolutely no trace of the mystery woman. He was wondering if the whole thing had been a dream, when he heard his squire Mara call out to him. The morning air was chill; Daeyus got to his feet and wrapped his cloak around him.

'The scouts have returned, my lord,' the boy told him.

Daeyus reached the camp and asked Vasu and Krupa to get the men ready. The scouts informed him that the Saka were three hundred strong and about four hours south of their position. They marched in the direction of the oasis. Daeyus questioned them about the physical condition of the enemy. He was informed that they looked like they had been without water for days. Daeyus smiled; some good news at last.

Although the enemy outnumbered them five to one, the desert would even the odds. He remembered how he had started this campaign with five hundred men, the finest warriors from his clan; now there were just sixty of them left. But these sixty men had been tempered in the furnace of the Karakum. They feared nothing. They would gladly march to the gates of hell and back with their raja. He watched them, proudly lined up in their bronze armour. They banged their lances against their shields as he approached. The round bronze shields had emblazoned on them a golden sun, the symbol of the Deva strength and power. Daeyus took his place at the head of the troops, flanked on either side by his two commanders.

It was noon when the Devas reached within striking distance of the Saka camp. The Scythians were all sprawled in the shadows thrown by their resting horses. Numa, the Saka chief, had decided to rest his men and horses during the hottest part of the day. He knew he couldn't ask any more of them. For ten days they had marched without food or water through conditions akin to hell, a phenomenal effort even by the Scythians' own high standards. The enemy had been forgotten, now only survival was on the Sakas' minds. Numa still hung on in the hope that the Oasis of Illum was a half-day's march away. The stars in the night sky had told him that, and he prayed he had read them right.

Daeyus saw clearly that the Saka did not expect an attack. They had made camp below a giant sand dune, which was a great spot to beat the heat but a terrible one to defend, especially if you were pitted against the greatest light cavalry in the world. The raja divided his forces into three; Vasu and Krupa took twenty-five men each to hit the Saka from either flank, and Daeyus held ten men with him in reserve and waited.

The enemy was completely unprepared when the first volley of arrows hit them from both the flanks. However, after the initial chaos, the Saka were quick to respond. They gathered their weapons, leapt on to their horses and started to give chase. Daeyus smiled as he watched the enemy play right into his hands.

Numa looked on helplessly as the Devas, on their rested horses, poured volley after volley of arrows into his men before they calmly rode out of range. Their accuracy astounded him. He mounted his horse and started to rally his men. Daeyus realised that he must act quickly or they would lose the crucial momentum that their surprise attack had brought. He led the ten men in an arrowhead formation with himself at point and charged right into the centre of the enemy camp. Before the Saka realised what was happening, the raja and his men were upon them.

Daeyus ran one man right through with his lance and knocked a second off his horse with a mighty blow from his shield; his horse did not even break stride as it ran swiftly towards the Saka chief. They were almost upon him when Daeyus felt the front legs of his steed buckle—a spear had been thrust into its chest. Daeyus toppled forward over the front of his horse. The soft sand broke his fall, but he lost his spear and shield. He drew his sword as the enemy swarmed around him.

Vasu, quick to spot the peril his raja was in, rallied his men and charged towards him. Daeyus hacked and slashed at the enemy as they surrounded him. One of his men tossed him his battle-axe. Daeyus caught the heavy weapon in mid-air and in one motion swung it at his nearest assailant, decapitating the man. The blood from the severed neck drenched Daeyus and enhanced his already frightening appearance.

Numa, the Saka chief, frantically barked orders to his troops. Daeyus noticed that the enemy was beginning to hurriedly regroup around him. The Devas were about to lose the advantage of their surprise assault. He shouted out a challenge to the Saka chief, whose response was immediate—he hurled his spear at him. Daeyus ducked and the javelin sailed over his shoulder. As he rose, two men barred his way. Daeyus caught one of them in the throat with his sword as he swung the axe at the other in an underhand stroke. The massive blade caught the Saka under the armpit of his sword arm and sliced it clean off.

By now Vasu and Krupa had reached him. They positioned themselves behind him, shoulder to shoulder, as they protected his exposed flanks. Daeyus grimaced; suddenly there was no room for him to swing his axe. Just then, another Saka spear was thrust at his face. Daeyus dropped his axe, grabbed the shaft of the spear and dragged the man off his horse right on to his waiting sword.

Numa watched this awe-inspiring display of strength and noticed the demoralising effect it was having on his men. He leapt off his horse, sword raised high in the air. Daeyus saw the movement from the corner of his eye and was ready. He turned towards the Saka chief and raised the spear. The weapon caught Numa in mid-flight right in the solar plexus.

Daeyus lifted the spear high in the air. Every muscle and sinew in his arm strained from the effort and a primal scream rose from deep within his throat. The battle stopped momentarily, all eyes on the mighty raja, his face and body splattered with blood as he continued to hold Numa on the point of his spear in an incredible display of raw power. Then he thrust the blunt end of the shaft into the sand.

The Saka watched in horror as the body of their chief jerked at the end of the weapon. Slowly, Numa's torso slid down the length of the spear, his agonised screams renting the air. All the fight seemed to leave the Saka. They jumped off their mounts, prostrated before Daeyus, and begged for mercy.

The prisoners and their captured mounts were taken back to the oasis where the young and strong were separated to be taken to the slave markets of Ecbatana. The older men, along with the wounded, were given a few horses and their freedom to return home. Daeyus saw the fear in their eyes as they thanked him for his mercy and left. They would spread the message far and wide across the Karakum. It would be a long time before the Scythians challenged the authority of Elam again.

It was well over six months and the beginning of winter by the time Raja Daeyus reached the Devas' camp at the south-western end of the desert. He and his soldiers were given a hero's welcome and a great feast was organised to celebrate the victory. The festivities went on for a week.

The first two days were devoted to the sacrifice; eleven bulls were slaughtered to honour the Sun God Surya and their ancestors for granting them victory. Then the high priest called out the name of each man who had fallen in battle. A goat was sacrificed for every dead warrior to help him on his journey to heaven where he would dine with the gods. After the sacrifice, the great feast began. The meat was barbecued in a huge, fiery pit and served with watery wine and unleavened bread.

After everyone had eaten and drunk to their heart's content, the bards came in. To die in battle was the ultimate honour for a Deva. The bards chose the most heroic stories from the battles and immortalised them in song. Then the wine got stronger and the music more frenzied as the dancing girls took over. Now the celebrations descended into endless hours of debauchery and sexual excess. Just as it was in battle, the raja took the lead in all the revelry and carried on till the very end.

It was another two days before Daeyus recovered and started to attend to his administrative duties. The gold from the sale of the horses and slaves was first used to compensate the families of the soldiers who had lost their lives in the Scythian campaign. Then the survivors of the campaign were rewarded for their bravery and their individual acts of heroism were recognised.

Over the next few months, through the winter, Daeyus paid particular attention to the training and rebuilding of his vastly depleted army. Fortunately, the Deva way of life provided him with a highly-trained and motivated group of young reserves to choose from.

Deva boys were weaned away from the comforts of parental love at the tender age of eight, divided into groups called dals, and put under the tutelage of an accomplished veteran, usually someone just retired from active service. The boys lived together in a boot camp. Their early military training included being tied to the backs of running calves and shooting arrows at stationary targets. They were also taught wrestling and fencing with wooden swords. All manner of sport was encouraged through their early development, with particular attention to archery, riding and combat.

When they were eighteen, they would compete amongst themselves, and the most promising young men would be taken into the reserves from where they would vie for a place in the raja's sena of five hundred. The rest would be put in charge of the security of their vast herds, till they distinguished themselves in the next trials.

Daeyus personally supervised these Spardhas, or trials of strength. The disciplines were archery, riding and combat. The competition was fierce; contestants fought tooth and nail and gave it everything to finish on top. The winners were given the biggest honour a young Deva warrior could hope for, a chance to ride into battle with the raja.

Daeyus also took a great deal of interest in the building and upgrade of his arsenal. He spent a lot of time with his weapon smiths, testing new weapons and giving suggestions to improve existing ones.

By early spring, he was able to devote time to his other great passion: horses. He had spent a few years on a breeding programme where he had introduced bloodlines from the Arabian Desert into his own collection of fine horseflesh. Now the pride and joy of that effort stood before him.

The young black stallion snorted and stamped the earth in annoyance as Daeyus approached him. He was as dangerous as he was beautiful. He had nearly killed the groom who had last tried to put a saddle on him. The man lay unconscious in his tent with a cracked skull.

As Daeyus approached the corral, he called out to him. The stallion recognised the voice; he had heard it from when he was a young colt and learnt to respect its authority. Daeyus walked towards the creature, saddle in hand. The horse whinnied nervously and tried to run. It took the combined strength of four men to hold the ropes and keep him steady. Daeyus asked the men to let him go. The horse bounded around the corral a few times and reared up in front of Daeyus in a gesture of intimidation. The raja was unfazed; he went up to him and spoke gently in his ear. The stallion bolted. Daeyus was patient and made repeated efforts to calm and cajole the young horse. Slowly the stallion began to calm down and at long last he shifted about restlessly and reluctantly allowed himself to be saddled.

As soon as the saddle was secure, Daeyus did not waste a moment. He grabbed the horn and leapt lightly into the saddle. This was too much for the young horse to take; he reared up on his hind legs and kicked backwards as he tried to dislodge the rider. Daeyus let the horse buck and weave its way across the open field. He continued to call to him in soft tones. Finally, the stallion decided to do what he did best. He moved from a canter into a fast gallop, his great mane flowing out behind him. Daeyus gave the reins some slack and the horse started to pick up speed. Soon the scenery around was a blur as they flew across the open plain.

Behind a rocky outcrop, a man squatted on his haunches and puffed on a pipe made of horn. The sticky sweet smell of cannabis lingered in the air. He finished his pipe and carefully peered around his sanctuary. In the distance, a black stallion bearing a rider approached. For over a month the man had patiently kept a watch on the Deva camp, staying out of sight of their patrols and scouts. Now, finally, he could see an opportunity.

The man held one end of a long bow between his toes and bent and strung the weapon with his powerful arms. The bow was made from the horns of an ibex and reinforced with strips of wood. It required all his strength to work it. He carefully checked the tension on the string. His eyes were the deepest black and his pupils had narrowed into pinpricks as he focused on the task at hand. From an ornate quiver, he pulled out a shaft made of the finest bamboo. The arrowhead was wrapped in soft leather, which he now carefully unravelled. He handled the arrow with extreme care as he checked it for balance. It was perfect.

A few hundred yards away from the man, the rider reined in his horse to allow it to drink at a little pond. The man narrowed his eyes as he estimated the distance. It was about three hundred yards. It would take a tremendous feat of marksmanship. He took a little fine sand between his fingers and let it run through them as he checked the direction of the fickle wind. He smiled as he noticed a gentle breeze blowing away from him, in the direction of his intended target. Clearly the gods were on his side. He placed the arrow on the great bow, the hard muscle in his chest strained with effort as he pulled the string back to his ear and focused on the target.

At the stream, Daeyus wiped down the flanks of the stallion and the horse whinnied with pleasure; both the raja and his mount were completely oblivious to the mortal danger he was in.

The man aimed for his victim's broad back, slightly to the left of his spine and below the shoulder blade. The bowstring sang in his ear as he let the shaft fly. The arrow had been fletched with the feathers of a Golden Eagle he had taken down in the Gobi Desert. It now flew true, in a lazy arc towards its intended target.

In her sanctuary in the jungle, a heavily pregnant Gaia sat up with a start. She let out a sharp cry.

As he tended to his mount, Daeyus suddenly felt a tremor as the earth shook around them. The stallion reacted sharply and reared up on its hind legs. Daeyus, who was holding on to the reins, was knocked off balance. The arrow that was intended for his heart, struck him high on the shoulder.

Daeyus struggled to control his steed as he felt an intense burning sensation in his shoulder, a pain unlike any he had ever experienced. It was as if somebody had slowly pushed a red hot metal rod into his back. He tried to shut out the pain as he gritted his teeth, grabbed the saddle horn and hoisted himself onto the horse. The stallion galloped away like the wind.

Daeyus struggled with the reins, trying to steer the horse towards the camp. He felt the left side of his body slowly start to go numb and realised with some degree of consternation that this was no ordinary arrow.

He felt something rise in the pit of his stomach as his body broke into cold sweat. This was something way beyond his understanding. He slackened his control on the reins. The stallion seemed to gallop with some purpose as if guided by an unseen force. Daeyus gripped the saddle horn with his good hand and closed his eyes as he tried to shut out the intense fire that coursed through the left side of his body.

The Marksman watched as the horse bore his victim away in the westward direction. He was not unduly perturbed; the goddess had treated the arrowhead with a potent poison before she had handed it to him. His victim would still die, only now it would be a long and painful death.

Gaia sat in a meditative trance as she willed the horse bearing her mortally-wounded lover to come to her. The forest nymphs or Apsaras had come to her aid and now prepared for the arrival of the wounded raja.

Daeyus opened his eyes and saw he was in a dark wood. His

horse had stopped and was stomping its feet, clearly uncomfortable with its surroundings. Daeyus raised his head and found himself face-to-face with a strange creature—it had the head and body of a man, but its legs and ears were that of a goat.

It was a Gandharva, a woodland spirit. The creature beckoned to the chief to follow him. Daeyus weakly kicked his heels against the flanks of the stallion and the horse slowly moved forward. For the second time that day, Daeyus felt darkness envelop him.

The Gandharva and the Apsaras helped Gaia get Daeyus to a bed made of soft branches of conifer and covered with flowers. They laid him face down on it. Gaia stripped off his clothes and examined the wound. She reached into her pouch and pulled out a smooth, round pebble, the colour of alabaster. The pebble had been energised with moonbeams, the source of Ishtar's power. Gaia had recognised the handiwork of the moonchild. She murmured an incantation in a long-forgotten language and placed the stone over the wound.

The Apsaras watched in fascination as blue veins began to appear in the stone. Gaia had to shoo them away to quell their excited chatter. Alone with her mortal lover, she laid her head gently on his good shoulder and felt his life force slowly return. Gaia ran her hand over her swollen belly and sighed deeply.

Daybreak found Mitra at the western border of the land called the Valley of the Five Lions. He had been on the move for nine months now, and every instinct in him compelled him to hurry. The mountain breeze blew his long hair back over his shoulders. It was the colour of the purest snow, yet his face had only begun to show the early signs of age. His white beard was also long, lying well below his chest. His eyes were dark and fierce and his gaze hawk-like. He rode bareback, holding on to the flowing mane of the wild mare.

He had ridden all day and all night for months now, stopping only to change horses. Yet he felt no exhaustion or thirst or hunger. Years of tapas had conditioned his body to sustain itself for long periods of time.

Ahead on the trail, he saw an old shepherd warming himself in front of a little fire. Mitra slowed his mount and scanned the man's aura for any untoward signs, but it seemed normal. The shepherd folded his hands in salutation.

'Greetings, Master Mitra! Please come and share some of my broth.'

Mitra was startled. How did a common shepherd know who he was? He examined the shepherd's aura a little more closely. The man watched him with a mischievous smile; Mitra now saw it flare brightly at its edges. This was a sage of considerable prowess, he had masked his aura and Mitra had fallen for the ruse. Embarrassed, he greeted the shepherd with bowed head.

'Forgive me, Master. I did not recognise you.'

The shepherd handed him a bowl of steaming broth.

'I am called Bhrigu, now drink.'

Mitra drank deeply; the broth warmed his body, sending a surge of pure energy through him. The shepherd studied Mitra; his gaze seemed to penetrate the deepest corners of his mind.

'You seem anxious, my friend. Is it your return to the world that you had once forsaken that troubles you?'

Mitra was glad to talk about something that had been on his mind for a while.

'I am troubled because I cannot understand the significance of this task for which I have been required to interrupt my tapas. I have done my time as a warrior, I've fulfilled my dharma.'

'That, I am afraid, is not for you to decide. You, Master Mitra, are to play a part in a series of events that are going to reshape the destiny of your people. This is something you cannot walk away from, so do not spend time dwelling on the reasons—do what must be done.'

Mitra acknowledged the wisdom in those words and bowed his head in humility.

'Thank you Master, you have set my troubled mind at ease.'

'The camp of Raja Daeyus is a two-week hard ride from here. Follow the trail across these mountains and then head due northwest.'

Mitra rose and bowed respectfully.

'Oh! Just one more thing before you leave.'

The shepherd reached into his robe and pulled out an engraved stone pendent on a leather string. Though he did not recognise the emblem, Mitra noted that the work on the stone was exquisite, from an era long gone.

'Sacrifice has always been the cornerstone of the faith and belief of your clans. A supreme sacrifice will be required for the success of this mission.'

He handed the pendent to Mitra.

'This will grant you safe passage when you need it most. Now go, for time is of the essence.'

Mitra thanked Bhrigu and was soon on his way.

Daeyus lay unconscious for weeks; the physical effects of the poison had disappeared from his body and the wound had healed well, yet traces of the potent toxin continued to ravage his mind. Daeyus moaned and cried out as he slipped in and out of consciousness. He saw the Apsaras make their way towards him, they licked their lips and stared at his body hungrily; he watched spellbound, as their beautiful hands reached out to caress his naked body. Suddenly, before his eyes, the hands started to change shape; they slowly turned into claws and talons that started to dig deep into his flesh. As they brought their faces near, razor-sharp beaks and canines tore into his body and ripped off large chunks of flesh.

Daeyus woke up with a start, his body covered in perspiration. The nightmare had felt so real, he examined his body, almost expecting it to be torn and bleeding. Daeyus allowed himself a smile of relief; he was never one to remember his dreams, yet every unpleasant detail of this nightmare was firmly etched in his memory.

His thoughts were interrupted by a scream. It was a woman. A few moments of silence and there it was again, only this time louder. Daeyus jumped out of bed and made his way swiftly through the trees in the direction of the cries. The screams intensified, and then there was silence.

Daeyus stopped, every muscle in his body tense. The forest was dark and sinister. He was not sure what would come out of those trees at any moment. All of a sudden, he heard another cry, this time it was of a newborn child. The raja squatted down on his haunches and let out a sigh of relief. Then he got up with a smile and slowly made his way in the direction of the sound.

As he came to a clearing, the spectacle stopped him dead in his tracks. Bathed in moonlight, the beautiful Apsaras were gathered around in a circle. In the middle, on a bed of white flowers, lay his lover. Her great beauty still shone through in spite of the exhaustion and rigours of childbirth. Next to her lay a beautiful baby. It gurgled with joy as it kicked its tiny legs in the air and stared up into the sky. Daeyus stayed near the trees, not wanting to defile this ethereal scene with his presence.

It was the magic hour before dawn, when night prepares to surrender to the day. A thick dark cloud had mysteriously appeared over the clearing. A beam of light emerged from the cloud; it enveloped the bed and the circle of nymphs. Gaia looked up at the cloud; her face broke into a gentle smile as she shut her eyes. Daeyus was transfixed as he watched his lover being gently lifted through the beam of light into the cloud.

Still in a daze, he made his way through the circle of nymphs and took the baby in his arms. It was a boy, a big heavy boy, with a shock of blond hair. The baby opened his blue eyes, looked at Daeyus and gave him a toothless grin. Daeyus felt a stab of emotion in his heart as he looked into the baby's eyes. They perfectly mirrored his own. There was no doubt in his mind; this was his son, a gift from the gods.

The Deva chief raised the boy high above his shoulder and shouted at the top of his voice. 'Long live Indra! Future king of the Devas.'

From the cloud above them came a resounding clap of thunder as if to punctuate the statement. The denizens of the forest cried out in alarm and the Apsaras ran for cover, but the baby only looked up into the heavens, clapped his tiny hands, and laughed.

2

Shalla awoke with a start. He pushed aside the naked woman who lay sprawled across his thighs. All around him were remnants of the previous night's orgy, now an array of beautiful motionless bodies strewn across the vast royal bed like corpses, in extremely lewd positions. The wine from the previous night lay heavy in his head and fogged his mind. As he struggled to regain his faculties, he heard it again.

'Thunder! It can't be, not at this time of the year. It's still spring and only the third day of the week-long Spring Festival of Susa,' Shalla thought to himself as he rushed to the doors of his balcony and threw them open.

Outside, the skies had turned dark. Thick clouds hid the sun, making it seem as if day had suddenly become night. Streaks of lightning snaked through the sky, followed by the deafening sound of thunder. In the streets, people hurriedly took down the festoons and the coloured canopies that had been put up for the festival. Shalla stared out blankly at the sky, not sure what to make of this strange phenomenon.

A slave approached and bowed low.

'Excellency! The high priest has sent word: the goddess is ready to speak with you.'

Shalla scratched his balls vigorously.

'Hurry up then, fool. Prepare me for the temple.'

In the great hall of the temple, at the feet of the marble statue of Ishtar, Braega sat naked and cross-legged, eyes closed. Shalla looked at his withered, old body in disgust as he was led to his seat opposite the high priest. One of the attendants came forward with a copper bowl filled with a strange powder. Another attendant put a glowing ember into it. The powder began to crackle as it caught fire and thick smoke started to rise from the vessel. The attendant held the bowl under Braega's nose, and the high priest inhaled deeply.

Shalla watched as the high priest's eyeballs began to roll back into their sockets. His head began to slowly thrash up and down. A strange noise began to emanate from his throat; it was a chant, in some alien tongue. Then suddenly Braega went still, his chin resting on his chest. The attendants silently melted away into the darkness, leaving the king alone with the high priest.

Slowly Braega raised his head. His eyeballs had moved up under his eyelids and only the whites of his eyes showed. As he opened his mouth to speak, his voice was thin and had a strange, quavering, high pitch.

'A child has been born to the Deva chief, Daeyus. The one who will unite the warring sons of Aditi. If he is left to live, he will grow so powerful that he will one day destroy our world.'

The high priest's next words were shrill and hysterical.

'Kill him now, Shalla, and save your people!'

Shalla listened carefully to the words of Ishtar, daughter of the moon. He had no idea as to who this Aditi or her sons were, but if it was Daeyus' child, he was within his grasp.

He bowed his head.

'Is that all you require of me, to kill a newborn child? You may consider it done.'

He paused for a moment as he waited for a reply, but the naked, bald man was still. Shalla tried to sound as humble as he possibly could.

'Now tell me, oh divine one! You, who are the queen of the night sky. What of my star? Does it continue to shine brighter than ever?'

Shalla watched in exasperation as Braega's chin dropped back to his chest. The goddess was no longer available for counsel. The attendants arrived and whisked the unconscious old man away. Shalla hid his irritation as he ordered one of the men to summon his general.

General Druma was a veteran soldier who had risen through the ranks. He had distinguished himself in the Sumerian campaign, and in return for his services, Shalla had promoted him to commander-in-chief of the Elamite army, a post usually reserved for the king himself. As he entered the temple, he found the king pacing about like a caged animal.

Druma saluted smartly with his right fist over his heart. Shalla hurriedly acknowledged it with a wave of his hand.

'What news do you have from Sumer?' he asked anxiously.

The news was both good and bad, so Druma chose his words carefully.

'Sargon the Asura has moved eastwards and taken the cities of Nippur and Adab.'

Shalla was quiet as he pondered this information. He saw Sargon as a bigger threat than any child from a prophecy.

'How long before he musters up the men and the courage to march against Elam?'

'The Asura king has already spread himself too thin in his campaign in Sumer. He is a long way from his capital Assur, and Sumerian rebels are constantly attacking his supply lines. It will take him a few years to consolidate his present empire. I do not think we need to worry about Sargon for some time, Your Majesty.'

Shalla was relieved to hear that piece of news. Just then Braega returned, decked again in his usual finery. Shalla turned to him.

'What did she mean by this prophecy? Who is this child I must kill?'

Braega was not his pompous old self that day. His tone was deadly serious as he addressed the king.

'My lord, the meaning is clear. You must kill the son of Daeyus. But to do that and leave the father alive would be catastrophic. Attack the Devas now while they are still weak and kill them all.'

Shalla considered the words of the high priest very carefully. Although there was no love lost between him and the Devas, he found it hard to believe that this ragtag bunch of savages would dream of taking on the forty-foot high stonewalls of Susa. Besides, he still had use for Daeyus and his mercenary army; they would be his first line of defence against Sargon the Asura.

He weighed his words carefully before he spoke. He did not care about this old fool but he did not wish to offend the goddess.

'Can't this wait a while, your holiness? If this child is as important as you say he is, I do not want history to remember me as a child-killer.'

'My lord! If this child is allowed to live, he will grow up to be a demon such as the world has never seen. He will unite the barbarian hordes that arrive from the northern plains. They will ransack our city and lay waste our lands. It will be as if the kingdom of Elam and this magnificent city never existed. Do you wish to go down in history as the king who let the destroyer of his city slip through his hands when he had the chance to kill him?'

Shalla gave the old man a look of pure hatred. Priest or no priest, no man could speak to him, the king of Susa, that way. For a moment he considered drawing his sword and loping off that wrinkly, old head. He imagined sending it back to the temple on a tray to be presented to Ishtar. But he quickly suppressed the thought. He used up every ounce of self-control that he possessed to douse his fury and turned to General Druma.

'Ready the troops. We march in two hours.'

The raja's safe return with his heir was greeted with great joy and relief. All sorts of rumours had abounded about Daeyus' sudden disappearance. Now they were replaced by demands for a grand feast.

On the appointed day, Daeyus sat on his ceremonial throne and awaited the festivities announced in his honour. To his left lay his son in a beautiful cradle made of dark pine and adorned with gold.

In keeping with tradition, a sacrifice preceded the festivities. Susena, high priest of the Deva clan, stood up to address the gathering. His thin and lanky frame was draped in a robe of white embroidered with gold thread—he was a man who took pride in his appearance. His face was narrow and lean and his raven black hair fell straight to his shoulders. His hooked nose and hooded gaze gave him a vulture-like appearance.

Daeyus watched him wearily. He had no patience for the high priest; he thought the man was a preening peacock who loved the sound of his own voice. He hoped the fool would hurry up so they could get on with the real celebrations.

Susena addressed the gathering in his deep voice, commanding attention.

'Devas, we are gathered here today to give thanks to Surya for delivering our raja safely back to us.'

A thousand voices rang out in praise for the sun. Susena waited for the excitement to subside. For all his vanity, he was a brilliant orator; he knew exactly how to hold an audience.

'The raja also filled my heart with rapturous delight by informing me of a new arrival to our clan. His son, your future king, Indra.'

The crowd erupted with joy at this announcement and began to press forward to get a better look at the baby. Rumours had abounded in the camp about the arrival of a mystery child; the official confirmation now drove them wild. Daeyus went up to the cradle, picked up his son and held him aloft for his subjects. The deafening roars of the crowd could be heard for miles.

Susena tried to restore order but in vain. Finally he called at the top of his voice.

'Let the sacrifice be presented.'

A quiet descended on the crowd as a giant, black bull was brought forward. The Devas were connoisseurs of cattle; it was the main unit of currency and the only true measure of a man's wealth and power in their society.

This bull was truly magnificent, standing at least six feet above the ground at its shoulders. Its coat of ebony shone with the radiance of health; it was lean in the flanks while its shoulders and haunches were bunched with heavy muscle. Daeyus looked into the creature's eyes; there was no fear in them, only a mild curiosity at all the fuss. It did not cower like sacrificial creatures usually did, but stood tall and proud, chewing on its cud and gazing at the open country beyond the camp. Daeyus summoned his master herdsman.

'This creature is not from our herds. Where did you find it?'

'This, my lord, is a fighting bull from Harappa,' the herdsman announced proudly. 'I have been grooming him for years, for an occasion such as this. He is truly a sacrifice meant for a great king.'

The raja and his subjects watched with interest as the bull was solemnly led to the altar. Susena began the incantations invoking the sun to accept the sacrifice. Four robust young men tried to force the head of the animal down onto the chopping block. The bull let out a loud bellow and shook its mighty head; the four men were thrown off the altar into the enthralled audience.

The crowd was highly amused as more men scrambled onto the altar to control the beast. The bull kicked out with its powerful hind legs. One of its hooves caught a man under his chin, snapped his neck clean and threw him back like a rag doll, into the now worried crowd. The other men on the altar slowly backed away.

The executioner, a pot-bellied giant of a man, dropped his axe and nearly wet himself in fright. Clearly, this was something he was not used to. A sacrificial animal fighting back—it was unheard of. The bull turned sharply towards him and one of its needle-sharp horns raked him across the belly, laying it open. He fell to the ground with his entrails spread all around him, screaming and writhing in agony.

Nobody in the crowd was laughing now. They watched horror-struck as the bull now turned around looking for an escape route. Standing directly in its path was the cradle with Indra in it. Daeyus leapt across from his throne to land directly between the bull and his son's cradle. The animal lowered its head and pawed at the earth with its front hooves. Daeyus stood his ground, his eyes locked into those of the beast.

For one brief moment they stood motionless, studying each other. Then the bull snorted, steam billowing from its nostrils, lowered its giant head and charged. Daeyus crouched low as he braced himself to grab the creature's massive horns. At the very last second, the animal swerved to a side and ran off through the crowd into the wilderness beyond the camp.

The raja restrained his huntsmen from chasing down the animal. The mood at the camp was now sullen, the festive air gone, replaced by a certain sense of foreboding. Susena and the priests huddled together in a corner and whispered to each other. Daeyus returned to his quarters, issuing orders that he was not to be disturbed.

After his long deliberations with the other priests, Susena lay in his tent, deep in thought. The sacrifice had not been completed and Deva blood had been spilt on the altar—the omen did not bode well for the tribe. Susena shut his eyes and sighed deeply, perhaps the next day would present a solution.

As he drifted off to sleep, he heard a sound. He was instantly awake, listening. The tinkling of tiny silver bells caught his attention, followed by a giggle. The voice was young, high-pitched and so sweet that it tugged at even Susena's cynical old heart.

He sat up, startled. Standing at the entrance of his tent was a vision of such rare beauty that it took his breath away. She was no more than sixteen, her skin the colour of wild honey. Around her waist, she wore a silver feather on a chain to cover the area where her smooth, sleek legs met. Her long, raven hair was straight and shiny and thrown in front of her shoulders. It did a very bad job of concealing her well-formed breasts. Susena struggled to avert his gaze from them and look her in the eye. Even as she bowed, her green eyes never left him.

'I am sorry I startled you, my lord.'

Susena's voice was hoarse with desire, and he struggled to muster some authority into it.

'Who are you? How dare you come in here unannounced?'

She walked towards the bed, her hips swaying rhythmically with each step. The silver feather hanging from her belly shifted and Susena's breath caught in his throat. He could not trust his voice any longer.

The girl came up and sat beside him. Her eyes were like that of a tigress, appraising her victim.

'I'm a gift, your holiness. Honour me with your acceptance.'

Her manner was so coquettish the high priest could not contain himself any longer. His breathing became hoarse and he made a clumsy grab at her breasts. She laughed as she pushed his hands away.

'Patience, my lord. Allow me the pleasure of pleasuring you.'

She reached under his robe and slid her hand up his thigh, running her fingers lightly across his flesh. He felt a shudder run through his body as her fingers reached their final destination, and he fell back on the bed in complete surrender.

Susena had never experienced anything like this before. The women he usually had were whimpering slave girls who did everything he ordered out of fear for their lives. While he enjoyed the power and control he had over them, this was something else altogether. She pushed his flimsy night robe away, bent down and slowly licked the length of his shaft, not taking her eyes off his face.

Susena grabbed a pillow and bit into it to stop himself from crying out loud. It would not do for the men to hear the high priest scream like a rutting animal. She laughed as she slowly strode him like a horse. She took off her belly chain and laid the silver feather on his chest. He looked at her, nearly delirious with joy, as she lowered herself on to him. Susena felt her delicate flesh tear as he entered her; she let out a sharp cry, further adding to his pleasure. She began to move, slowly at first. Then her hips began to find a rhythm of their own. Susena moaned with pleasure.

She gradually increased the pace and he felt his belly tighten as he began to gasp. She grabbed him by his neck and drew him towards her. Susena marvelled at her strength; he opened his mouth to scream as he reached the pinnacle of his orgasm. She tightened her muscles and drew his seed into her. His mouth opened in ecstasy, and she pressed her mouth against his and breathed deeply into it. Her breath was as sweet as her appearance. Susena's body convulsed several times in pleasure and then was still.

As the night wore on, in his royal tent, the raja was unable to sleep. He stepped outside and the crisp night air immediately made him feel better. He asked Mara to saddle up his steed. The squire returned leading the horse and Daeyus rode out into the night alone. As he thought about the events of the evening, he was overcome by a sense of apprehension. The gods had refused to accept his sacrifice . . . this had never happened before.

The ground ahead broke into a gully formed by a dry stream. As he neared it, he saw a pack of wolves and vultures ravaging a carcass. He slowed the stallion to a walk, not wanting to disturb the feeding frenzy. As he approached, he recognised the massive carcass. It was the sacrificial bull.

It was early in the morning when Susena awoke. The events of the previous night felt almost like an eminently pleasurable dream. He felt something on his chest: it was a silver chain with a feather pendent. Susena smiled in satisfaction, the reason for the failure of the sacrifice had come to him in a dream; he was amazed at the clarity he now possessed. He called out to one of his attendants and asked him to seek an immediate audience with the raja.

Daeyus sat up in his throne as he prepared to receive the high priest. He had been unable to sleep a wink the whole night.

'What does that pompous ass want so early in the morning?' the weary raja thought to himself.

As Susena walked in, Daeyus noted that the priest was not his usual self. While he was decked in his usual finery, he was not wearing white, the symbol of his priesthood, but a robe of blue. He seemed nervous, trembling with excitement.

'Greetings, Susena. What brings you here this early in the day?'

Daeyus used his name and not the formal title of address for the high priest, letting the man know that he expected this intrusion of his privacy to be for an issue of paramount importance. He noticed that the high priest was nervously fidgeting with something around his neck. It was a finely worked silver feather.

Susena bowed low.

'I would never dare to commit this transgression if the situation did not demand it, my lord. I request that you lend me a patient ear as you might not like to hear some of the things I have to tell you.'

Daeyus nodded impatiently, asking him to continue. Susena now chose his words very carefully.

'My lord, sometimes in our ignorance as mortals we commit certain acts, the repercussions of which can have a terrible impact on humanity.'

He hesitated for a moment.

'For god's sake, stop beating around the bush and say what you have to say,' Daeyus cut in impatiently.

The words now blundered out of Susena's mouth. A high-pitched quiver replaced his normal deep baritone.

'My lord, the child you think is your son is actually a demon. He will be responsible for the destruction—'

Daeyus did not let him finish. He leapt off his chair, grabbed the man by the throat and lifted him off his feet.

'One more word and you die.'

He flung him across the tent. Susena hit the ground and once again started to protest. Daeyus drew his sword and advanced menacingly towards the high priest. The words froze in Susena's throat. He abandoned all dignity and scrambled on all fours for the door.

The arrival of Krupa saved the high priest from further harm.

The commander had an urgent message, he said. 'Lord Mitra of the Aditya clan has just arrived at the camp and requests an immediate audience.'

Susena took the opportunity to make good his escape. Daeyus sheathed his sword and hurriedly ordered arrangements to be made to receive his honoured guest.

Raja Mitra was a legend among the warriors of the northern tribes. Once a great chief of the Aditya clan, he was renowned as much for his wisdom and counsel as his skill in warfare. Daeyus remembered how he had led a mercenary army in the siege of the Sumerian city-state of Ur.

The night before the battle, Daeyus, then a young captain, had watched the raja ride alone to the top of a hillock that overlooked the city. Out of concern for the safety of his general, Daeyus had followed him at a safe distance.

On top of the hillock sat a man with matted hair piled high on top of his head and ash smeared all over his body. He had the appearance of a sage, but his body was built like that of a warrior in peak condition. Daeyus watched from a distance as Mitra bowed down to the man, who raised his right palm and placed it above the general's head. A bolt of blue energy emerged and entered Raja Mitra's head.

As the battering rams of the mercenary army broke down the mud brick walls of Ur, Mitra led the cavalry in a triumphant dance of death and destruction through the city. He slew scores of Sumerian warriors and made his way to the centre of the city to the magnificent temple of Baal, the patron deity of Ur. A god with an insatiable appetite for human sacrifice.

In the temple, the high priests of Baal watched spellbound, their hearts filled with superstitious awe, as Mitra, divine energy coursing through his body, brought down the forty-foot statue of the god with one well-aimed kick to its chest. That was enough for the defenders of Ur; they laid down their weapons before Mitra in surrender.

Daeyus, who had been assigned to the rearguard, did not actively participate in the battle. He was with the troops still garrisoned outside the walls. A movement on the hillock caught his attention.

Silhouetted against the full moon was the man with the matted locks, dancing with a trident in one hand and a rattle drum in the other. The hill seemed to shake with every step of his wild, yet rhythmic dance. His laughter seemed to echo all around as the tongues of flames from the burning city rose high and licked the night sky. Daeyus did not speak to anyone about what he'd seen; he could scarcely believe his own eyes.

Later, at the victory celebrations, the chiefs of the various tribes gathered to divide the spoils of war. Raja Mitra shocked the gathering by announcing that he was abdicating his throne. He appointed his brother as the new raja of the Adityas. He then divided his share of the spoils among the kin of his men who had fallen in battle and rode off alone in the direction of the rising sun.

Daeyus was brought back to the present by the announcement of Lord Mitra's arrival. He smiled as the old man approached; Mitra still carried himself with the air of a military man.

'Once a soldier, always a soldier,' Daeyus thought to himself, noting that age had not slowed the old warrior down one bit. He went down on one knee and bowed his head in respect.

Mitra took him by the shoulders and raised him to his feet. His grip was still strong.

'Greetings, Raja Daeyus! Time is running out so I must come straight to the point. You and your clan are in grave danger. Even as we speak, Shalla marches against you at the head of a sizable, fast-moving force.'

Daeyus was stunned. From any other source he would have dismissed this as slander. It did not make sense to him. Why would Shalla make a move against him?

'There is no time to be lost, my king. You must break camp and get ready to march.'

The tone dispelled all doubt from Daeyus' mind; he went outside and barked urgent orders to his men. The hustle and bustle started around the camp as the raja's orders were passed on. He returned to Mitra.

'Should we take the south road, my lord? It will be easier on the wagons and the livestock.'

'No! They will be expecting that. They will ride us down in no time.'

Mitra drew a line on the ground towards the northeast.

'We will make for the Amu Darya River here and ford it.

From there we can make our way through the Pass of the Wolves, and if fortune favours us, it will be a two-day journey from there into the Cloud Mountains where we will be safe.'

Shalla cursed out loud as he rode at the head of his cavalry. His generous posterior, now used to the silken cushions of his throne, ached from the days of hard riding. However, he had used the time in the saddle to evaluate the situation. Perhaps a political advantage could be extracted from this campaign. His spies, who were scattered across the land in the guise of merchants, had brought him news that more and more tribes were leaving their northern lands near the Caucasus Mountains and moving into Central Asia. These newcomers were not content living as pastoral nomads and soldiers of fortune. One of them had occupied the land called Mycenae and was now building city-states there to rival his own.

Shalla knew that it would not be long before Daeyus also began to harbour such ambitions. By wiping out the Devas, he could send a strong message to the arriving northern tribes, to avert their avaricious gaze from his beautiful city. He ignored the pain in his arse and screamed at his captains to increase the pace.

Sunrise found that the caravan had made steady progress through the night. The constant drizzle, though unpleasant, would sufficiently obliterate their tracks and buy them a little time. Daeyus rode ahead alone, using the time to collect his thoughts. He had always been a pragmatic man when it came to religion.

As long as the will of the gods did not conflict with what he thought was best for his people, he obeyed it. If not, the priests were asked to reinterpret gods' will to go along with the raja's plans. Susena's interpretations of the omens had angered him then, but now he could not but help think, what if the high priest was right? Daeyus dismissed the thought even as it entered his mind. Indra was his son. His flesh and blood. For better or for worse, that was the way it would always be.

He tried to bring his thoughts to the immediate threat that was closing in on them. Shalla's duplicity was unexplainable but not altogether surprising. The Elamite king was known to shift allegiances and turn friends to foes to suit his needs. Daeyus did not share Mitra's optimism on the success of their present endeavour. It would be impossible to outrun the Elamite cavalry with wagons and herds of livestock. Shalla might be a pompous ass, but he commanded an extremely efficient fighting force, and they would be riding hard. The Devas could not allow themselves to be caught on open ground to be picked off by the enemy archers and then be ridden down by their vastly superior numbers. He rode back to the lead driver of the caravan and instructed him to pick up the pace. He looked around for Mitra, but the seer had gone ahead on a scouting mission.

Shalla arrived at the deserted Deva campsite in a rage. He looked at their sacred sacrificial pit, the only indication left of their presence in the area. He cursed the rain as he parted his tunic and urinated copiously into the pit. The outriders he had dispatched had returned one by one. The Devas had not made the obvious choice and taken the south road, which meant that they expected to be pursued.

Shalla suddenly had a feeling that this was not going to be as easy as he had expected. He turned to General Druma.

'You have ridden and fought with these barbarians before! What do you think they will do?'

Druma carefully weighed his options; to hazard a guess and be proved wrong would not be a good idea at this moment. Shalla was looking to vent his anger and frustration on somebody. Druma was too crafty an old fox to fall prey to that. He looked east, pensively. The arrival of the last outriders at that moment saved him. They had found the caravan tracks heading towards the river Amu Darya. Shalla screamed in triumph and ran for his horse.

Druma followed his king, still lost in thought. He had fought many a campaign alongside the Devas. He had also been present when the first intelligence reports of the Deva strength had arrived. Daeyus had three hundred soldiers, of which about two hundred and fifty were new recruits who had not seen any action. Druma had not shared in the general amusement that went around with this piece of information. These numbers could not be more misleading when it came to measuring the true strength of these men. The Elamites were about to corner an angry lion; the results might just not turn out according to plan.

Daeyus stood in the narrow cleft between two massive cliffs. This was the Pass of the Wolves. At its narrowest point, four men could ride through, shoulder to shoulder. In the distance ahead, Daeyus could see the thick clouds that gave the mountains hidden behind them their name. Slowly the wagons and livestock made their way through the narrow confines of the pass. Daeyus now assembled his fifty veterans. He asked them to pick up their battle gear and say goodbye to their families. The men obeyed without question. Daeyus kissed his son's forehead and gave him back to his wet nurse. He was afraid to prolong the physical contact lest it make him weak.

Mitra silently watched the exchange between father and son; he put his hand on Daeyus' shoulder reassuringly. The raja turned to him.

'He is in your care now, my lord, as are my Devas. I know they will thrive under your wisdom.'

Mitra's face did not betray his emotions. He clasped the king around his shoulders.

'Farewell, Daeyus. May the gods heap their glory upon you.'

Daeyus then called Vasu and asked him to assist Mitra for the rest of the journey. He also appointed him regent and guardian of Indra's legacy till his son came of age to take his place at the head of the Devas. Vasu accepted the honour with little joy. He would rather have taken his place alongside his raja. Both men knew this would be a fight to the finish, and Vasu could not think of a better way to end his illustrious military career.

The fifty veterans watched the caravan snake away down the path. One of them, a brave but dim-witted fellow, Atar, remarked loudly, 'But they haven't left any horses for us. How in Surya's name are we going to join them after victory?'

His comment brought a smile to the raja's face.

'We will ride back on the horses of the Elamites after we have slaughtered them all.'

Cries of affirmation rose from fifty throats. Daeyus continued on a more serious note.

'Men, you have done for me more than any raja can ask of his soldiers. We have fought many battles. Savoured many sweet victories together. But today we do not fight for wealth, women, power or glory. Today, we fight for survival. Survival of our clan! Our future! And our way of life!'

The men banged their swords against their shields. Most of them had families in the departing caravan. They knew exactly what had to be done.

'I do not promise you a glorious victory. For all you know we will die here unheralded, unsung. No bards to record our valour, no survivors to recount our deeds. But these Elamites will remember us. They will remember this day for the rest of their lives. They who have lived under the shelter of our blade, will now feel its edge. Fight well today men, for tomorrow we will dine with the gods.'

He raised his sword high in the air and fifty voices screamed out in unison.

'YEEEE-AAAH!'

Captain Nehat heard the cry as he crossed the great river in haste, at the head of three hundred cavalry. They had ridden like the wind to get here ahead of the main force. His orders were to engage the enemy and slow down their escape. The battle cry could mean only one thing: that the Devas had decided to stop running and make a stand.

Nehat looked on at the Pass of the Wolves with a certain degree of trepidation. He had been through this region a couple of times before and had sufficient knowledge of the terrain. The Devas had chosen their spot well. The pass with its overhanging rocks and narrow passageway was perfect for an ambush. He was in a dilemma. His instincts told him that he should wait, but the king's orders had been clear. The young officer did not want to be the one responsible for the caravan getting away. He did not hesitate. Leading the charge into the dark recesses of the pass he found that the passage narrowed at the centre, which forced the cavalry to slow down. Then it widened again. The overhanging rocks afforded little or no light in there, enhancing the already sinister atmosphere within the pass.

As they exited the narrow passage and tried to pick up speed, the Deva line hit them. Two rows of ten warriors each, standing shoulder to shoulder with spear and shield, charged at the horses. Nehat felt his horse collapse under him with a spear thrust in its chest. He fell to the ground, his leg pinned under his dead horse.

From the overhanging rocks, a stream of arrows poured into the rear of the Elamite cavalry. Nehat watched in stunned silence as his men dropped like flies all around him. With a superhuman effort, he freed his leg and crawled into a corner from where he had an uninterrupted view of the mayhem that was being unleashed.

Daeyus had given specific instructions to kill the horses, knowing as he did so just how difficult it would be for his men to carry out his order. There was nothing a Deva soldier loved more in the world than a good horse. They prized it above even a beautiful wife. Now, perched precariously on ledges, his archers strived to carry out his bidding.

As the men and horses at the rear of the column fell, the Elamites were trapped with no room to manoeuvre their steeds. Now Daeyus led twenty of his men who had been waiting in reserve through the line into the confused throng, screaming encouragement and swinging his battle-axe. When the bloodlust waned, Daeyus looked around him; the three hundred-strong Elamite cavalry had been butchered down to the last man and horse.

Covered in blood and gore, Daeyus and his men looked around at the carnage with grim satisfaction. There had been no fatalities in their ranks; five men were wounded, but still able to wield their arms. But the Devas did not exult in their victory—they all knew that this was only the beginning.

One of the men found Nehat hiding inside the slashed underbelly of one of the horses. He had scooped out its innards with his bare hands and crawled into the cavity. There he had spent the last couple of hours crouched in terror, watching the men in his command being systematically hacked to pieces. He could not speak; he stood there and stared at the raja with a blank expression on his face. Daeyus was a great believer in the impact of psychological warfare. He looked into the man's crazed eyes and realised that this soldier would be far more useful to him alive than dead.

It was the latter part of the day by the time Shalla and his men reached the pass. The eerie silence and the circling vultures that greeted them did nothing to lift the sagging morale of the Elamites as they lined up and awaited orders.

Suddenly, a scream was heard from within the pass, and an Elamite soldier emerged. He ran towards them, shrieking about being attacked by demons from hell that ate both men and horses. It was Captain Nehat. Druma knew of the captain by reputation, he was a brave man. Something terrible must have happened within the confines of that pass to scare the living daylights out of the young soldier.

Druma acted quickly. He walked over to the captain, struck him on the head with the hilt of his sword and knocked him out. As he ordered for him to be taken away, he hoped the officer's delirious rants had not affected the morale of his troops. He sent a rider out to the commander of a nearby garrison, asking for a division of infantry and archers. He was not going to take any more chances against these men.

A furious Shalla ordered another attack. This time the Elamite cavalry's approach was more gingerly. As they entered the pass, slipping and sliding over the blood and entrails of their own people, even the seasoned war-horses were spooked by the stench of death. The Devas made short work of repelling this attack. Through the day and well into the night the Elamites launched four more unsuccessful forays into the pass.

Inside the pass, as night fell, Daeyus instructed his men to pile up the dead horses at the entrance. They then poured clarified butter over the corpses and set them ablaze. The reeking smell of death inside the pass was unbearable, but the Deva soldiers did not seem to be bothered by it. They were in a zone, their senses completely tuned to the task at hand. They tightened their grip on their weapons and waited.

With half his cavalry gone, Shalla waited for the flames to die down before he sent in the freshly arrived infantry. They poured into the pass wave after wave, trampling over their own dead men and horses. Daeyus and his men, wounded and thoroughly exhausted, fought on gamely.

Shalla now instructed his archers to take position outside the pass. Druma watched in horror as Shalla, uncaring about the safety of his own men, ordered his archers to fire volley after volley of arrows into the pass. By the time the rain of arrows stopped, three men were left standing.

Daeyus broke off the shafts of the arrows that stuck in his body and looked around at his men. It had been a long, hard night. One of Krupa's legs was sliced off at the knee. He used a red-hot sword to cauterise the wound and leaned on his spear to stay upright. His breath came out in raggedy gasps. The third Deva standing, Atar, had a gaping wound in his abdomen. He had tied a piece of cloth tightly around his waist to prevent his entrails from falling out. He still wore his dumb smile.

Daeyus was bleeding profusely from numerous wounds on his chest. He staggered out of the southern end of the pass and gazed anxiously into the sky. Morning had just broken and he saw the signal he had been waiting for. A plume of green smoke appeared through the clouds near the top of the mountain. The caravan had finally made it.

Daeyus smiled wearily. The sun rose from behind a distant hill and bathed the three survivors in its light. Their mission accomplished, he turned to Atar.

'I think it's time for you to find us some horses.'

The mood in the Elamite camp was far from belligerent. They had lost one-and-a-half divisions of cavalry and a full division of infantry. Shalla was furious as he digested the bitterness of his failure. The caravan had already crossed his borders; Daeyus' demon whelp would live.

As Druma rallied his men for the final assault, he heard the sound of a conch shell booming out of the pass. He stopped in surprise; that was usually the sound that preceded a Deva cavalry charge. The Elamites watched, some in shock, some in open-mouthed admiration, as three men rode out of the Pass of the Wolves.

Daeyus, lance in hand, led them in an arrowhead formation, with himself at point, as he made straight for the centre of the Elamite line.

Shalla could not believe his eyes. He shouted out to his archers. The three riders looked up to see the sky filled with hundreds of arrows in flight. Daeyus reversed the grip on his lance and, bending his back, flung it into the air with all his might. It flew straight towards Shalla. Fear lent the Elamite king wings as he threw himself off his horse in the nick of time. The lance flew over his shoulder and struck a soldier behind him in the middle of his chest. The impact of the throw unseated the man from his mount and pinned him to the ground.

The volley of arrows caught the three riders in full stride. They were lifted off their horses and flung to the ground where they lay like human pincushions. Shalla recovered his composure and picked himself off the ground. Sword in hand, he rushed towards the prone figure of the fallen raja.

Sixteen arrows protruded out of Daeyus' torso, yet his great spirit still clung to his body. He laughed as Shalla ran towards him, which only served to infuriate the Elamite king.

'You rejoice in the knowledge that your son lives. But rest assured, barbarian, I, Shalla, swear that the day I face him, he will die an even more terrible death than his father.'

Daeyus spat out a mouthful of blood as he raised his head and summoned his last reserves to speak.

'INDRA! Remember his name. The next time you hear it, your empire will crumble to dust before your eyes.'

Shalla screamed in rage, raised his sword and brought it down towards Daeyus' neck. An inch from the target he stopped his blade. He was disappointed to see that there was no fear in the raja's eyes, only a grim sense of acceptance. Shalla sneered at him.

'I will not make this so easy for you.'

He sheathed his sword and walked away.

Daeyus lay there, his eyes shut. Slowly the sounds of the departing army faded. The Elamites marched quietly, displaying no exuberance at their victory. It had come at too dear a cost. When Daeyus opened his eyes, he saw that a group of vultures circling overhead was slowly beginning to drop in a lazy downward spiral.

Closer to him on the ground, he heard another sound. It was the muted scratch of claws over hard ground. Then he heard a low growl; it was the call of the alpha male telling the pack that it was time to feed.

As the wolf pack cautiously made its way forward, he took a deep breath. The omens, the dream, it all seemed to finally make sense. Daeyus, raja of the Devas, closed his eyes as he prepared to accept his fate.

From her vantage point atop the ziggurat, Ishtar watched the scavengers ravage the carcass of the defiant raja. The child had escaped, but Ishtar was not troubled. She had one more trick up her sleeve, and this time she would not fail.

3

The caravan continued to make slow progress up the narrow mountain trail. They had been on the move for several days now, and the horses and cattle were near the end of their tether. Mitra allowed the pace to slacken, but did not stop. Although he did not expect any more pursuit, he knew that if they stopped on the trail, they were sitting ducks for an ambush, or even worse, an avalanche.

The thick cloud cover made it hard to guess the hour. Mitra sensed that it was well approaching dusk. The light disappeared very quickly in these mountains. Mitra strained his eyes. Through the thick mist he saw a dark shape emerge—it was Vasu. He had taken a patrol ahead on a scouting mission. He had good news.

'Up ahead is a snowfield. The ice is thick; we can rest there for the night.'

After they'd set up camp, Mitra and Vasu walked around, reviewing the situation. The journey had taken its toll on the old and the sick and also on some of the young. The dead were carefully wrapped in blankets and piled into a single wagon. Mitra then went to check on young Indra. Mahisi, the widow of Krupa, had gladly assumed the responsibility of bringing up the child when Mitra had offered it to her. She was childless and vowed to look after Indra like he was her own. She had already organised a small army of wet nurses. Indra now lay on the lap of one of them, calmly sucking on her breast. The rigours of the journey had not seemed to affect him at all.

As night fell the mist cleared, only to be replaced by a howling wind that cut through their robes, chilling them to the bone. Vasu and Mitra warmed themselves around a fire and discussed their future plans. This was only a temporary respite while their food reserves were plenty; they needed to find shelter desperately. With the snow melting, the trail ahead could easily prove to be a death-trap.

After Vasu retired for the night, Mitra sat for a long while and stared into the fire, lost in thought. Shalla had very good reason to abandon the chase into these mountains. A few years ago, an entire Elamite army, down to the last man, had vanished here. Apart from the landslides, flash floods and avalanches, there was one more serious threat to consider—the Pakhtu, a hill tribe known for their valour and aggression. Mitra knew they were well within their lands, but it was still early spring and he hoped the Pakhtu raiding parties had not ventured this far north yet.

The next morning, there was excitement in the camp. The scouts had returned with a captive, a boy of ten. Mitra studied him carefully from a distance, but the boy's aura was unreadable. He asked one of the men to bring the boy to him.

As the tribe broke camp around them, Mitra tried to question the young boy. He appeared very calm, and the only excitement he showed was when he spotted the cattle. He stared at them, fascinated. Mitra showed him how to stroke their sleek flanks as they passed him, and the boy laughed happily. They soon had an effective communication system going with hand signals. The boy conveyed to them that the trail ahead was still blocked with heavy snow, and it would take a few weeks for it to melt. He agreed to take them to a safer place where they could camp for a few days.

As the mist thickened around them, the boy led them down a narrow path that descended steeply into the valley below. The Devas struggled with their wagons down the slope. It was so steep that at places the wagons had to be hitched to the front of the bullocks and lowered down. A few agonising hours later, they were in a secluded canyon, sheltered from the elements by the steep cliffs around. The boy made a sign that they should camp there.

Vasu looked around. He realised that it was a box canyon— one way in and one way out. There were many little fresh water streams that crisscrossed the canyon floor, which was covered by short, green grass. It was a great campsite, except for the fact that it was also an ideal place for an ambush. Vasu was about to convey his misgivings to Mitra, when the older man asked him to look up. On the cliffs directly ahead, a bunch of wild-looking men were staring down at them. They were big, with thick hair and shaggy beards, and wore large cloaks of bearskin. They had wide grins on their faces, the kind hunters have when a fat antelope falls right into their lap. It was the Pakhtu.

They were careful not to reveal their exact number, but Vasu knew that they didn't need too many men to pick them off one by one from those cliffs. They clearly had the upper hand. Now all the Devas could do was wait and hope that the intentions of the Pakhtu were friendly.

A rope suddenly dropped from the cliff and a man swiftly rappelled down the face. He reached the bottom and made his way towards the boy, the thick fur cloak draped around his broad shoulders giving him an ursine appearance. He ruffled the boy's hair fondly and had a quiet word with him.

Vasu tried to make a sign that they came in peace. The man watched him for a moment, amused.

'I speak your tongue. It was taught to me by a wise man who travelled through these parts a long time ago.'

Vasu let out a sigh of relief.

'I request an audience with your chief. We would like permission to camp here till the weather improves and subsequently, safe passage through your lands.'

The man had lost interest in the conversation—he was focused on the cattle.

'We have had a long and hard winter, our elders and children are nearly starving to death. Now you show up here like this with so much meat on the hoof. Surely this is a gift from the gods.'

Vasu hid his irritation at the man's insolence.

'We will be glad to share some of our meat with you, enough to fill all your hungry bellies many times over.'

The man looked at the tired, exhausted faces that stared at him.

'What do you know of our hunger? Why should we be content with a little share when we can kill every one of you and take it all?'

Although his tone was matter of fact, there was no mistaking the menace in his words.

Mitra decided it was time to intervene before the situation got out of hand.

'Forgive me, but I have something that might be of interest to you.'

He took the stone Bhrigu had given him off his neck and threw it to the man, who caught it in mid-air.

As he opened his palm and beheld the pendent, all the arrogance seemed to drain out of him. He bowed to Mitra.

'Forgive me, my lord. The stars told us of your imminent arrival, but I did not expect so many of you. I, Thora, chief of the Pakhtu, welcome you to our land. You and your people are now our honoured guests.'

There was a marked relief amongst the Devas when they heard these words. While not ones to shirk from a fight, the punishing journey had left them in no shape to do battle.

'On behalf of my people, I thank you Chief Thora. Please accept this little gift as a token of our gratitude.'

Mitra summoned the chief herdsman.

'Bring out a hundred of our fattest bulls.'

The Pakhtu chief could not hide his joy. In a land with precious little resources, this much meat was a bonanza.

'Our hungry children will sing your praises. Make this place your home; in a few weeks, when the ice thaws, I will be back to guide you on your journey ahead. Farewell till then, my friends.'

The chief and the shepherd boy left the canyon with their new herd.

The canyon served them well as a camp. The high cliffs sheltered them from the icy wind, and, though they were still well above the tree line, it afforded them plenty of fresh grazing for the horses and cattle.

Mitra organised the funerals for the people who had passed away during the journey. In the absence of wood, the bodies were doused in clarified butter and set ablaze. Mitra then called out the names of the fifty warriors who had fallen at the pass. All the members of the tribe greeted each and every name with loud cheers. The loudest cheer was reserved for Daeyus. Every Deva screamed at the top of his voice, in the hope that their raja would hear them in his heavenly abode where he dined with the gods and their ancestors who had fallen in battle.

Mitra then sat down and watched the high priest take centre stage. Susena started with a prayer for the departed souls. He then thanked the Sun God Surya for delivering them through this trying ordeal. Once he was finished, he turned to address the gathering. Mitra noticed that the high priest's voice seemed to change, acquiring a strange high-pitched quiver to it.

'My people! The gods have been kind to us thus far, but I think it is unwise to test the limits of their generosity. The omens had foretold this great peril and I had tried to warn our great king.'

Susena took one of his dramatic pauses and began to pace up and down as the crowd waited anxiously for him to explain what he meant. Mitra noticed a feverish glint in the man's eyes, almost like he was under some kind of spell.

'Our great Raja Daeyus, may Surya grant peace to his soul, was the victim of a cruel deception. This child he believed was his son is actually a demon born to rid Earth of humanity. That is why the Elamites pursued us. They had nothing against the Devas; it was this cursed child that they wanted.'

He paused and surveyed his audience. There was no sign of protest or dissent; they seemed enthralled by this astounding revelation. Susena continued triumphantly. 'As long as this demon is in our midst, our hardship will never end. If he is allowed to live, he will be responsible for the destruction of not only our clan, but of the entire human race.'

In her temple, Ishtar waited with bated breath. It was she who had presented herself as a gift to Susena on the night of the failed sacrifice. It had been child's play for her to draw out his power along with his seed and to plant in him a tiny essence of herself. It was this she used now to control him. Susena, the high priest of the Devas, was now her plaything, with a single point agenda inscribed in his mind: death to the demon Indra.

However, as with all human beings, there were certain aspects of the mind she could not control. In this case, it was the man's ego and his penchant for grandstanding. She had also not taken into account the presence of Mitra. She had a healthy respect for the seer and she now hoped that her minion had not taken things too far.

Mitra looked towards Vasu in shock. Daeyus' trusted lieutenant said nothing. Mitra stood up, his eyes flashing with anger. 'Enough! I will not stand here and have the memory of a great raja insulted.'

Susena quickly lost all his bluster and hurriedly stood aside. Mitra gave him a withering look as he continued. 'Devas! I am not of your clan, yet I, an Aditya, stand here amongst you in the service of this boy. It has been written in the stars. This boy, Indra, will be a great warrior such the world has never seen. He will unite the northern tribes to fight as one nation. He will be a greater raja than his illustrious father.'

Loud cheers greeted this statement. Mitra looked at the high priest, who stood there with his head down, humility personified. The seer realised there was very little he knew about Susena; he decided to soften his stand until he could learn more about the high priest and his true intentions.

'The wise Susena is right—the omens did foretell the birth of a destroyer. But it is the cities of your enemies that this child will destroy. They will cower within their high walls and tremble at the very mention of his name. He will etch the name of the Devas in letters of gold on the pages of history. It is I, Mitra, who speak these words.'

Mitra sat down to the rapturous applause of the crowd. Susena gestured for the crowd to be silent; he then bowed low to Mitra and spoke once again, this time in his deep baritone.

'Forgive me, great master! I made a mistake in my interpretation of the signs. My knowledge is merely a drop of water against the ocean of your intellect.'

Mitra looked at the bowed head and realised that he had made an enemy for life. Susena now raised his voice in a chant.

'Long live Prince Indra, future king of the Devas!'

All around him, the crowd took up the chant. Mitra watched Vasu echo the chant and then look towards the seer with a smile. The smile did not reach the regent's eyes.

Mitra was not pleased with himself. He had allowed his anger to show, and he knew that he and Indra had now made a powerful enemy. Luckily for him, in spite of their current predicament, the great love that the Devas had for Daeyus was intact. Mitra would have no trouble finding trustworthy men to guard young Indra, but that alone was not going to be enough. As an Aditya, he had no real say in matters concerning the Deva clan. For the young prince to survive, he would need a powerful ally from within his own people.

The solution presented itself to Mitra a few days later. Vasu invited him for a great feast to celebrate the birth of his daughter. After a scrumptious meal, an emotional Vasu hugged Mitra.

'My lord, please forgive me if I offended you in any way. I look forward to your continued guidance on our perilous journey ahead.'

'You shall have that, my lord regent. Now if you will excuse me, it is time for my meditation.'

Vasu, a little drunk from all the celebrations, was not willing to let Mitra go that easily.

'You will have to do me one more honour, my lord. I would like you to bless my daughter and give her a suitable name.'

He asked for the child to be brought forward. As Mitra held

the beautiful baby girl in his arms, a solution presented itself to him.

'I name this child Indrani, and on behalf of His Majesty the young prince Indra, I ask for her hand in marriage.'

There was a moment of silence. Nobody had expected this announcement. Vasu was the first to react. He clapped his hands in joy.

'Wonderful! My daughter could not have got a better match in the entire wide world. Thank you for doing my family this great honour, my lord.'

A loud cheer greeted this statement.

Mitra studied Vasu carefully; the regent seemed genuinely pleased with the unexpected turn of events. He now looked around for the other principal player in the equation, but the high priest had left as soon as he heard the announcement.

The next couple of weeks were filled with bright sunshine. Vasu put his young army through its paces by arranging a series of drills and mock combat. Mitra too joined in the war games, and everyone clamoured to cross swords with the legend. It was a story they would be able to tell their grandchildren one day. The master soon proved that age had not diminished his skills as a warrior in any way; he was still a superlative swordsman with boundless stamina. He ran through at least four or five opponents in a session. His victims, less than half his age, dropped their weapons in exhaustion and requested to be relieved.

Susena watched Mitra in action, resentment simmering in him as Ishtar fed his insecurities. In the old days, priests had been highly respected and feared in their tribal society. King and commoner alike consulted them in the all-important decisions of life. Daeyus, however, had shown a scant disregard for priests and all their rituals and divinations, and the Devas had followed his lead and slowly begun to turn away from them. Susena knew that with Indra on the throne, Mitra would be his advisor on all matters concerning the divine, and there would be no place for the high priest in the scheme of things.

Ishtar let these thoughts fester along with the constant reminder of the threat Indra posed to the survival of his tribe. She had underestimated Mitra again; his announcement at the birthday celebrations had been a political masterstroke. Now Ishtar would have to make sure that this egotistical ass that was under her control proceeded with extreme caution.

Indra, now old enough to crawl, was a child with boundless energy. The slightest chance he got and he would be off, chasing butterflies, beetles or any other form of creepy crawlies. If these unfortunate creatures happened to get caught, they found their way into his mouth very quickly. A worried Mahisi employed a small army of young slave girls to watch over him and he in turn made sure he kept all of them busy.

One of these girls had caught Susena's fancy. He now watched as she finished her duties and made her way through the camp. Unlike the other girls, she did not head straight back to the slave encampment but followed one of the streams in the opposite direction where it disappeared behind a circular formation of rocks. Susena made a mental note to himself that this one would bear watching.

The young girl entered the stream near the rock formation, still clad in her dirty, knee-length tunic. She dived into the water and made her way through an opening in the rocks. As she came up for air she was within the circle in a still, deep pool. This place offered her total privacy. She swam to a ledge and took off her tunic. A cloth was tightly wrapped around her chest, which she now proceeded to take off hurriedly.

Basit let out a deep sigh as the last bit of cloth was unwound, and her perfectly-shaped breasts emerged. She massaged them gently to allow the blood to circulate. This deception, though painful, was necessary. She had started her moon sickness over a year ago, yet she had cunningly concealed it from everyone. Even the unusually sharp eyes of Mahisi had not been able to detect anything.

Every month she gritted her teeth and bore the severe cramps, showing no outward signs of any discomfort. Her childhood was the only shield protecting her from the inevitable fate that awaited every beautiful slave woman. If her secret were discovered, Basit knew that the very men who now joked with her and laughed at her antics would turn on her like a pack of wolves. She hated her breasts and the fine down of hair that was now growing between her legs. She lay back on the ledge and allowed the sun to soak into her honey-coloured skin. These were the only few moments she got to enjoy being a young woman, and she was going to make the most of it.

She closed her eyes and thought about her days as a child, in her land along the banks of the great river Nile. She had been one of the privileged girls who had been selected as initiates to the temple of the great goddess Isis. She remembered the first few years she had spent in the temple, days filled with play and lots of religious study. Until the day the arrival of an army of horsemen had turned her perfect little world upside down.

Basit had watched from a little hiding place behind the altar as these men rushed into the sanctum sanctorum with drawn swords, showing utter disregard for the sanctity of the temple. The priestesses were rounded up and raped right there in the presence of the giant statue of the goddess. One by one the men took turns on the women, and Basit had spent the whole night listening to the screams of young priestesses who were like her older sisters.

The survivors and all the initiates were rounded up and marched across the desert along with the other men and women of the town. Along the way, Basit realised that she'd been left alone because the men saw her as a child. She'd barely survived the long and arduous journey that ended at the slave markets of Ecbatana. There she was bartered for a good Scythian horse and she found herself in the hands of Krupa, commander of the Devas.

Basit opened her eyes with a start as she came awake. The sun had disappeared behind the tallest rock. She gathered her clothing hurriedly and started to get dressed.

Vasu watched as the men finished their training for the day; it got dark very quickly in these mountains. He took a deep drag of the hemp pipe he was smoking and leaned back against a rock, allowing the smoke to slowly drift through his lungs. He had spent some time thinking about what Mitra had said. Could Indra be the child of the prophecy? He had heard it discussed once around the campfires when he was a child. It was a prophecy lost in the annals of time.

To unite the northern clans was an impossible task. Yet if it were accomplished, the man who did it would have under his command the most powerful fighting force in the world. But to lead them and earn their respect, he would have to be the greatest warrior the world had ever seen.

His mind then went to his daughter's birthday celebrations. The political ramifications of the betrothal had not escaped

Vasu. Now, away from Daeyus' shadow, he felt that he was coming into his own as a leader. He enjoyed the responsibility of leading the Devas, and it had started to bother him that the arrangement was only a temporary one. But when Susena had come to him with his stories about ill omens and demons, Vasu had gone along only because he thought there was a possibility that the high priest was right.

Vasu was a simple man; he had no wish to oppose the will of the gods. Mitra's position in the matter and the reminder of the prophecy had now made Vasu change his stance completely. As long as Mitra and Indra had the support of the clan, they would have his support.

True to his word, Chief Thora arrived in a few weeks with his men to inform the Devas that the road ahead was clear. The Pakhtu then escorted the caravan to their southern border. When the time came to part ways, the chief presented them with ten bundles of strong rope made from hemp, a plant that grew wild in the valleys.

'You will find it useful on the ride ahead. Have a safe journey, my friends. May the gods protect you.'

The Devas left the Pakhtu with another hundred head of cattle and went their way. The few weeks of good weather had vastly improved conditions and the mood of the caravan was remarkably upbeat as they continued their journey southwards. The trail wound downwards until they were soon well below the tree line. The Devas now marched through beautiful forests of rhododendrons and pines. The melting snow had transformed one of the larger streams into a gushing mountain river, and as they camped along its banks, the men ventured into the water filled with giant salmon. They speared the fish in vast numbers and grilled them at the campfires; it made a welcome change from the usual fare of meat and dairy products.

They made good progress in the summer months. On occasion they came into contact with other mountain tribes and traded with them. Since fresh meat was the most precious commodity in these parts, they were always able to negotiate with them for the best campsites on their land.

Mitra chose to withdraw from his administrative duties and spent a lot of time alone on the trail. Sometimes he would be gone for days, riding well ahead of all the scouting parties. He was a little anxious: the months of good weather were going by fast; it was time for them to find a more permanent settlement, where they would be able to comfortably ride out the brutal winter. All the valleys they had encountered thus far had not been large enough to accommodate them and their vast herds for that length of time. Finally, he decided to make camp in one such valley for a few days while they awaited the arrival of their scouts, who had gone ahead to reconnoitre the trail.

Basit woke early one morning and made her way through the forest, she was extremely happy—her hard work had paid off and she was now part of Mahisi's personal staff. This meant that she did not have to live in the slave encampment anymore. Finally, her life was starting to look up.

She made her way through the trees as she looked for a secluded spot on the banks of the stream where she could bathe. At a safe distance, Susena followed her. He watched her as she moved gracefully through the trees, his mouth dry with excitement. He was going to enjoy the task at hand.

Basit shivered as the cold water enveloped her naked body. She proceeded to wash herself as she hummed a song from her childhood. The sound of a pebble clattering against a rock startled her and she turned sharply. Only a few feet away, resplendent in his robes of blue, stood the high priest Susena. Basit covered her breasts with her arms and slowly made her way towards the rock where she had laid her tunic, but the high priest beat her to it. He placed one foot on her tunic and beckoned her to come towards him.

Terror stricken, Basit complied. She had seen the victims of the high priest's amorous advances return torn and bleeding to the slave camp and heard their horror stories of Susena's perversions. She shut her eyes and prayed to the divine mother for protection.

The high priest's eyes ran appreciatively up and down her body. 'Surya be praised! The little bud has transformed into such a beautiful flower and I did not even notice it.'

He brushed her arms aside, held one of her erect nipples between his fingers and squeezed hard. She let out a gasp of pain. He laughed and continued to fondle her nipple, but this time he was gentler.

Basit felt them harden, and she tried hard to control her arousal, ashamed of it. Susena watched her squirm, revelling in her discomfort. Basit now felt his fingers move slowly up her thighs. Fortunately for her, it was not Susena's boorish ego that controlled his hand; it was controlled by another, peerless in the art of love.

She felt his fingers between her legs, strumming her like a harp, sending shivers of pleasure through her body. Her breathing began to get ragged as she hungered for more. Susena expertly guided his index finger into her moist interior. He was very gentle.

By now Basit had lost all sense of modesty. She began to push herself against his hand. Susena watched her closely, her eyes were shut and her head was thrown back. She ground her hips against his hand as she moaned in pleasure. Then she stiffened, her beautiful face contorted in rapturous joy, she felt herself about to explode into a mind-numbing orgasm, when Susena suddenly stopped.

Her eyes snapped open. She had been soaring towards the gates of heaven only to be brought crashing down to the earth. Susena stared deeply into her eyes. She watched fascinated as the high priest raised his still moist finger to his mouth and slowly sucked on it. Basit shuddered in pleasure looking at him. He moved his face close to her ear and whispered huskily. 'This is a mere drop compared to the ocean of pleasure you will experience if you do my bidding.'

Basit hesitated, unsure what the man had in mind. Susena sensed her misgivings. 'Of course you could refuse, but I will still have my way with you and I promise you I will not be so gentle. Then I will leave you to the soldiers. After they are finished with you, I don't know if you would be fit to serve a fine lady like Mahisi.'

Ishtar had sensed her deepest fear and used it to force her hand. His words had the desired effect. Basit fell at his feet and kissed them. 'I am the dust at your feet, my lord, I live only to serve you.'

Susena smiled smugly, as he leaned forward and told her exactly what she would have to do.

It was late afternoon on a particularly beautiful day in the valley. Under a pine tree, Mahisi sang Indra a lullaby and put him to sleep. She laid him down gently on a little bearskin mattress and asked the guards to keep watch. She then quietly made her way into the forest. Basit watched her mistress leave; she knew exactly where she was headed.

As Mahisi hurried through the woods, humming a pleasant tune, somewhere ahead a young soldier was waiting for her. To the other members of the clan she was still the grieving widow, so she had to be discreet; but she had needs, and this young man fulfilled them more than adequately.

The guards were also caught up in the laziness of that lovely afternoon. One of them noticed Basit making her way towards them. In her hand the beautiful girl was carrying a clay pot full of mead appropriated from Susena's fine stocks. She greeted the guards in her usual shy way.

'Good day my brave warriors, I have brought you a gift, a little something to enjoy this beautiful day.'

She held the vessel out to them. The guards looked at each other hesitantly, and finally the older one reached for it and took a swig; the liquor was vastly superior to any he had tasted before. He handed the pot to the young man who looked apprehensive but gingerly took a small sip. He enjoyed the sweet liquor so much that he put it to his lips again and drank a big mouthful. The heady liquor induced a coughing fit; the older man snatched the pot away and gave his companion a contemptuous look. He then took an equally big draught. Basit watched this exchange impatiently.

'My brave warriors, perhaps you should find a place a little more discreet. If the regent found you drinking on duty, he would skin you alive.'

The two men were quick to spot the wisdom in her words and they sauntered off into the nearby trees bearing the pot of liquor with them.

Basit watched them leave. She had added a powerful sleep-inducing narcotic to the liquor. It wouldn't be long now before the two men would start to feel its effects. She had all the time she would need to accomplish her task. She looked at the ring on her finger, a gift from the high priest. She carefully tugged at the shiny black stone set in the middle of it. It came away in her fingers, revealing a tiny, sharp needle. She carefully turned the ring to face her palm. All she had to do now was inflict a tiny scratch on the baby as she picked him up. The poison would instantly find its way through his blood stream into his tiny beating heart and stop it forever.

Susena watched his beautiful assassin ready herself for the task at hand. In spite of the risk involved, a morbid sense of curiosity had dragged him towards the scene of crime. He wanted to savour his moment of triumph at close quarters.

Just then, a shadow passed over him and caused him to look up. A magnificent eagle flew overhead, bearing a sinuous black reptile in its talons. A little ahead, Basit looked at the baby fast asleep on the ground. His golden ringlets moved gently in the breeze. Her heart broke as she prayed. 'Forgive me, sweet Isis, for what I am about to do.'

Tears rolled down her cheeks as she bent towards Indra.

The eagle was now flying directly over her. It suddenly dropped its prey and the snake landed on Basit's shoulder, coiling itself around her neck. Basit stood up in shock. The snake raised its hood and its tongue flicked out, gently caressing her cheek. Basit recognised the reptile, it was one of the most feared creatures in her homeland. How it had found itself so far away in these frozen mountains was beyond her understanding. The Egyptian cobra struck her on the cheek and she fell to the ground, writhing in agony.

Basit tried to scream but only bubbles of froth came out of her mouth. The last thing she saw was the pair of lidless black eyes that stared blankly at her.

Susena stood transfixed as he watched the horrific scene unfold in front of his eyes. Two mortal enemies had colluded to thwart his plans. The eagle had alighted on a branch of a pine tree; it now stared impassively at him. The message was clear to Susena, the earth and the sky stood watch over this child. Now no one could do it harm.

The cobra turned towards the high priest who stood there, terror petrifying him. As the snake opened its mouth and hissed at him, two tiny jets of venom flew out of its fangs, striking Susena squarely in the eyes. The high priest fell to the ground, his hands clutched to his face as he screamed in agony.

From her vantage point high above her magnificent city, Ishtar sighed wistfully; she had played her last hand. Now she resigned herself to the inevitable.

The screams brought men and women running out of their tents; even the two guards were woken from their induced sleep. They arrived to see no sign of the snake; only the bodies of the high priest and the slave girl lay on the ground, their faces twisted in acute agony. Indra, who had woken up with the noise, was waving his tiny hands and kicking his legs in the air happily. Above them, the eagle sat on the high branches of the pine tree and proceeded to finish his interrupted meal.

Oblivious to the dramatic developments around them, Mitra and Vasu were locked in conference in the regent's tent. The scouting party's return was long overdue. The Deva scouts prided themselves on their discipline and sense of duty, and Mitra knew that if they had not shown up yet, there was probably good reason. He feared the worst.

A young squire rushed into the tent, head bowed, all breathless with anxiety.

'My lords! Please come quick.'

Mitra and Vasu rushed to the spot to see a red-faced Mahisi clutching Indra to her bosom and showering him with kisses. Irritated with the excessive attention, the child started to cry.

As Mitra surveyed the ground where the horrific event had occurred, it became clear to him what had happened. The two victims had died of snake-bite but as far as he knew, there were no venomous snakes in this region, at least none capable of delivering this kind of a death. He smiled as he realised that he was not alone in looking out for the welfare of the child. Unseen forces were at hand to aid him in his efforts. He turned to the regent.

'My lord, I don't think it's wise to remain here any longer. Let us march on and hope that we meet up with the scouts along the way.'

The green forests were soon left behind as the trail once again snaked upwards. The smiles now started to disappear as the strain of the climb began to tell on the faces of the Devas. Mitra, now satisfied that all the immediate threats to Indra's life had been removed, once again began to ride out alone on scouting expeditions. On one such trip, with the caravan at least a day's journey behind him, he topped a rise and reined in his horse. Ahead of him the mountainside was covered with a thick blanket of snow.

Mitra alighted and looked around for an alternate route. Across the snow, he noticed some movement. It was a horse. From the look of its saddle trims and reins, Mitra knew that the horse belonged to one of the missing scouts. He called out to the animal; it neighed as it heard his voice but stood its ground. Mitra thought perhaps its rider was lying around nearby, hurt. He started to lead his horse carefully across the snow. It was hard and slippery; the horse wasn't too happy with the situation and whinnied its displeasure.

Mitra was halfway across the snowfield when he heard a loud sound, like thunder. He looked to the heavens, expecting rain, but the sky was clear. Then he heard it again and looked up at the face of the mountain. The entire slope that he was standing on was breaking away and starting to slide down the mountain. His horse panicked and tried to bolt back. Mitra turned to grab it but he was too late, the ice slid under the animal and knocked it off its feet. He watched helplessly as the hapless creature tumbled down the mountainside.

The block of ice Mitra was balancing on was travelling at a good speed now. He looked ahead, rapidly surveying the situation and saw fairly stable ground to his left. There was a ten-foot gap in between which was increasing very quickly, and Mitra knew he needed to act fast. He took a couple of paces back, ran forward and took a long desperate leap. He landed on the stable block of ice with a couple of feet to spare, but there was no time to celebrate as this block too broke away and hurtled down the slope.

Mitra struggled to retain his balance; he knew he had to stay on his feet if he wanted to survive. Ahead to his left, he saw a fairly large boulder protruding out of the snow. He timed his jump to perfection, hit the ground and rolled on his shoulders twice to reach the boulder. As he rested his back against it and looked up, he saw a gigantic wall of ice rushing towards him. He hugged his knees to his chest, tucked his head down and prepared for the inevitable.

When he came to his senses, Mitra found himself buried in a tomb of ice. Both his shins were broken from the impact of the avalanche. He managed to create a little space to move his right hand and started to claw at the snow with his fingers. As his hand brushed past his ribcage, he felt a stab of pain as though somebody had inserted a dagger into his side. He realised that he had broken a couple of ribs. He slowly reached towards his waist for his dagger. He felt the hilt and smiled with relief—now he had a fighting chance. He drew in his breath as he pulled it out of its sheath. His broken ribs grated against each other and caused him to cry out sharply.

Mitra took a moment to survey the situation. It was only the intense physical conditioning from his tapas in the Himalayas that had kept him alive till now. It would not be long before the intense pain and the cold rapidly drained his energy. He had to get off this slope and quickly. As a seer, Mitra had no great attachment to his body; he saw it as a vehicle for his soul. Death was not something he feared; to him it was merely the culmination of one journey and the start of another. But now he forced himself to stay alive, if only for the sake of the boy Indra. He gritted his teeth and started to dig.

A few agonising hours later he broke through the surface of the snow. The night sky was clear, filled with a billion stars. Their astounding beauty gave Mitra another reason to stay alive. As he dragged his broken body out of what could have been his tomb, he realised that both his legs were broken. He would have to use the strength of his arms to pull himself up the slope and back towards the trail. Using the dagger like an ice axe, he dragged his broken body across the snow.

Mitra tried to get his mind off the excruciating pain that coursed through his body and made slow but steady progress up the slope. He had to find some kind of shelter soon or he would not live to see another sunrise. After five hours, he was completely exhausted. He could no longer feel his arms. He took a few moments' rest. By his estimate, the trail would be another two hours' climb from his current position. He wiggled his fingers and rubbed his hands together to keep them warm, but the break was only causing his body to freeze up again, so he grabbed the hilt of the dagger and started to climb again.

He had only gone a few more paces when, somewhere high on the mountain, he heard another loud, cracking sound. He forced himself to a sitting position, pain shooting through his broken shins as he looked around frantically for some shelter. Then he saw something that gave him a sliver of hope.

Ten paces up and to his right, there was a deep crack in the ice. From his current position it looked just about big enough to offer a man shelter. All exhaustion was forgotten as the adrenaline kicked in and Mitra started to move. After a few excruciating minutes, he reached the crack and fell through it, rolling into a cave below. He screamed both in pain and triumph—he was alive. Another cracking noise came from the outside and Mitra saw tons of ice sliding over the mouth of the cave. He closed his eyes and let himself drift off into blissful oblivion.

A cold draught of air woke him up in the morning. He noticed that it was coming from the back of the cave. It could only mean one thing; there was another way out. Curious, Mitra started to pull himself in the direction of the draught. As he made his way, he realised that this was not a cave but a tunnel, probably created by running water.

A few paces inside, the tunnel started to slope downwards. It was wide enough for Mitra to lie down across it. He now tucked his arms into his sides to protect his shattered ribcage, and rolled down the tunnel. By the time he got to the end of it, the ground had levelled out again. Mitra crawled out to the mouth of the tunnel and peered outside. What he saw made him forget his pain. He laughed, till he had tears rolling down his cheeks.

Outside, the sun had just begun to rise over the distant hills on the horizon. Bathed in its golden light were miles and miles of green grasslands interspersed with wooded thickets; a wilderness paradise of unparalleled beauty. It was the plateau of Gandhar. Mitra lay on his back and said a silent prayer to the Sun God. Their long and arduous journey was about to come to an end.

4

It was a sun-kissed afternoon on one of the beautiful open meadows of Gandhar. Mitra took his mare through her paces as he headed south across the endless grasslands. In front of him on the saddle, his tiny fingers clutching the flowing mane of the steed, sat Indra, now a boy of four. His curly blond hair billowed in the breeze, and his cheeks were red, flushed by the thrill of the ride. He was screaming in excitement.

'Faster, Mitta! Faster!

Mitra indulged him by digging his heels gently into the mare's sides. As the mare increased her pace, it only served to excite the child more.

'Faster, Mitta! Mysi told me my father could ride as fast as the wind. I want to ride as fast as the wind, Mitta.'

Mitra laughed.

'You will one day, my prince. But not today, I'm an old man and I'm scared.'

The boy was quiet as he digested this piece of information. After some thought, he spoke.

'Don't worry, Mitta. When I'm king, you will ride with me into battle. We will ride like the wind and destroy our enemies.'

Mitra laughed. Growing up with Mahisi and her constantly

gossiping women folk, had helped the boy's vocabulary immensely. But Mitra hoped Indra didn't pick up on every conversation those women had; some of it could make even the crudest of warriors blush.

'I shall wait eagerly for that day, my prince. Now we must slow down, the mare is tired and she needs to drink.'

'Okay, Mitta.'

As the mare slowed down to a walk, Indra stroked its neck and hugged it.

Mitra led the horse up a slight rise in the land from where they could get a view of the terrain ahead. The child was quiet as he watched a herd of antelope speeding into the woods away from them.

Ahead lay a stream and a thicket of woods, beyond which, as far as the eye could see, was a wetland teeming with crocodiles, poisonous snakes and other dangerous creatures. It had been four years since Mitra had ridden this far south. He had come here during their first summer in Gandhar to mark the borders of their land. The wetland marked the southern boundary of Aryavarta; that was the name Mitra had given their settlement.

He alighted from the horse and gently led it down to the stream. There he helped Indra down and watched as the child ran around in excitement. He sat down under the shade of a tree; his hip ached a little from the long ride, a reminder of his encounter with the avalanche. It had taken him three months to recover from that ordeal.

Mitra had chosen to live away from the settlement, a little further upstream along the banks of the river. He built a little hut there and soon had a garden to grow his herbs and vegetables. After the first year, he left the administrative duties of Aryavarta in the capable hands of Vasu, and spent his time doing tapas. Any spare time he had, he spent at Mahisi's home with Indra, telling and retelling the old stories of the northern tribes.

He suddenly remembered the child and looked around for him. There was no sign of the boy. A worried Mitra got to his feet and called out to Indra. A rustle in the nearby bushes drew his attention and he saw the child walk out carrying what looked like a big bundle in his hands.

'Mitta! Mitta! Look what I found.'

Whatever it was, it was alive and had Indra tottering under its weight. Then suddenly, it let out an indignant little growl. Mitra's eyes widened with surprise as he realised what it was—a lion cub. It looked no more than a week old by the size of it. Mitra drew his sword and looked anxiously about. The last thing he wanted was to be confronted by an angry lioness. The child now sat down and hugged the cub tightly to his chest. Mitra went up to him.

'You must let it go, my prince; a lion cub cannot be your pet.'

Indra held the cub closer to his chest.

'No! He is mine. I found him.'

Mitra knew how stubborn his little ward could be, so he tried a different approach.

'The cub's mother must be looking for him, my child, you must let it go.'

Indra was not ready to buy that.

'But it was alone when I found it. What if it has no mother or father, like me? Please Mitta, I will look after him well.'

At this point, the lion cub took matters into its own hands or paws. It struck out at Indra's hand and scratched him on his forearm. The child let out a sharp cry and let go. The cub ran into the bushes. He turned to Mitra, fighting back his tears.

'Why did he do that, Mitta? I only wanted to be his friend.'

Mitra took the child in his arms and gave him a hug.

'He will never be your friend, my child, the next time you see each other, one of you will kill the other.'

Indra broke free from the hug and said indignantly, 'Kill each other? Why?'

'Because, one day, you and he will want the same thing: to be king of this land.'

Mitra watched the child silently absorb this piece of information.

The sound of an approaching rider stopped the conversation going further. It was one of the young warriors assigned to protect the prince. The man alighted and bowed formally.

'My lord, the lady Mahisi has sent me to request that you and the prince return immediately.'

Mitra was puzzled at the urgency in the man's voice.

'Why? What seems to be the problem, young man?'

'It is a mist, sir. It has risen out of the east and threatens to cover the whole plateau.'

Mitra picked up the child and hoisted him on to his mount. As the two of them rode back, Indra was unusually silent, lost in thought.

The young herdsman stood on a little grassy knoll and called out in a low voice to his cattle. The mist was coming in thick and fast, visibility was already very poor and the herd was still a long way from the stockade. The young man strained his eyes as he looked for the lead bull; once he got his attention, the rest of the herd would fall in line.

From his elevated position, he could see the blanket of mist approach and soon it was all around him. He called out again to the lead bull. There was no response. The boy was worried at this rather uncharacteristic development, he wondered if he should use his horn and sound the alarm. Just then he heard a loud bellow; it was the bull.

The boy was worried as he hurried down the slope in the direction of the sound. This had clearly not been an acknowledgment of his call; this was a cry of alarm. The boy gripped his staff and ran through the thick fog. The last time he had heard a bull make that sound was when he was very young and it had preceded a wolf attack. Around him, he heard the cows and calves start to panic and run helter-skelter. He called out to them and was pleased to see the immediate calming effect his voice had on them.

Ahead, he heard a thud; it was the sound of a heavy body hitting the ground. The boy hesitated for one brief moment, it would be foolish to run into a pack of wolves armed with only a staff, but he was a Deva, he would never be able to face his tribe again with the knowledge that he had just stood there and done nothing to save the animals in his charge. He gripped his staff tighter. Maybe he could crack the skull of the pack leader. That might persuade the rest to leave.

Although he knew that his plan had only a slim chance of success, the boy bravely moved forward. He crouched low in the grass, straining his eyes, hoping to catch sight of the cursed beasts before they saw him. A shape loomed large ahead of him. He recognised it through the mist and tears ran down his face, it was the carcass of the lead bull.

The young man tried to control his grief and anger at the loss even as he realised something was very wrong. There was no sound of the feeding frenzy that usually followed a kill. In fact, except for the restless sounds of his herd, there was absolutely no sign of wolves.

The herdsman knelt beside the carcass and looked for any sign of the predators. There were no pugmarks—the only tracks around, other than that of his cattle, seemed human. Suddenly the young man became aware of a strange smell around him, it was the smell of blood and rotting meat. He felt something warm against the back of his neck. It was hot breath.

The herdsman turned sharply, swinging his staff, but something grabbed it and ripped it out of his hands as if it were a toy. He found himself staring into a pair of malevolent red eyes. Even as he opened his mouth to scream, a sharp pair of canines closed around his throat and tore away his windpipe, silencing him.

Mitra stood outside his hermitage and looked out into the mist. He had never seen anything like this in the four years they'd been at the plateau of Gandhar. It had been a few days since it had come in, and now the mist hung like a thick blanket over the entire plateau.

Mitra hated this weather. He'd barely moved out of his hut the last few days, preferring to devote the time to his meditation. Only an urgent summons from Vasu had got him out today. He whistled for his mare and leapt onto her back. As he made his way along the river, he soon spotted the dull glow of the oil lamps that told him that the settlement was near.

In the short time they had been there, Vasu had proved to be a more than capable administrator. Aryavarta, the first permanent settlement of the Devas, had been planned very well. The houses were arranged in three concentric semi-circles along the bank of the river. At the centre stood the Sabha, a sixteen-pillared wooden structure, under the roof of which the tribal council met. In front of the building was a massive clearing, at the centre of which was the sacrificial pyre. Around the clearing, tiny stalls had been erected for the weekly market. Further down river to the west were the farms and the military barracks, along with the slave quarters.

As Mitra rode through the settlement, he could see small groups of people gathered around fires in front of their homes. It was evening, and bards and storytellers had got together to sing and recount tales of valour. As he passed close to a group, Mitra caught the words of an old ballad; it was sung to ward off evil spirits. The last four years had been the most peaceful the tribe had ever known. Barring a few skirmishes with lions and wolves, there had been hardly any chance of action. He smiled as he thought to himself, 'Evil spirits! With no enemies around, that was the best thing the storyteller could come up with to scare folk!'

He guided his mare through the two rows of torches that lit the path to the Sabha's entrance.

Mitra was surprised by the silence that greeted him in the hall. Usually it echoed with light banter and idle boasts. Today, though, the atmosphere was surprisingly sombre. A young officer stood in the well of the house. He appeared tense and uneasy. As soon as he caught sight of Mitra, Vasu rose and walked across to greet him.

The last few years of inactivity were starting to tell on the old warrior: his fine robes could not conceal the belly that was starting to assume enormous proportions.

'Greetings, Master Mitra! Thank you for honouring us with your presence at such short notice.'

He ushered Mitra to a seat next to his own and turned to address the gathering.

'You may begin.'

The young officer bowed respectfully.

'I am Paras, son of Atar.'

A murmur of appreciation went through the sixteen members of the Sabha; his father had been a brave soldier and a vital member of Daeyus' army.

'I was leading the night patrol yesterday on our eastern border near the Forest of Cedars when we came upon a dead bull. On examining the carcass, I found that its windpipe had been crushed. The bite marks around the wound were unlike that of any lion or wolf.'

Paras hesitated for a moment, unsure about how to continue.

'No attempt had been made to eat or drag the carcass away either, my lords.'

Murmurs went up among the members. Mitra said nothing. He looked at the young warrior, who clearly had something more to say. He held up his hand for silence as he addressed Paras.

'So what did you do?'

Paras bowed respectfully to Mitra as he answered.

'We scoured the area for tracks. In spite of the mist, the signs were quite easy to read. Thirty head of cattle had been led away into the Forest of Cedars.'

Paras hesitated for a moment before he continued.

'The tracks were almost human, my lord.'

'Almost! What do you mean almost?' one of the members asked in a hushed voice.

The Sabha was now rife with speculation: enemy tribes, monsters, ghosts and ghouls, all manner of explanations were offered. Vasu did not like where the conversations were heading. He asked the assembly for order as he turned to Paras.

'The herdsman, where is he?'

Paras' voice choked with emotion.

'Missing, my lord. I request permission to lead a patrol into the forest to find him.'

Vasu cut him off.

'No, you have done more than anyone can ask, now leave it to us.'

Paras' eyes welled up.

'Please, my lord! I must try to save him. He is my brother, the only family I have left in this world.'

Vasu was shocked.

'Why didn't you try and find him immediately?'

Paras had tears running down his cheeks.

'Our orders were to patrol the border, my lord. The men under me are still in the reserves, they have not seen any action, and I did not want to risk their lives chasing an unknown enemy into the mist. But please, my lord, allow me now to get together a team of volunteers and look for my brother.'

Vasu and the rest of the members leaned forward to confabulate. Mitra looked at the young man, admiring how he had not let emotion sway him from his duty.

'Brave Paras, I require a saddle for my mare please. Will you see to it?'

'Right away, my lord.'

Mitra waited for the young man to leave before he turned to address the Sabha.

'With your kind permission, my lord regent, I would like a couple of days to look into this matter.'

Vasu smiled with relief. He had racked his brains as to whom he could entrust with this mystery. He could not have come up with a better choice.

'My lord, my elite guard is at your disposal.'

Mitra smiled. 'I will need only Paras.'

A perplexed Vasu signalled to the guard. In a moment, Paras rushed in, his face flushed with excitement. Mitra turned to him.

'Go gather your weapons and a couple of days' supplies for the two of us and wait for me outside.'

Paras eagerly ran to do his bidding. Vasu adjourned the Sabha. As the members left one by one, he turned to Mitra.

'A word with you, my lord, before you leave.'

Mitra sat down as the rest of the members wished him well and left. When they were alone, Vasu turned to him.

'Master, three years ago you asked me to declare the Forest of Cedars on our eastern border out of bounds for our people. What exactly was it that you saw there? You did not explain then.'

Mitra thought back to that bright summer's day. He had been on one of his exploratory missions around the plateau. None of the Deva patrols had ventured that far east yet. He had ridden into the Forest of Cedars and, almost immediately, sensed something strange about the place. There'd been an almost foreboding silence within it: none of the usual birdcalls and cries of animals; in fact, there had been no signs of life.

A half-day's ride later, the forest started to slope downwards into a deep valley shrouded by mist. As Mitra slowly started down the steep incline, he heard the cry of a deer. The animal seemed mortally wounded.

Mitra made his way in the direction of the cry and came upon the deer lying on the forest floor, bleeding from a wound on its neck. The hunter was nowhere in sight. As the mist slowly rose, enveloping him and the dead animal, Mitra cast his awareness around into the valley, seeking out any presence or aura.

It came to him like a reeking smell—a strong, malevolent presence. It seemed to be all around him, watching his every move. Then he heard a voice in his head; there was no mistaking the menace in its tone.

'Stay away, stranger. This is our land.'

Mitra had looked around, but all he could see was the rapidly rising mist.

'My lord! Is everything all right?' Vasu's voice brought Mitra back to the present.

The seer got to his feet quickly.

'Yes, my lord regent! I have no answers for you right now, but I intend to find them. Now, I shall take your leave.'

There was an hour or so still left to daylight when Mitra and Paras found themselves standing on the banks of a stream. They had ridden hard through nearly zero visibility. Both Paras and his horse knew their way through the mist and Mitra had been glad to follow the younger man's lead. Across the stream, now hidden behind thick layers of fog, lay the forbidding Forest of Cedars.

Mitra alighted and knelt on the bank. He could see the tracks of the cattle leading into the stream.

'I think it would be best that we wait for first light.'

'As you wish, my lord.'

The two men tethered their horses and sat down under a tree. Mitra could see that Paras was anxious, but he did not want to give the young man any false hopes regarding his brother. Weighing his words carefully, he said, 'If they haven't killed him earlier, they are not going to do it now.'

'I pray to all the gods that you are right.'

Paras knew it was unlikely his brother was still alive, yet he preferred to let hope guide him on this quest, rather than vengeance.

'Well, they have thirty head of cattle to butcher. That will take some doing. Now get some rest.'

Mitra stretched out under the tree and immediately fell asleep.

Early the next morning the two men broke camp quickly and were soon across the stream on the narrow trail that cut through the forest.

As they ventured deeper into the forest, the mist thickened and soon it was dark as night. Paras shivered as he felt a chill in the air. Next to him, Mitra was a dark shape on a horse. He gripped his lance tightly; Mitra had asked him to leave behind his armour and shield before they set off, and now he felt strangely vulnerable.

As they approached the point where the forest floor began its steep incline, Mitra asked Paras to slow down. They stood on the lip of the slope and peered down, again Mitra got wind of that strange malevolent presence. Even Paras' uninitiated mind seemed to sense something. He spat on the ground in disgust.

'The air in this place reeks of evil, my lord.'

The sound of something crashing through the branches behind made both men turn around sharply. On the forest floor lay the corpse of a young man. Paras cried out in shock as he recognised his brother. All the blood seemed to have been drained from his body.

Mitra was furious as he scanned the forest with his mind. He soon detected the presence, a short distance away, perched high above them on a tree. The creature seemed to be alone. Mitra used telepathy to communicate with it.

'For three years we heeded your warning and did not set foot in here, not because we feared you, but for the sake of peace. What was the need for this provocation?'

'Provocation! You brought your vast herds of animals and drove away all the deer and the wild goats from these lands. My people have nothing to hunt and are starving!'

'So you attack and kill defenceless young boys?'

There was no immediate reply; the creature seemed to be pondering what Mitra had said. Mitra grabbed Paras by the shoulder and pointed with his staff the precise location of the creature.

'The boy was brave,' the creature finally said. 'He stood his ground and tried to fight. He did not give us a choice.'

As Mitra released his shoulder, Paras leaned back and flung his spear in the direction pointed out by Mitra. A sharp cry told the two men that the weapon had found its mark. The creature hit the ground with a thud. Through the mist, they saw the dark shape stand upright and wrench the spear out of its shoulder. Then it bounded towards Paras on all fours and, with an incredible burst of speed, leapt for his throat.

Mitra was the first to react. He swung his staff at the beast. The hard knot of wood at one end caught the creature on the side of its head, just as its jaws were a few inches from Paras' throat. The impact threw it to one side, where it lay breathing heavily. Paras advanced towards it, sword raised.

The creature shook its head as if to clear it and turned towards them, sitting in an upright position. Mitra was surprised to observe how it naturally assumed the lotus position, a sitting position favoured only by seers and holy men. Its skin was pale and transparent, so its veins and arteries could clearly be seen. Its hairless, naked body did not seem to be affected by the cold. The face was feral, with a slightly protruding nose and jaw. Its eyes, with its red pupils, were perfectly adapted to see in poor light. It had big pointed ears and an impressive set of canines, which it revealed as it grinned at them.

Mitra, looking into the creature's eyes, caught a glimpse of the human being within.

Paras watched in shock as the wound inflicted by his spear on the creature's shoulder miraculously closed up, leaving no scar in its place. The creature turned to Paras, and he could hear its thoughts clearly in his head.

'It is I who killed your brother. Take my head by all means if you must, young man, for that is the only way to kill one of us.

But before that I pray that you listen to my story, for it might be useful to you and your kind. You, who are about to rule this land that once belonged to my tribe.'

The creature looked at the two men, amused by the shock on their faces.

'I am Uruk, of the Pisacha tribe, who once ruled this beautiful plateau. Many years ago, when I was a young warrior, I led a hunting party to one of the mountain slopes to the east. There we saw a bright pillar of light appear in the heavens, shining down on the mountaintop.

'While the others were scared, I was of a curious bent of mind, so I climbed the mountain to investigate. When I reached the top, I came upon seven beings, priests of some kind. They wore robes with hoods that kept their faces covered. Their leader touched me on my forehead and spoke to me using his thoughts. He forbade me to speak of what I saw there or ever return. I had no idea how they had got up there or how they survived with no food and protection from the elements. The only way to the top of the mountain was through our land and our tribe had never come in contact with them, ever.

'I went back and spoke to no one, not even my family, about what had happened up there. But almost immediately I noticed the change that had occurred in me. I was able to read thoughts and communicate with others mentally. I also received the gift of healing. For a while I tried to keep it secret, but it was hard to conceal such powers for long from the other members of the tribe. Soon my hut was always filled with people wanting to be treated for all sorts of ailments.

'As my popularity grew, it began to worry the chief and he

decided to send his guards after me. While I got wind of the plot early, I was unable to save my family. They were ruthlessly slaughtered. A few faithful companions and I escaped and made our way up the mountain. We were hit by a blizzard that raged for days. While it warded off our pursuers it left us exposed on the mountain face, completely cut off from our land.

'For days we waited for the weather to yield, but to no avail. With no food and faced with the prospect of freezing to death, I made the decision to disobey the beings and make our way once again to the summit. This time at the top there was no pillar of light to greet me. Instead I saw a crude temple made from the huge rocks lying there. Inside, the seven of them sat in a circle engaged in some kind of a ritual. The leader politely requested us to leave, as they did not have any food to offer us.

'We looked at these beings. They seemed to be in perfect physical condition. How was this possible if they had no food to eat? We became angry that they did not want to share their food with us. Tired and starving, I do not know what madness overcame me. I gave the order to attack.

'The beings offered no resistance. As their hoods were swept aside, we saw that they had huge, oval-shaped heads, completely devoid of any hair. Their eyes were large, with pupils that were dark blue and seemed to gaze into the very depth of our souls. Though their bodies looked young, they seemed to carry the wisdom of the ages in their eyes.

'Hunger had pushed me beyond the limits of reason where I could pay attention to any of these signs. I had become a savage beast. I struck the leader on the head with my club. He did not cry out, but fell down and continued to stare at me. His eyes, strangely enough, seemed to be filled with pity.

'With no wood to make a fire and no strength left to butcher their carcasses, I gave the order to slit their throats and drink their living blood. In my madness, I told myself that if their mere touch had given me these powers, drinking their lifeblood would turn us into supermen or even gods. As we drank to our heart's content, a deep sleep overcame each one of us. This is the way we found ourselves when we awoke. As for those beings, their bodies had vanished without a trace.'

Uruk's savage face underwent a startling transformation and he started to weep. Mitra watched him in silence, amazed by his story. He scanned the creature's mind, looking for signs of deceit. There were none. Who were these beings? Why were they living on this remote mountaintop?

'So do your men share your regret at their fate?' Mitra asked Uruk.

The creature spat on the ground in disgust. 'They have become mindless beasts whose lives are governed by the thirst, for that is our curse. We have been forever dismissed from the light to skulk in dark corners and suffer this insatiable thirst for fresh blood.'

Mitra realised that, for his part as the principal in the incident, Uruk had to carry the burden of his human conscience within this grotesque body. He felt only pity for this unfortunate creature as he asked him to continue with his tale.

'We found another way down the mountain, a secret passageway through its depths. There we waited, fearful of the sun, all the while suffering the thirst. I blamed the chief for our plight and decided to exact a terrible revenge on him and his supporters within the tribe. But the village was more than two days' march from the mountain, with no protection from the sun on the plateau.

'I waited patiently for months, till one day fortune finally favoured us. A mist descended on the plateau. We waited for the cover of night and then attacked our old village. However, I did not bargain for the bestiality of my companions. Once I unleashed them on the village, they proved to be impossible to control. The end of the carnage left not one male member of our tribe alive. They were all slaughtered, down to the last child. I selected a few young and fertile women and fed them with my own infected blood to turn them. We needed them to breed the next generation of the Pisacha.'

Uruk took a deep breath, it was as if a great weight had been lifted off his shoulders. He had a faraway look in his eyes.

'We have lived and hunted here ever since, never leaving this forest except once every four or five years, when the mist comes in and the entire plateau of Gandhar becomes our hunting ground once again.'

He stood up and bowed his head.

'My people lack the intelligence to see the futility of our present existence. But I have no desire left to live like this anymore. So take my head, warrior, and avenge your brother.'

Paras was calm as he said, 'I have no wish to go against the gods who have condemned you to this existence. But know this, man or beast or whatever you may be, if you ever venture into our lands again we will hunt down every last one of you. It will be like you and your kind never existed on this earth.'

Mitra was pleased with the young warrior's restraint. He knew how much Paras wanted to avenge the death of his brother. He now stood up and addressed Uruk.

'Let us now come to an understanding. The stream that flows through the western border of the Forest of Cedars marks the end of your land and the beginning of ours. Let that line never be crossed.'

Uruk clenched his right fist and placed it on his heart, his savage face now almost serene.

'The Pisacha will always honour this pact, Master.'

He turned and leapt in the air, and then all they heard was the rustling of leaves as the mist and the trees swallowed him up.

They rode back in silence, each man lost in thought at all he had heard and witnessed.

'Do you think the Pisacha will keep their word?'

Mitra took his time to reply.

'It is not the Pisacha I worry about. It is us.'

5

It was the first hour after dawn and the clanging of bronze from Mitra's hermitage carried far across the quiet plain. In the little courtyard, Mitra sat with four young men watching a duel in progress. The boys were engrossed in the fight.

Varuna, the oldest, was leaning back on his elbows, affecting disinterest, but following every move closely. Next to him, Agni jumped up and down, screaming encouragement. He had to be restrained physically by Mitra as he nearly fell into the combat area in his excitement. Vayu, the third boy, was physically the largest. His shoulders and neck were thick with muscle and belied his youth. He was a good-tempered lad with a sense of humour to match. He taunted the two fighters, questioned their manhood, and made ribald jokes. Soma, the youngest, was silent as he watched the two fighters carefully and studied their every move. His face was a picture of concentration.

In the middle of the courtyard, fourteen-year-old Indra circled his opponent warily. He held his sword steady, pointed at his opponent's head, and peered over the rim of his shield as he looked for a weakness in his defence. His adversary, Paras, watched his younger opponent carefully. They had been sparring for an hour now and neither had been able to create an opening.

Indra was quick on his feet as he launched an attack. He darted forward with a couple of swift lunges and forced his opponent to give ground. Then he launched himself high in the air and brought his sword down hard in a chopping motion. Paras took the blow high on his shield; the impact jarred his arm. He could not but admire Indra's stamina as he continued to take evasive action.

Indra realised his opponent was getting tired and did not let up. He continued to follow him as he rained blows on his shield. Finally, he got the opening he was waiting for. Paras, now exhausted, dropped the hand that bore the shield slightly. Indra's eyes lit up: this was exactly what he had been waiting for. He lunged forward eagerly.

Even as he shifted his weight forward, he realised that his more experienced opponent had baited him, but it was too late. His momentum carried him forward, unchecked. Paras though prepared for the manoeuvre, was still taken by surprise at the speed of the strike. At the last minute, he twisted his body out of the way and swung his shield. The blow was late as the blade passed through his defences, but the bronze shield caught Indra on the wrist and forced him to drop his sword. In a flash, Paras leaned in and tapped Indra on the shoulder with the flat part of his sword. The contest was over.

Paras realised how close Indra's blade had been to his exposed flank and heaved a sigh of relief. Although they were using training swords, that blow could have given him a painful injury. Mitra was the only other person to notice what a close call it had been for the young warrior. Indra threw his shield aside in anger and stormed off. His wrist hurt, but he resisted the urge to massage it. Soma was about to go after him, but a stern look from Mitra made the young boy sink right back down. Paras bowed, left the combat area and took his place on the side.

Mitra now called Varuna and Vayu to the arena. Their weapon of choice was the mace. As the two of them faced off, Vayu had a big smile on his face. He shrugged his massive shoulders, warming up as he watched his adversary. Varuna just stood, face expressionless, mace at the ready; his dark eyes were inscrutable as he stared at his opponent.

Indra was now outside the courtyard as he heard the maces clash together, announcing the beginning of the next duel. He let the tears of disappointment flow down his cheeks. He could not believe how he had walked into that one. He'd had his opponent right where he wanted him, and then he had handed over the victory on a platter.

While all these thoughts were racing through his mind, he heard movement nearby. He turned sharply in the direction of the sound and hurriedly wiped his face. He realised that it was coming from the shrubbery that fenced Mitra's courtyard. He rushed towards it, reached in and dragged out a screaming, protesting girl.

'Sachi! What are you doing here?'

The girl was beautiful, with delicate features and skin the colour of pale ivory. Her long, black hair fell straight and cascaded down to her hips. She turned to him, her dark eyes flashing.

'I am the regent's daughter. I go where I please.'

As Indra let go of her, his tone became gentler.

'You cannot be here. If Mitra sees you, you will be in a lot of trouble. What do you want anyway?'

'I came to see the champion of the next Spardha in action, and I have to say, things don't look too good,' she laughed.

Indra was about to protest angrily when he looked at her and realised she was teasing him.

'Oh, be quiet. Go home. You have no place here among warriors.'

He turned and walked away with her laughter ringing in the background. Sachi was the girl who was to be his bride. Mitra had named her Indrani and fixed the alliance when she was born. Sachi was the name her family had given her, the name she would use till the day she married him. They had been playmates since childhood and although at times she talked too much, Indra loved to spend time with her. But now, with the trials so close, it would not do for Mitra and his companions to see him hanging around with a girl. He made his way back to the courtyard and quietly took his place by the side as he watched his two friends in action.

Varuna, unruffled, was stalking a tired-looking Vayu, staying close to his bigger opponent and not giving him an opportunity to swing his mace. He had not even broken into a sweat. When he was able to get close enough, Varuna used a series of quick jabs and short swings to knock his bigger and stronger opponent off balance. Vayu's armour was dented in several places and his shoulders were bruised. His breathing was ragged as he staggered and fell.

Varuna hung back and waited for him to get up, Vayu rose and immediately swung his mace. Varuna deftly sidestepped the blow. Vayu cursed under his breath as he went after him, aiming one massive blow after another at his elusive opponent till finally, exhausted, he stood there gasping for breath. Varuna moved forward and goaded his opponent with his weapon, taunting him. With a huge grunt, Vayu raised his mace and swung it. Varuna stepped back as the blow landed in front of him and then quickly moved in. He stepped on the shaft of Vayu's mace as it hit the ground. Vayu lost his grip on the weapon; Varuna struck a light blow on his back causing him to fall over. The duel was over.

Varuna offered his fallen opponent his hand to help him get

to his feet. Vayu laughed as he grabbed it in an arm lock and wrestled Varuna to the ground. The two of them then got to their feet and made their way back to their seats, smiling.

Agni rushed to the combat area even before Mitra could call him. He was mortified to hear that he and Soma would be wrestling. He started to protest.

'But Master, I cannot wrestle this runt—it won't be a contest.'

Mitra smiled.

'If you concentrate a little, you might defeat him.'

Agni laughed loudly.

'Defeat him! Hah! I will teach him a lesson he will not forget.'

Soma, lean and muscular, built like a whiplash, was already in preparation for the bout. He anointed his arms and legs with animal fat and watched his opponent quietly. Agni got more and more impatient as he waited.

'Oh, come on Soma. This fight is not going to last as long as your preparations.'

Soma now stretched his limbs and took his time; he knew this would irritate Agni further.

Finally, after what seemed to Agni like an eternity, Mitra announced for the fight to begin. Agni rushed in. He hoped to use his superior height and build to good effect. Soma was prepared; he crouched low and did not allow Agni to get his arms around his lean frame. Agni tried to grab his shoulders, but Soma wriggled away—the grease on his body making it difficult for Agni to get a grip. The two of them circled around for a while, prompting Vayu to shout, 'Come on ladies, this is a duel, not a dance.'

Agni paused to catch his breath and gave Vayu a dirty look. Soma darted in and pushed him, causing him to lose his balance. Vayu hooted with laughter.

Agni's temper came to the fore. He hissed, 'I'll get you, you little weasel.'

He rushed forward, arms raised. Soma stayed low and slapped his hands away. Agni tried again, only to get the same result. The slaps served to infuriate him further. Soma noticed that his friend's face was going red and almost matched the colour of his fiery hair.

Agni bent his head and charged at Soma, who showed superb agility; he leapt in the air and, using Agni's head as leverage, vaulted neatly over him. Agni's charge nearly carried him into the spectators, who laughed at him. Even Indra, in spite of his surly mood, had a big smile on his face. The laughter of his companions drove Agni into a blind rage, he turned and charged again.

Soma was revelling in the moment and did not expect the same move again. He was a little late to step aside, and one flailing arm caught him with enough force to knock him off his feet. With a growl of triumph, Agni leapt on to his fallen opponent. Soma saw him coming and raised his legs in the air. His feet caught Agni on his chest and Soma used the momentum of the bigger boy against him and threw him over his head.

Agni did a somersault in the air and landed hard on his back. The impact knocked the wind out of his sails. In a flash, Soma was on him. He used his knees to pin the shoulders of his opponent to the ground. Mitra called the end of the fight and Soma was lifted off his feet and carried by a jubilant Indra for a lap of honour. It was not often that the slightly built Soma prevailed in a one-on-one encounter with his friends.

Vayu continued to taunt Agni as he helped him to his feet. Agni took it in his stride and smiled as he dusted himself and called out to the victor.

'One of these days I'm going to knock that crafty little head right off your shoulders with my mace.'

Indra went to Paras and clasped his shoulder.

'You fought well, my friend. Please forgive my behaviour. I should learn to be more graceful in defeat.'

Paras smiled. 'Don't worry, my prince. The way you fight, you will not have to worry too much about defeat.'

Mitra called for their attention.

'You have acquitted yourself well, my boys, and as a reward I would like to inform you that Mahisi has arranged a grand feast tonight. So enjoy yourselves and don't stay up too late as I expect you here at dawn for your riding lesson.'

The announcement was followed with hoots of appreciation. In the last seven years of training and study, they had been forced to get used to Mitra's cooking. Though their teacher was extremely skilled in a lot of disciplines, culinary science wasn't one of them.

Just as they were gathering their things and preparing to leave, Mitra made one final announcement.

'Just so the ones who lost don't feel they got away scot free, they can carry the victors on their backs to the feast.'

A groan escaped from Indra's lips, at the thought of hauling Paras all the way to Mahisi's farm.

Mitra sat down and lit his hemp pipe as he listened to the sound of excited voices recede into the background. For the last seven years, he and Paras had trained these boys and honed their martial skills. Indra's companions had been handpicked from Mahisi's orphanage, their fathers had fought and died with Daeyus at the Pass of the Wolves. These boys had now sworn a blood oath of allegiance to Indra. Their fate was now inseparably bound to his.

The boys had their own distinct personalities, yet they seemed to get along very well together. Now, in a week, their skills would be put to the ultimate test. It was time for the Spardha.

For a tribe that had been at peace for several years—something quite unusual given the way of the Devas—the Spardha assumed great significance, allowing young warriors to assess their true potential in combat and win some glory.

The rules for the tournament were simple. The best young warriors were chosen to represent their groups or dals. These groups were pitted against each other in the various disciplines of skill and combat. The top two dals would compete for the trophy. They would also nominate one warrior from their group for the ultimate face-off to decide who would be the individual champion. This was the prize that Indra wanted above everything else.

The natural thing for Indra to do would have been to join his father's dal, the Lions, but Mitra had advised against it. The Lions were now led and trained by Pusan, Vasu's son. Pusan was the reigning champion of the Spardha and the foremost warrior amongst the Devas. He had his own ideas as to who should be the leader of the tribe, and it did not include Indra.

Mitra knew how important this victory was for his young ward's future, and he'd made the decision to start a new dal. Their symbol was the swooping falcon, which was emblazoned in silver on a purple banner that now fluttered proudly on a pole in Mitra's yard.

While the older dals, like the Lions, the Bears and the Wolves had a faithful following, a large alumnus and a number of candidates to choose from, the Falcons had a pool of only five young warriors. But Mitra was not just training them for a competition, but for a life of war. He did not want these boys to just win the Spardha. He was training them to conquer the world.

There was great anticipation in the clan regarding this Spardha. During Daeyus' time, it had been an annual affair. But now, in times of peace, it had been three years since the last tournament. The enthusiasts and the punters hung around the training areas, trying to assess the potential of each of the dals. While there was enough information available on the other dals and the candidates they were likely to field, the Falcons were a mystery as they trained and lived away from the settlement at Mitra's hermitage. They had not participated in the last tournament, preferring to watch from the sidelines as Pusan and his Lions took the prize.

In the Lions' training yard, Pusan had just finished putting his wards through the wringer. They stood before him, led by his protégé Atreya. Pusan gripped his shoulder proudly.

'Well done, my champion. Once again the Lions will devour the opposition in this Spardha.'

Atreya, his muscular frame covered with sweat, raised his training sword high in the air and led the boys in their war cry.

'Victory to the Lions!'

Just then a messenger rushed in and bowed low.

'Greetings, Captain Pusan. The regent has asked for you to meet him in the Sabha as soon as possible.'

Pusan dismissed his squad and hurried to meet his father.

At Mahisi's residence, the Falcons were treated to a feast far beyond their expectations. After the intensive training session, the boys fell upon the food like a pack of ravenous wolves. There was venison stew served with unleavened bread, succulent catfish caught fresh from the river and grilled on coals, quail eggs and thick cream cheese. In keeping with their current standing as young warriors, they were also served a portion of watered-down wine along with the food. By the end of the feast, the boys were ready to pass out. They were escorted to their old dormitory where they had lived as children.

Paras waited for them to fall sleep before he quietly made his way back to Mahisi's hut. Unlike Mitra, who seemed comfortable with his celibacy, Paras had needs. Both he and Mahisi had this discreet arrangement that worked well for both parties.

It was still an hour before dawn when five horsemen led by Pusan made their way southwards from Aryavarta. Though still a few months short of his twentieth birthday, Pusan had developed a formidable reputation as a warrior. It was why his father had entrusted him with this task.

For the last few months, a lion had terrorised farmers in the southern lands. It had taken several horses and cattle and recently killed a young farmer and his wife. The people had named him Baldar, the strong one. Pusan had vowed that he would bring back the lion's skin and sit on it to watch the Spardha.

To the south, near the great swamp, the first rays of the sun revealed the animal, with its distinctive black mane, as he prepared to feast on a young heifer. Baldar was in his prime, yet he did not live in a pride. He preferred to live and hunt alone. The advent of the Devas into Gandhar had driven the lion prides further and further south beyond the swamps, yet Baldar had chosen to stay. He was the real master of this land and no human would take that away from him.

Although Baldar was big and strong, as his name suggested, his real strength lay in his cunning. An expert at camouflage, he had made his home in the treacherous swamp amongst poisonous snakes and giant crocodiles, and he chose his battles very carefully. This was why, in spite of numerous efforts by the Devas, no arrow, blade or spear had ever marked his tawny hide. Now, as daylight arrived, he dragged the carcass of the heifer back through the reed beds, well into the protection of the swamp.

Pusan and his band arrived at the spot where the lion had made the kill. The tracker read the signs and pointed in the direction of the reed beds. Pusan, on a magnificent black stallion, was accompanied by five of his closest cohorts, men from his own dal who had helped him win the last Spardha. Pusan gave the order for them to enter the swamp in single file. The tracker led the way on foot, hacking away at the reeds that grew almost to the height of a man. He was followed by Pusan.

As they made slow progress through the treacherous terrain, the mosquitoes began to attack and the men cursed as they slapped the stinging insects off their bodies. The tracker suddenly sensed something and gave the signal for them to be quiet. He heard the alarm call of a thrush—it was a warning that a predator was near.

The man was about to make the sign of imminent danger when suddenly, out of the stinking morass, Baldar rose like a primeval monster, covered with black, sticky mud. With one mighty blow of his paw, he crushed the skull of the tracker, and before the rest of the hunting party could react, he disappeared once again into the reeds. Pusan watched helplessly as the tracker lay in front of him, writhing in pain. There was nothing he could do for the man, so he drove his lance through his heart and gave him a quick and merciful death.

Now Pusan was confronted with the dilemma of going ahead without the tracker, a decision fraught with danger, or turning back and losing face at the Sabha. But Baldar took the decision out of his hands. He let out a loud roar that made the horses rear up in fright. One of the men was unable to control his steed and the animal bolted wildly across the swamp.

The horse had only gone a few paces when the black ooze started to slow him down and swallow him up. The more the horse and rider struggled, the quicker they began to sink into the mud. Pusan screamed for the man to get off the horse and lie flat on the quicksand with his limbs spread out. The others then threw him a rope and dragged him to dry land while his steed slowly sank into the dark depths of the swamp.

So engrossed were they in the man's rescue that they failed to notice that the lion had crept up behind Pusan. The great beast sprang at the warrior. Fortunately for Pusan, the soft mud did not give Baldar the purchase to leap high enough. However, the claws of the great beast ravaged the hindquarters of his horse.

As Pusan turned to meet the threat with his lance raised, Baldar attacked again. This time his claws raked across Pusan's thigh and laid it open to the bone. Pusan gritted his teeth and tried to ignore the white-hot pain that shot through his leg. He thrust his lance at the beast and the spear grazed a heavily-muscled shoulder. Baldar quickly disengaged from battle and disappeared into the reeds.

Pusan looked at the wound on his thigh: the lion's claws had laid open the femoral artery. This meant that he needed to get help quickly or he would bleed to death. He bound his wound tightly using strips of leather from his saddlebags and reluctantly gave the order to turn back.

Baldar watched the men leave with the body of the dead tracker. He made no attempt to stop them; there was an unfinished meal that awaited him in the reeds. He had sent out a strong message to the men who occupied the northern lands.

The marshes were his kingdom. The authority of man would not be recognised here.

Over the next few days, news of the failed lion hunt spread like wildfire through Aryavarta. Mitra was summoned to Vasu's house. When he got there, a worried regent met him at the door. Pusan lay inside surrounded by physicians. In spite of being sedated heavily, he was in agony and delirious with fever. While the physicians had been able to stem the loss of blood, they were unable to do anything about the infection in the wound.

The chief physician, a grizzled old man, turned to the regent, his head bowed in resignation.

'My lord, we are running out of time, so I must ask you again. Allow us to amputate his leg. That is the only way to save his life.'

Vasu shook his head. He was firm in spite of his grief. He looked towards Mitra and beseeched him with folded hands.

'My lord, save the boy's leg. I know you can. Please save my son, for I know he will take his own life rather than live the rest of his days a cripple.'

Mitra looked at Pusan. His once radiant face was pale and gaunt. He had lost a lot of blood; only his robust constitution had helped him survive this long. Mitra examined the wound carefully. The physicians had done their job well; they had sealed off the severed artery, cleaned and dressed the wound. But the claws of a carnivore carried all manner of dangerous infections. Mitra sniffed at the wound; he could smell the mild rot that had set in—it was gangrene.

He asked everybody to leave the room. Only Vasu's wife,

Madri, was allowed to be present. He pulled out a bunch of tiny leaves from his bag; in the dim light, they shone with a pale green luminance. He chanted a mantra and crushed them in a bowl with some spring water. This was sanjeevani, a herb that was native to only these mountains; it was unknown yet to the physicians of the time. His master had revealed its secret to Mitra. It was said to have the power to bring a man back from the dead. He mixed the fresh paste with some warm water and administered it to Pusan. He asked Madri to feed Pusan the remainder of the contents of the bowl during the night and left.

The next morning, the Falcons were taking a break after a rigorous riding session when one of the slaves from Vasu's household rushed there with news for Mitra. Pusan's fever had broken; the physicians had examined him and discovered that the infection was now under control. Vasu's son would live, and keep his wounded leg.

Varuna was not too pleased with their master's decision to save Pusan. He was the first to break the silence after they heard the news.

'I hope the Master does not regret his decision one day. Pusan is the only obstacle between Indra and the throne.'

Soma immediately jumped to Mitra's defence.

'What would you have him do, Varuna? Let the man die? Mitra will not let such a petty situation sway him from the path of his dharma.'

Varuna turned to Soma, his dark eyes flashing in anger.

'Petty! That man has boasted publicly that he will be the next chief of the Devas. Atreya and his Lions have been strutting around like the roosters in Mahisi's hen house ever since. If they win the Spardha, we will have to leave Aryavarta with our heads bowed in shame.'

Vayu laughed.

'Looks like our friend here is getting a little nervous before the competition.'

Varuna turned to him angrily.

'Nervous! Why don't you pick up your mace and I'll show you how nervous I am.'

'Come on then.'

Vayu, still smiling, reached for his weapon.

Soma hurriedly stepped between the two.

'Save your strength, my friends, we need it for the tournament tomorrow.'

Indra had been quiet all this while. He now stood up and spoke. His voice was gentle, but there was no mistaking the determination in it.

'If it is my destiny to be the raja of the Devas, no man is going to take that away from me.'

Paras, who had been setting up the targets for their archery practice, called out to them. Indra picked up his bow and twanged the string. The sound resonated through the tense atmosphere and diffused it. The Falcons readied themselves for their next round of training.

It was late in the evening when Mitra got back from the house of the regent after checking on Pusan. The young man looked rested and well on his way to recovery. Mitra sighed as he thought of the consequences his action would have on the future of his young ward. The past few weeks, Mitra had spent a fair amount of time in Aryavarta. There was open talk now of Pusan being the next chief of the Devas. Some of the seeds of discord that had been sown by the former high priest Susena had taken root and grown among the populace.

The laws of leadership among the Devas were simple: the chief of the tribe had to be of pure blood, and his right to the throne had to be acknowledged by the former chief or the Sabha. Daeyus had endorsed Indra's right to the throne. But his bloodline was questionable, because they did not have a clue as to the identity of his mother. In addition to this, Vasu's able administration and Pusan's performance in the last Spardha had won them many admirers among the influential members of the tribe.

While Daeyus' deeds of valour were remembered on special occasions by nostalgic veterans and bards, it was the prosperity that Vasu's short reign had brought that the common folk appreciated. Mitra realised that if Indra was to ever sit on that throne, they would all have their work cut out for them.

As he approached the hermitage, he spotted Indra sitting outside by the fire and staring out into the distant horizon. The boy saw Mitra and stood up to greet him. The rigours of his training had chiselled his body to perfection. It was built for speed and endurance, and those were Indra's strengths in combat. His long, blond hair was swept back from his face and tied in a loose braid. His blue eyes had that piercing intensity which reminded Mitra of his father. His features were more delicate though; Mitra assumed he had inherited this from his mother's side. While Daeyus had not revealed her identity, the boy's aura and the perfection of his features told Mitra all he needed to know about his mother.

'It is late Indra, why haven't you gone to bed like the others?'
'I could not sleep Master, my mind is troubled.'
Mitra put his arm around Indra and led him back to his hut.
'What is it, my boy?'
Indra stopped and turned to him.
'I have to win. That is the only way I can be chief of the Devas.'

Mitra looked into the boy's eyes and saw the quiet determination in them.

'You will, my young falcon. Now apply your mind to what you have to do tomorrow and give your body some rest. I will see you in the morning.'

Mitra watched the boy trudge back reluctantly to his hut. He knew Indra would have rather stayed and asked him a hundred more questions.

The old sage's heart swelled with pride as he thought back on the years. He had watched Indra grow from a spoilt little boy into this strong young man, bred for greatness. He sighed as he looked up at the stars. They told him that the journey for Indra was about to begin, and it would be a long and arduous one.

Aryavarta was decorated like a newlywed bride for the Spardha. For the next five days, life would come to a standstill in the city. The area in front of the Sabha had been cleared and an arena built for the martial contests. It was now decorated with festoons and colourful banners. The various dals had their own dugouts where the contestants could limber up and await their bouts. Behind them were enclosures for supporters to cheer their heroes as they arrived for the contest.

The Falcons entered the arena to an extremely muted reception. They looked splendid enough in their tunics of purple with the silver falcon emblazoned on them.

Varuna, who was well versed in the politics of their world, was the first to come up with a reason.

'What do you expect? We are a bunch of orphans being trained by an Aditya. Why would they switch loyalties from their old dals and support us?'

Agni jogged up and down impatiently.

'Who cares about support? Let's just go ahead and do what we have to do.'

Vayu was his pleasant self as he went towards the audience enclosure and acknowledged whatever little support they had. The people from Mahisi's farm and orphanage had gathered behind their dugout, along with a few slaves. He swung his mace in a series of breathtaking moves, causing a cheer in their small ranks. Soma ignored the crowd and concentrated on limbering up.

Indra looked about him and then called for his friends to gather close in a huddle.

'Falcons, by the end of these five days, each of you will be carried in glory, on the shoulders of these very people who ignore you now. I, Indra, son of Daeyus, swear this. Now let's put on a show they will not forget in a hurry!'

'Yeah!' they cried in unison and pumped their fists in the air.

Their modest support cheered them lustily. The Falcons now settled down to do their warm-ups and awaited the arrival of the other dals.

The Wolves walked in, brightly attired in green and yellow, amidst rapturous applause. Nala, a young man with a growing reputation as a peerless archer, led them. They acknowledged their considerable support and settled down.

Now the crowd erupted in jubilation—the Lions had entered the arena. In their flamboyant colours of red and gold, led by the magnificent Atreya, the defending champions announced their arrival with a breathtaking display of acrobatics.

The applause took a few minutes to die down. When it did, Vasu stood up to address the gathering from the steps of the Sabha.

'Devas! It gives me great honour to present to you the

Spardha. To the participants, I say do your dals proud and always remember that this is a contest. The very opponents you face in competition today you will fight alongside in battle tomorrow. So fight with honour and follow the rules. Good luck and may Surya shower his blessings on you all.'

The announcer then took over and informed the crowd that they would start with the equestrian events, which would take place in a large meadow on the outskirts of the settlement.

Aryavarta resembled a ghost town as nearly every able-bodied man, woman and child left to watch the equestrian trials. In his father's home, Pusan woke up from the effects of the pain-killing potion given to him. His family had left him in the care of an attendant and gone to watch the Spardha.

Pusan was thankful for the peace and quiet. He had gotten weary of the anxious faces hovering around him all the time. He cursed out aloud at his fate. He had failed in his task to kill the lion and now he owed his life to Mitra, someone he despised almost as much as he did Indra. Just then the attendant entered with news of a visitor.

'Master Makara is here, my lord.'

Pusan was surprised to hear that his old tutor had come to see him. Makara rarely left his home outside the settlement. In his own words, there was no place in Aryavarta for true men of god. He asked the attendant to usher him in with the utmost respect.

During the reign of Daeyus, Makara had been one of the rising stars of the Deva priesthood. He was being groomed by Susena as his successor. Unfortunately for Makara, on the death of his mentor, Mitra took over the duties of priesthood and the Deva clergy suddenly found themselves totally redundant.

Makara's pride did not allow him to eke out a living performing household rituals like the other Deva priests. Instead he retreated into the shadows, away from public life. He then waited and watched for an opportunity to restore the Deva priesthood to its former glory.

In order to make ends meet he was forced to work as a tutor for the children of the wealthy and influential families of Aryavarta. At long last the opportunity he craved presented itself—he was made tutor to Pusan, son of Vasu.

Now years later he entered the bedchamber of his ward. Pusan watched his old tutor as he made his way into the room. He was surprised to see how kind the years had been to Makara. His shaven head and eyebrows along with his kohl-lined dark eyes gave him an ageless androgynous look. Tall and thin, he dressed and carried himself just like his mentor, Susena. Garbed in the white and gold robes of the old high priest, he cut a fine figure as he sat at Pusan's bedside and greeted him.

'I am glad to see that you are well, boy. The rumourmongers of this town had written you off a while ago.'

'I wish those rumours were true, Master. I have no desire to live. I have failed my father.'

Pusan got no sympathy from Makara.

'Stop your whining, boy! I told you a long time ago to give up trying to please your father. He has no time to laud your achievements. He is too busy being a slave. He was a slave to Daeyus, now he is a slave to Mitra and he will die a slave to Indra.'

Pusan did not say anything, he just lay there with downcast eyes. Makara looked at him, his eyes flashing fire.

'But you, my boy, have a choice. Do not be a slave like your father. Wrest the leadership of this tribe from that demon Indra who will only lead the Devas to destruction. Banish the dark sorcerer Mitra from Aryavarta. Then you and I can usher in an era of prosperity such the tribe has never seen or will ever see again.'

Makara watched Pusan carefully, he knew the young warrior better than anybody else. Pusan had first come to him a troubled boy of six. It had not taken Makara long to realise that the boy craved his father's attention, which was at that time divided between Indra and the affairs of the tribe. Makara nurtured the jealousy Pusan felt for Indra, adding fuel to its fire till it grew into a full-blown hatred. Through the formative years he had been the young warrior's only true friend, philosopher and guide. Now Pusan was a puppet in his hands. He looked at Makara blankly.

'What must I do now, Master?'

Makara softened his tone.

'First you must ensure that Indra does not become the champion of this Spardha.'

The Falcons watched Nala and the Wolves run a perfect course. The obstacle course for the equestrian trials had been cleverly laid out. It included several wooden fences of varying heights and the final hurdle was a burning cart that the contestants had to leap over. Nala was the last of the Wolves trio on show. He expertly guided his horse over the burning cart. The Wolves' supporters roared in triumph.

It was now the turn of the Falcons. Mitra chose Soma, Vayu and Indra to run the course. The cart was set ablaze. Soma started and went through the course quickly, timing each of his jumps to perfection. He finished the last one beautifully, calming his mare and gently coaxing her to leap over the burning cart. He was faster than all the previous riders. Even some of the rival supporters cheered this display of brilliant horsemanship. Vayu followed and soon ran into trouble; his horse was a little bit of a nervous starter and he lost some time before he managed to finish the last hurdle.

Indra took the course next and moved smoothly over the first few obstacles. He finished the last water jump with feet to spare and made his way towards the final obstacle. The fire on the cart was about to die down so one of the referees threw some clarified butter into it. The flames flared up brightly. Indra's horse, a feisty young stallion, saw this and reared up. Conscious about making up the time Vayu had lost, Indra whispered encouragement to his steed and forced it forward. They raced towards the burning cart.

Just as he made the leap, Indra realised something was wrong. The stallion had panicked and jumped too early. Its front legs crashed into the burning cart and Indra was thrown over its head and through the blaze. He hit the ground hard, rolled over and got to his feet. He ran to check on his horse, his concern for the animal making him forget his own injuries.

The poor creature lay on its side and looked at him wild-eyed in terror. Its front legs had shattered on impact with the cart. Indra tried hard to hold back his tears as he drew his sword and thrust it through the heart of the mortally-wounded animal.

The Lions, who were up next, went on to finish second behind the Wolves in the event, much to the joy of their supporters.

The final events of the day were the duels. Contestants from the various dals would charge each other on horseback, armed with blunt lances and shields. The objective was to unseat one's opponent from his horse.

The Falcons gave a good account of themselves in this event: Agni and Varuna won all their duels. They were neck and neck with the Lions when Mitra did something unexpected—he did not let Indra participate in the duel but left it to Soma to fight Atreya. The diminutive Falcon was no match for Atreya's superior strength and he was knocked down from his horse. The Lions won the event.

An excited Sachi rushed home to give Pusan the news. He was elated to know that the Lions were leading the competition. As Sachi washed and dressed his wound, Pusan asked about Indra. When he heard about his mishap, he laughed.

'And that fool wants to be chief of the Devas.'

Sachi was quick to retort.

'He *is* going to be the chief, brother. But before that he is going to be the next champion.'

Pusan scoffed at her remark.

'You are as big a fool as he, my dear sister. Our parents have filled your head with this stupid idea that he is going to be the king and you his queen. That is never going to happen.'

Sachi was shocked at her brother's insolence.

'How can you say that? He is the son of Raja Daeyus and his legal heir. Would you go against your father and Mitra?'

Angry, Pusan tried to sit up, but was still too weak.

'I will follow the laws of our tribe—only a pure blooded clansman can lead the Devas. Not some bastard who might be the spawn of a demon. Our father is blinded by his loyalty to Raja Daeyus. As for Mitra, he has no right to an opinion in this matter—he is not of our tribe.'

Sachi could not believe what she was hearing. She tightened the bandage in anger, causing her brother to wince in pain.

'I think your injury has affected your brain, my dear brother, you sound like a madman. Do not forget that if it were not for

Mitra, you would have been forced to spend the rest of your life as a cripple,' she said and left the room.

Mitra had just finished an inspection of their supply of arrows for the archery trials the next day. He asked the weapon smith to deliver the arrows to his home and was stepping out of the smithy when he met an anxious Sachi. She had with her a jar of salve.

'My lord, I know you will not let us meet, so would you please give this to him? He hurt himself at the trial this morning.'

Mitra smiled.

'His burns have been treated, my child.'

He saw her crestfallen expression and hurriedly added.

'Don't worry, when you are married you can have the sole responsibility of taking care of him. Surya knows, with the amount of trouble he gets into, you will be kept very busy. Now let him be for the next few days, he must keep his mind on the Spardha.'

'Spardha! All you people care about is the Spardha. I think it is time to put a stop to these barbaric customs,' Sachi said and walked off in a huff.

Mitra watched her leave, amusement writ large on his face. She was a feisty one; Indra would have his hands full with her. He chuckled at the thought as he made his way back home.

In his hut, Indra lay on his reed mat, unable to sleep. The loss of his horse had affected him far more than he had let on. He knew he alone was to blame for what had happened. He should have ensured that the horse had been trained to face a fire jump. Only Mitra had seen how badly shaken he was, and wisely decided not to put him in the jousting contest. In his state of mind, it was possible that he might have lost to Atreya, thus giving his opponent the psychological advantage in the battle for the individual championship. He closed his eyes and forced himself to sleep. Tomorrow would be a decisive day for the Falcons.

The second day of the Spardha started with the archery trials. Targets of varying sizes—from that of an apple to the size of a horse's head—had been set up all around the course. This was an eagerly-awaited contest: the cavalry archers were an important, perhaps *the* most important part of the Deva war machine. The Devas prided themselves on their skill as archers. So the crowds had arrived early in order to get vantage positions, with the latecomers even risking seats that would put them directly in the path of arrows if they missed their targets. But it was a measure of the trust the Devas had in the skill of their archers.

The contest began with all the dals nominating three archers each. Each archer was given ten arrows, and would have to shoot down ten targets while riding his steed at full gallop. Indra was pleasantly surprised when Mitra loaned him his mare to use for the trial. She had carried Indra on her back as a child and he knew her well. The Falcons were among the first to take the field. Varuna, Agni and Indra rode with the reins gripped between their teeth as they shot arrow after arrow at their respective targets.

Indra was the last to finish and he chose the most difficult target to end his routine. The crowd watched with bated breath as he discharged his last arrow at an apple, placed fifty paces away. The arrow sliced through the fruit and divided it into two near-perfect halves. The audience rose as a man to applaud the feat. All three archers had got a perfect score—something that had never happened in the entire history of the Spardha.

The Lions had a disastrous outing with Atreya being the first to succumb to the pressure of chasing three perfect scores. From the other dals, only Nala of the Wolves achieved a perfect ten. He helped his group finish a creditable second. The Falcons had won the contest handsomely.

Vasu, amazed at the skill of the Falcons and Nala, remarked to his generals, 'It's heartening to see that our legacy of being the greatest archers among the northern tribes is intact. I have never seen such a brilliant display of archery in all my years.'

The generals nodded in agreement. One of them remarked, 'I agree, my lord. It is a pity we have no wars to fight to put these sublime skills to the test. Like us, they will have to live with the boredom that peace brings.'

'Yes General, but at least they can grow old like you and me and watch their sons become men.'

A loud cheer went up from the crowd as the commencement of the krida was announced. The area had been divided into two halves for this contest. Two teams of four riders each carried five-foot long wooden poles and faced off against each other. Each team was allowed to send two riders into the opponent's territory. The objective of the contest was simple: whoever made their way first across their rival's half and collected their opponent's flag would be declared the winner. Anyone who fell to the ground would be deemed disqualified.

The Lions were particularly strong in krida—their red and gold flag had not fallen into the hands of their adversaries yet. Now they needed only one more perfect defensive game against the Falcons, and victory would be theirs.

Led by Varuna and Soma, the Falcons made a foray into their opponent's half but were beaten back. Vayu and Indra managed to hold off the Lion's subsequent counterattack. Both sides fought doggedly as they fended off each rival attack. Then, the Lions made their first mistake, a crucial error in strategy. They opted to hold back their four players in a defensive line. With no offensive line to worry about, Indra made an unexpected tactical change. He and Soma made their way into the Lion's half. Mitra looked at Paras and raised his eyebrows in surprise. These two together were not part of their offensive line-up. Usually Vayu or Varuna paired with them. The two bigger boys used their strength to keep their opponents at bay, while Indra or Soma made the run for the flag.

Atreya watched the two Falcons approach steadily; he was unsure which one would make the run. The shadow from the massive sundial was nearing its mark, which would announce the end of the game.

Suddenly, Soma broke away sharply to his left and made a dash for the flag. Atreya screamed out a warning to his teammate, Khara, and the boy prepared to meet Soma's charge. Soma swung his stick at Khara, who blocked the blow. Before he could counter, Soma dragged his stick along his opponent's and struck him on his fingers.

Khara dropped his stick in pain but quickly recovered and threw himself at Soma. He hoped to sacrifice himself and take Soma down. Soma watched his opponent come at him and, at the very last second, he swerved out of the way. Khara flew harmlessly past him, hit the dust and was eliminated.

Soma turned his horse once again towards the red and gold flag that fluttered in the distance. So intent was he on his task that he failed to spot the imminent danger. Atreya swung his stick in a wide arc and it struck Soma on the back of his helmet. The force of the blow was enough to knock the young Falcon down and put him out of the contest.

Atreya turned to see Indra make his way towards the other two Lions. The two boys watched Indra as he headed straight for them. This was going to be easy. They tightened the grip on their sticks and waited for him.

As he approached the two boys, Indra's feet left the stirrups and he wrapped them around the neck of his mare. Atreya's eyes widened with shock as he realised what his rival was about to do. He pushed his steed in a wide arc to cut off Indra's path to the flag and screamed a warning to his two teammates.

'Watch out! He's going to—'

But his words came too late. As the two Lions swung their sticks at Indra, he let go of the reins and threw himself backwards till he was flat on the back of the mare, using only his feet to anchor himself to her neck. The two sticks flashed above him and the mare broke through. The crowd clapped in admiration at the horsemanship of the young Falcon.

As Indra sat up, he saw that now there was only Atreya between him and the flag. Atreya charged towards him and swung his stick ferociously at Indra's head. Indra brought his own stick up to block it, but the strength of the blow knocked the weapon out of his hands.

Atreya gave a yell of triumph and swung his stick in a backhanded arc. He hoped to take Indra by surprise, but the Falcon was ready for him. He skilfully weaved out of the way and the momentum of the strike carried Atreya forward, causing him to lose his balance for a second. Quick as a flash, Indra leapt from his horse on to Atreya, taking the Lion's captain and his own team by surprise.

As the two young warriors fell, Indra made sure his opponent's body was between him and the ground. He landed on Atreya's broad back and pinned him to the ground. With Atreya out of the contest, Indra whistled to his mare and she came around towards him at full gallop. Atreya screamed to his teammates as he realised that Indra's body had not touched the earth. The

Falcon was still in the game. The two Lions had already turned their horses and they now sped towards the two fallen boys. Indra's mare reached them first. He leapt off the back of his fallen opponent and grabbed the reins of the mare and hoisted himself onto her back.

The two Lions were almost upon him. One of them swung his stick and hit Indra on the back of his neck between the helmet and his padded armour. He ignored the pain, bent his head and spurred the mare on with his heels. She responded splendidly with a burst of speed that left his two remaining opponents standing. Out of the corner of his eye, Indra could see the referee lifting the bugle to his mouth to announce the end of the krida. The pain in his neck brought tears to his eyes, but through the blur, he spotted the red and gold flag. He reached out and grabbed it. The bugle sounded a second after thunderous applause broke out from the crowd. They had done it. The Falcons had won.

The contestants got a well-deserved one-day break after the horse trials. Indra spent a good part of it in bed nursing his sore neck. Soma, who had taken a heavy fall, was also in pain, as were Varuna and Vayu, who had a few niggles and sprains themselves. Only Agni was relatively unscathed. He finished his training and rushed into the hut.

'You know, I think I have been underutilised the last two days.' He pointed to Soma who lay flat on his back and said, 'Look at that squirt, why did he have to go in at the end with Indra?'

Soma threw his pillow at him and groaned with the effort. 'Maybe because this little squirt is a better rider than you are, you big oaf,' he said.

Agni caught the pillow and flung it back. It was a wild throw.

'Bah! The krida is not only about riding, it is also about staying on your horse. All it took was a feather touch to knock you over.'

Varuna, who had been taking a nap, was woken by the argument.

'Shut up you two and take your quarrel outside. I can't remember when I last had a day of rest and I'd like to enjoy it.'

At the house of the regent, Pusan was still in a fit of rage over the results. Atreya bore the brunt of his ire, yet he offered no excuses and allowed his mentor to vent his fury. Finally, exhaustion and pain made Pusan fall back on his bed. Atreya went to him, head bowed.

'The Lions will win the Spardha, my lord, even if I have to give my life for it.'

Pusan grabbed him by the tunic and pulled him close. Atreya was shocked to see the venom in his eyes.

'I do not care about the Spardha anymore. Swear to me that I will not have to crown that bastard Indra champion.'

Atreya nodded fearfully. He could not believe the extent of Pusan's hatred towards Indra.

'I swear, my lord.'

The next day, the action shifted back to the arena for the combat trials. Pusan, against the advice of his physicians, insisted on being present. He lay in the dugout of the Lions and directed proceedings from there. Unfortunately for Pusan, the day belonged entirely to the Falcons. Agni and Varuna were invincible with the mace and the sword. They destroyed the opposition with a stunning display of martial prowess. So dominant were they in the trials that Mitra decided to rest his best fighter, Indra.

While the Devas laid great emphasis on their cavalry training and archery, their close combat techniques left a lot to be desired. They relied heavily on physical prowess, and their skills were designed to finish off a fight in the quickest possible time. This worked well for them in battle as, more often than not, the Devas only got off their mounts to finish off an already vanquished enemy.

It was this weakness that Mitra had exploited when he trained the Falcons. He taught them breathing techniques designed to conserve energy during a fight and build stamina. Indra and the other boys were given special exercises that built strength, as well as speed and endurance. The results were now plain for all to see: the Falcons seemed one step ahead of their opponents at all times during combat.

The Lions had a disastrous outing, with all their fighters being defeated. The Wolves had fared only marginally better. The other dals were now out of the reckoning, and their supporters had now openly shifted allegiance to the Falcons. As the end of the day's proceedings was announced, the loudest cheer was reserved for the Falcons as they left the arena.

Pusan was at his wits' end that evening. Like the rest of the crowd, he had been blown away by the Falcons' performance. Like Mitra, he had gambled and rested his champion fighter. He had hoped to keep Atreya fresh for his battle in the final, but now for the first time, there was a serious danger that the Lions would not make that final. Agni had taken Khara apart, and his other fighter Puru had taken a blow to his head from Varuna's shield that had knocked him out.

The next day, more disappointment awaited Pusan and the Lions. Khara lost to Aruna of the Wolves in the spear trials. Soma did them a favour with a brilliant display of spear fighting, which saw him defeat Aruna. So far the Falcons had won everything, and far too easily.

The stage was set for the final event—the mace trials, a weapon that was very popular with the tribe. Left with no choice, Pusan entered Atreya as his fighter. The brave Lion had only one more hurdle to cross to get his dal into the final. Vayu, of the Falcons.

The two fighters circled each other warily. Vayu had had a much easier time in the trials and won all his fights easily. Atreya's journey had been much harder, the mace was not a weapon he was really comfortable with; like Indra he favoured the sword. In spite of this, he had done well so far. His natural instincts as a fighter had helped him win a close fight with the Wolves. Now a victory would get the Lions into the final and give him a chance to challenge Indra for the championship.

Vayu went on the offensive immediately, testing his opponent with a few powerful blows before he broke away. Atreya went after him, eager for a quick victory. Restraining himself from using the slam-bang method he usually adopted, Vayu hung back, circling the arena as he kept a close eye on his opponent. He darted in and out, employing a few light blows to test Atreya's defence, but focused on conserving his strength, knowing he could use it to good effect later. Atreya's earlier bouts, coupled with the unfamiliar weight of the weapon he wielded, began to take its toll and he started to grow weary of pursuing Vayu around the arena. Impatiently he approached Vayu, who blocked the blows thrown at him with ease.

Suddenly, Vayu sprang forward and his mace came down on Atreya, who raised his own weapon to block the blow. It had all of Vayu's weight behind it and Atreya was a little late in bringing up his guard. Vayu's mace crashed through his defence, struck him on the shoulder and shattered his collarbone.

Atreya dropped his mace and fell to the ground in agony as he clutched his broken shoulder. His dream of being champion was destroyed. A tremendous roar went up among the Wolves' supporters. It was Nala who would challenge Indra for the individual championship.

As he had promised, the Falcons and Indra were carried up and down the arena on the shoulders of their jubilant supporters. Vasu and the entire Sabha gave them a standing ovation. The Falcons had won the Spardha, with the Wolves finishing second. It was the first time in the history of the tribe that a new dal had emerged victorious in its first outing.

Sunset did not halt the proceedings on the final day of the competition. Oil lamps were lit and the announcement was made for the final challenge to determine the individual champion. Unlike the other fights, in this one the contestants were allowed to carry weapons of their choice. Indra opted for the sword and the war club, while Nala chose to go with the more conventional sword and shield.

As the two contestants warmed up, Pusan sent word to Nala through one of his trainers, promising him two of his best horses if he defeated Indra. Nala's eyes lit up—Pusan bred the best horses in Aryavarta; he was now all the more determined to win.

The fight began and Indra attacked Nala with a fury that shocked the crowd. He rained blows on Nala's shield with his sword as well as the club. Nala slowly gave ground at the furious assault and looked for an opening in his opponent's defence. The arm that bore the shield was numb from the numerous blows it had received. Yet Indra did not let up in his offensive, constantly moving so Nala did not have a stationary target to aim at. Soon the exhausted young Wolf made his first mistake:

he batted aside Indra's club with his shield as he leaned forward and thrust his sword at Indra's torso.

Indra twisted sharply. Nala's momentum carried him forward, and as the Wolf passed him, Indra turned and swung his club. The blow caught Nala square on his back. In spite of his padded armour, it knocked the wind out of him and he fell on his face in the arena. As he rose slowly, Indra rushed forward and with one mighty blow of his club, he knocked the shield out of Nala's hand.

In desperation, Nala raised his sword and struck out at Indra's head. His opponent avoided the blow easily. An exhausted Nala made one final thrust; Indra pirouetted out of the way with the grace of a dancer and tripped his opponent. As he fell to the ground, Indra put his foot on Nala's sword and tapped him on the shoulder with the flat part of his blade. There was a whoop of joy from the Falcon dugout as his teammates rushed out and hoisted Indra on their shoulders. It was finally over. Indra was the champion.

In the absence of Pusan, the previous champion, who was conveniently indisposed, Vasu presented Indra with the champion's trophy, a magnificent golden dagger with a gem-encrusted hilt. The crowd roared their approval.

Indra waited for the applause to subside before he addressed the gathering.

'Devas! My lord regent! I thank you for this honour. But before I truly become your champion there is one thing that I must take care of.'

Vasu and the crowd waited, perplexed by this announcement. Indra continued.

'The great lion Baldar still roams the marshes of the south unchecked. Only when I have killed him can I be your champion and the true son of my father.'

The crowd erupted in joy.

'Long live Indra, a worthy son of Daeyus!'

A worried Soma watched the crowd celebrate and whispered in Indra's ear, 'Was that really necessary?'

'Yes. To be their raja, it is not enough for me to be a champion. I must prove that I can succeed where their previous champion failed.'

He raised the golden dagger aloft and watched the crowd go delirious with joy.

6

It was morning in a thicket of woods that bordered the great swamp. A young man was huddled next to a small fire on which a wild hare was being roasted. Soma swatted a mosquito and cursed under his breath. It had been ten days since they had set off from one of the farms south of Aryavarta. Indra had insisted on making this journey on foot. He had also declined Vasu's offer of an armed escort and opted to only have Soma for company.

The two of them, much to Soma's distaste, had lived the last few days like savages, and Soma had woken up that morning very irritable, longing for a bath and a real bed. The swamp, a wetland formed by the great river Mittani, was full of mosquitoes and other stinging insects, not to mention giant crocodiles and venomous snakes. Over the last few days, they had combed the stinking morass for any sign of the great lion. Although they found plenty of tracks and remains of his older kills, there was still no trace of Baldar.

That day, Indra had woken up early and gone out alone. Covered from head to toe with the black mud from the swamp, he was now lying absolutely still, confident that he was perfectly camouflaged among the reeds. A deer was standing upwind from him. It twitched its tail nervously and looked up. It was a young stag that had separated from its herd to feed on the sweet, succulent grass that jostled for space among the reed beds of the swamp.

Now it paused and looked directly at Indra who did not move from his place in the reed bed. The mud did nothing for his aesthetic appeal, but it afforded protection from the mosquitoes. He waited for the deer to look away before he stealthily moved forward a few paces. Suddenly something burst out of the undergrowth on the far side. It was the biggest lion Indra had ever seen.

The deer started to run, but it was too late. One swipe of a giant paw shattered the hindquarters of the hapless creature. Even as it tried to drag itself away, a pair of massive jaws closed in on its neck. The stag was a full-grown red deer at least two hundred kilos in weight, yet—Indra was shocked to see—the great lion shook its head and tossed it around like a rag doll. Within a few seconds, it was all over. The lion stood over its kill poised to feed. Suddenly, something made it look up. Indra lay absolutely still, holding his breath and trying to keep his excitement under control. To be spotted now would mean one thing only: a swift death.

The lion looked around cautiously; something had made him uneasy. Indra shut his eyes for a few tense moments afraid his pounding heart would give him away. Then after what seemed to Indra an eternity, it picked up the carcass and dragged it away into the undergrowth, out of sight. Indra waited for a few minutes before he stealthily retraced his steps and quickly made his way back to the camp.

Soma saw Indra arrive and curled his nose in disgust.

'If only the Sabha could see you now, they'll crown you raja immediately.'

'I've found him!' Indra said excitedly, ignoring Soma's sarcasm. 'He's made a kill not far from here. This is our chance Soma, we must hurry.'

'What's our strategy?' Soma asked nervously.

'Just carry your dagger and a throwing stick and let's go. We must travel light and move fast.'

Soma held up his dagger and stick, a quizzical expression on his face.

'What are we going to do with these? Tickle him to death?'

It was nearly noon by the time they reached the spot where the lion had made its kill. It was not easy to track the beast through the wetlands, but Indra had learnt from the best. Mitra, before he had given up the consumption of meat, had been an expert hunter and tracker. As they followed the trail, Indra was glad that he had already familiarised himself with the terrain ahead. He knew exactly where the lion was headed. He had scoured this area and had discovered a spot where Baldar frequently used to feed. Now his tracks were pointing right to it. He turned to Soma and explained to him what he had in mind.

Soma could not believe his ears.

'This is your plan? You expect me to put my life on the line, when *this* is your plan?'

Indra smiled.

'Didn't you swear an oath or something to that effect, or have you forgotten?'

'No, I haven't forgotten, but I was thinking about battles, valour and glory. Not ending up in the belly of a lion, and that too in this stinking hellhole!'

'Don't be so dramatic, Soma. This plan is going to work. Now take the lead, and whatever you do, don't step off this trail.'

Baldar was busy with his kill under a tree in the middle of his swamp when he heard a sound. Then Soma came into view, dagger in one hand and throwing stick in the other, running at an even pace. To hide his nervousness, he was singing one of the tribe's marching songs. Behind him, Indra matched him step for step, using Soma's body to shield himself from the eyes of the lion.

When he was about fifty feet away, Soma stopped. Next to him was a pool of wet, sticky mud. There was no sign of Indra. Baldar watched the young man; he did not perceive him as a threat, not as yet anyway. Soma knew that to go closer would be to invite trouble, yet he somehow had to get the lion to charge at him. He whispered a silent prayer and threw his stick at the great beast. Soma did not wait to see the effect of his throw; he just turned and ran. The stick whirled through the air and struck Baldar right in the middle of his snout. The lion let out a roar and charged after Soma.

Indra was certain he had chosen the right man for the job. His friend was by far the swiftest runner he had seen. But even with his head start, Soma was no match for the lion as it quickly reduced the gap between them. As he sped down the narrow trail, Soma began to feel the beast's hot breath on his back. He frantically struggled to increase his pace.

The lion was almost upon him when something rose out of the mud pool next to the trail. A hand reached out and grabbed the lion's mane; it was Indra. The forward rush of the lion lifted Indra clear out of the pool. He swung himself onto the back of the beast and used his heels to dig into its haunches.

The lion let out an indignant roar and reared up on its hind legs. Indra clung to the creature's mane with one hand and with the other he reached for his dagger. As he raised the weapon, he knew he only had one chance to get this right or he and Soma would end up in the belly of the beast. He aimed for the spot on Baldar's neck where the spinal cord met the skull and drove the bronze blade in with all his strength.

Baldar roared in pain as Indra sharply twisted the weapon, severing its spinal cord. The lion stopped dead in its tracks and Indra was thrown over its head. He hit the ground hard, tumbled and rolled over to face the beast.

Baldar took a couple of awkward steps and dropped to the ground, his face only inches from that of his killer's. As the lion stared into those deep blue eyes, there was a flash of recognition. He had seen those eyes many years ago, when he was a cub. Those same blue eyes had gazed at him then with so much love and affection. Now they stared at him with the ferocity of a wild beast, as they willed him to die. Baldar, the king of the swamp, took one last deep breath and then his indomitable spirit left his body and soared to the heavens.

It was another week by the time Indra and Soma, tired and unkempt, rode into Aryavarta. They went straight to the Sabha where the weekly market was taking place. Their appearance invited curious glances from the citizens. Indra alighted at the steps of the building and lifted a huge bundle off the packhorse that he led. The onlookers began to gather around as he unfurled the bundle and revealed the pelt and head of the great lion.

Among the crowd was an old farmer who had lost his son to the beast. He walked forward and looked at the head in awe.

'It is Baldar. He has slain the great one.'

That was all the affirmation the crowd needed. The news spread like wildfire through the market as everyone thronged for a glimpse of the giant beast and its slayer. Cries of praise for Indra rent the air.

Vasu and a few members of the Sabha stepped out to see what the commotion was about. The old warrior had tears of joy as he embraced Indra.

'My boy, today you have proven to be a worthy son of your father. You will be a great raja and it will be my privilege to crown you.'

Unnoticed, Pusan had made his way through the crowd. He looked carefully at the pelt and ran his fingers through it. He soon found what he hoped he would not. Where the lion's shoulder had once been, there was a scar. It was the wound made by his spear. There was no doubt in his mind now. Pusan stood in silent rage amidst the revellers; his dream of leading the Devas appeared more distant than ever.

The pelt was hung on four poles at the entrance of the Sabha for a full week before it was sent to Mitra's hermitage as a gift to the master from his star pupil.

The next few weeks found Indra and Soma as honoured guests at the dinner tables of several prominent families of Aryavarta. Soma was made to recount the story over and over again till every man, woman and child in Aryavarta knew the tale of the slaying of Baldar by heart.

Over the next few years, Indra and his friends continued their martial training and, along with this, Mitra prepared them for their place amongst the nobility of the tribe. For the boys, this proved more difficult than fighting—they found things like decorum and protocol much harder to take to.

One day, watching the boys leave after training, Mitra thought about how the years had forged their friendship and loyalty to one another. It was around these warriors that Indra would build an invincible force and craft an empire such as the world had never seen.

In Indra, though, there lay something deep in the dark recesses of his mind. A dark energy that Mitra could not measure, understand or fathom. It simmered like a dormant volcano within the young man and Mitra used everything in his power to calm it. He taught the boy several meditation techniques to quell his short temper, for he knew that if the boy ever unleashed that energy without having learnt to control it, it would consume everything around him, friend and foe, without discrimination.

On some days Indra was made to stay back for his lessons on kingship. He learnt the laws of his tribe and was also given situations where he had to pass judgment without fear or favour. It was during one of these classes that, for the first time, Indra asked about the circumstances of his birth.

'Tell me Master, did you know my mother? What was she like and why did she not live with my father?'

Mitra had prepared himself for this day. 'Your father did not tell me who she was,' he said. 'I don't think he told anyone.'

'Was she of the northern tribes?'

Mitra shook his head. Indra was quiet for a while as his eyes slowly welled up.

'Then it is true what Pusan says, I do not deserve to be raja.'

Mitra held him by his shoulders and looked deep into those soulful blue eyes.

'My boy, your mother might not be a Deva or from any of the other northern clans, but she belonged to a race far older and more illustrious than ours. You are a gift to our people, the man who will unite our warring tribes into one great nation. I saw this in the night sky at the time of your birth. It was this that brought me back amongst your tribe. No one is more suited to lead the Devas than you and don't let anybody tell you otherwise.'

Indra's face brightened at these words.

'Then as the stars are my witness, I will not let anyone stand between my destiny and me.'

He bowed to his master and left.

That night, Mitra could not sleep, he thought long and hard about the prophecy. Part of his initiation as a seer and mystic involved learning the technique of past life regression. It was a task not recommended without the supervision of another adept, but Mitra decided that the circumstances demanded he take the risk. He decided to travel back in time and reconstruct the exact events that led up to the prophecy.

He reached into his bag and removed a little pouch that contained the seeds of the dhatura plant. He crushed it in a bowl with some warm milk and honey. Then he invoked the blessings of his master and emptied the contents of the bowl down his throat. Almost immediately the powerful narcotic began to take effect. He lay back on his reed mat and shut his eyes. As his body drifted into deep sleep, his mind began to move back through time. He saw his childhood flash before his eyes. Then the images began to move at a rapid rate as he was taken further back through several past lives till he saw himself on a small grassy mound near the shores of the Black Sea, the young chief of a tribe of savage hunters.

Nura, the new chief of the Aie tribe, stoked the dying embers of the fire; it was that time when night surrenders to the day. Around him lay his hunting party, fast asleep. They had been through a long, hard winter, followed by the great flood that had wiped out half the tribe. Only the youngest and the strongest had survived. Before he died, Nura's father had handed over the reins of the tribe to him. Now it was up to him to look after and provide for his people.

It had been months since the floodwaters had receded. The Aie scoured their lands for the great herds of deer that once abounded in these plains. But the rising waters of the Black Sea had destroyed the sweet grass, leaving very little grazing for the herds. So the once proud hunters had to live on roots, berries and small creatures that had survived.

Nura knew that, as chief, the people looked to him to lead them through these trying times. The grumbling had already started amongst a few disgruntled young hunters. Discussions were being held on whether the land would be able to sustain a population as large as theirs. Nura knew that if they did not find any meat soon, he would have a rebellion on his hands. He prayed to the gods for a successful hunt.

Nura looked up as the first light of dawn spread across the sky. Something on the ridge ahead caught his attention and he looked on, amazed. Silhouetted against the sky was the most magnificent pair of antlers he had ever seen. He woke his tribesmen, who quickly readied themselves for the hunt. Expert hunters, the Aie moved swiftly and silently towards the ridge. The herd of deer, still oblivious to their presence, was engrossed in their feeding. The hunters silently fanned out in a semicircle as they ran in, and Nura signalled to the men on the extremes to flank the herd.

The hunters at the flank cast their spears, bringing down a couple of deer. Nura saw the stag lift its head. It looked around anxiously for an opening to break through, but he had set the trap well, the hunters had cut off all escape routes.

Nura watched the stag turn towards him and realised that it was readying to stand and fight. Nura smiled; this creature would make a worthy adversary. He braced himself as the stag lowered its magnificent antlers and charged towards him.

The young chief stood perfectly still as the stag neared him. The distance was too short to cast his spear. He saw its antlers loom large in front of him; it had six sharp prongs on either side. Each one of them was capable of running through a man. Nura pushed his spear out in front like a staff and jammed it into the antlers and held on with all his strength. The stag shook its head and tossed Nura about. He dug his feet into the earth and tried to wrestle the creature to the ground. The spear broke in his hand and knocked him off his feet.

The stag stopped to shake the pieces of wood from its antlers, which bought the young chief some time. One of his men tossed him a short, heavy stabbing spear. Nura hefted the weapon and got to his feet. He was on top of the ridge now. The animal had to run upwards to meet him. He turned to the beast just as it began charging.

Nura timed his jump to perfection. As the beast lowered its head to disembowel the man in front of him, he leapt forward, head first, over the great antlers. He felt the sharp horns of the creature pass inches under his belly. He readied his spear and thrust it deep into the back of the creature, aiming for the spot between the heavily-muscled shoulders. The spear bit deep into its flesh as Nura's momentum carried him over the body of the stag. He hit the ground hard and rolled to his feet.

The stag, now mortally wounded, stood on the ridge, blood streaming down its flanks. Yet it did not flee, but turned around to face the man once again. Nura drew his skinning knife and waited, bracing himself for the next charge, but it did not come. The spear had found the heart of the beast, and its knees slowly buckled and it fell to the ground. The Aie raised their spears and yelled in triumph.

The sun had almost set by the time the Aie finished with the skinning and the butchering of most of the carcasses. Fires had been lit everywhere to roast and smoke the meat. So engrossed were they in their task that they failed to notice a small raft floating through the gentle waters towards them.

A man stood on the raft and looked towards the land with relief. He had floated across the sea several months now. The waters of the great flood had swamped his native land, an island in the western ocean. As far as he knew, only he had survived. It was up to him now to ensure that the legacy of his people was preserved.

In the fading light, he noticed a group of savage tribesmen butchering the carcasses of a few deer. The man gently dropped into the water and pushed the raft away. He did not want to be seen as a castaway who had been adrift for a while. The first impression was everything and in this case it could be the difference between life and death. The man took a deep breath and dived below the surface.

Nura looked up from his task of skinning the great stag. The sun, an orange orb, had almost disappeared into the dark waters. Suddenly he saw something in the water that made him sit up. It was a man unlike any he had seen before. His hair and long beard was the colour of snow. His body was covered with bronze armour and shone in the fading light. To the Aie, who had never seen metal, he looked like a creature from another world, a god. One of the young men in the tribe panicked and cast his spear. The flint tip struck the metal armour and bounced off. The god did not draw his sword or make any threatening gesture; he merely continued to walk out of the water towards them. The Aie looked at each other in shock. Nura shouted out to them to lower their weapons; he had no desire to provoke the god any further.

The stranger walked up to the man who had cast his spear; he had been struggling with the carcass of a deer. The primitive flint knife made the butchering of the animal extremely taxing work. As the god drew his gleaming sword, there was a hush among the Aie; they expected the god to punish the man for his folly. But he picked up one of the limbs of the animal in one hand and swung the heavy bronze blade. The sword sliced through flesh, bone and tendon almost effortlessly. He held up the severed limb in his hand. There were cries of wonder and astonishment among the tribe; they had never beheld such a weapon before. The stranger went to Nura and presented the severed limb to him as he spoke.

'I am Kasyapa.'

Nura did not understand, but head bowed, he accepted the offering from the god. Now it was his turn to appease their divine guest. He cut out the heart of the great stag and offered it to him. Kasyapa accepted the offering, trying hard to hide his disgust. His people had shunned the consumption of meat a long time ago. They believed that it increased the development of the baser instincts within the mind. He gagged at the prospect of tasting flesh, but he knew that it had to be done. He bit into the soft rubbery organ and tore off a piece of it. Blood dribbled down his chin and stained his beard. It took all his will to prevent himself from throwing up as he forced himself to swallow the vile-tasting chunk of flesh.

A cry of appreciation went up among the Aie. The god had accepted their offering. The tribe had no doubt in their mind that it had been he who had blessed them with such a successful hunt. The man who had thrown the spear prostrated at his feet, begging for forgiveness. Kasyapa lifted him to his feet and handed him the remaining portion of the animal's heart. More shouts of joy erupted at this gesture. Their god was as generous as he was compassionate.

Many years passed. Kasyapa lived among the Aie; he learnt their tongue and their ways. He taught them to grow crops, domesticate the cattle and the horses on the wild steppes and how to extract metal from the earth. He did not allow the grateful Aie to worship him as a god. They began to refer to him as Arya, or noble one. He took as his wives Aditi and Diti, the beautiful sisters of Nura. Aditi bore him four sons: Ikshvaaku, Yavana, Aditya and Deva. Diti gave him one, his favourite, whom he called Asura.

Kasyapa's sons grew into fine young men and their indulgent father opened his vast treasure trove of knowledge to them, promising them that their children would rule the world one day. This did not go down well with the gods in heaven. Blinded by paternal love, even the wise Kasyapa did not see that his sons had only inherited his physical form, one of great strength and beauty. Their nature was of their mothers, that of the savage Aie.

The sons of Aditi soon proved to be the scourge of the northern steppes, subduing all the other tribes of the land. They captured vast territories, killing the men and enslaving the women and children. These women bore them many sons, and they soon established their own individual clans. The gods in heaven watched with consternation. They knew that if these warriors were left unchecked, the entire world would soon become their battleground. They appeared to Kasyapa in his dreams, asking him to control his savage progeny. But the Arya did not heed their warnings. He was blind to the faults of his offspring. He spent his days in the company of his youngest son, Asura, who had not let the promise of wealth or women sway him from the side of his noble father. It was then that the gods decided to teach Kasyapa a lesson.

It was the fiftieth year since Kasyapa had first appeared

amongst the Aie. Nura announced a grand feast to honour the Arya and invited the five sons and their clans to participate. The feasting and merrymaking went on for days. On the final day, the gods sent an emissary, the great sage Narada. Kasyapa and his sons, along with Nura, gathered together in the great hall of the palace to welcome him. Narada presented the Arya with a flask of wine and informed him that he had an act of entertainment to present for the feast, a gift from the gods. He then bowed and left.

The wine was presented to the audience. Kasyapa was not sure of the motives of the gods; he made a sign to Nura and his sons to not touch the wine. His sons, however, ignored their father's warning and drank the wine with gusto. Even Asura, who until then had stayed away from all manner of intoxicants, helped himself to a cup.

A veiled woman appeared in the hall and began to dance. So graceful was she in form and in movement that she soon had everyone in the audience spellbound. Her skin was the colour of alabaster, her body was sculpted to perfection and her sheer clothing showed off her full breasts and finely-shaped limbs. As she moved, the tiny bells on her exquisitely-worked anklets produced the most enchanting music. She finished her act by taking off her veil and revealing her face to the enthralled audience. Kasyapa recognised her, even as her great beauty took his breath away. It was Menaka, the divine enchantress.

The sons of Aditi leapt to their feet, their eyes crazed with lust. Each of them claimed the woman for his own. Before their father could say anything, three of them had drawn their swords and fallen upon each other. Deva, who had not drawn his sword, watched in horror as his three older brothers hacked each other to death. He fell to his knees in front of his dead brothers and wept.

Asura, the son of Diti, had not moved from his seat. Through the carnage, he had not taken his eyes off Menaka's face. She looked at him and smiled. Asura stood up and walked over to his stepbrother. Kasyapa watched, a mute spectator, as his favourite son drew his sword and plunged it into Deva's back. Asura then seized Menaka by the waist and carried her off on his horse towards the distant lands in the south.

Outside, the clansmen heard of the terrible event that had occurred within the palace. They abandoned their celebrations, drew their weapons and fell upon each other. By now the gods had decided that Kasyapa had learnt his lesson. A mist descended from the sky, enveloping the warring clansmen. They dropped their weapons and fell to the ground, unconscious.

When the fog lifted, they came to their senses and huddled together. They had no memory of the terrible events that had just come to pass. Kasyapa came out to address them; his heart was broken yet he kept his voice firm. He told them to leave these lands forever and never return. They meekly gathered their belongings and branched out in different directions.

Nura, who had been a hapless spectator until now, turned to Kasyapa angrily.

'How could you let this happen, Arya? Is this the legacy you promised your sons? You said their children would one day rule the world. Today you have left them with nothing. With no land, no tribe and no future.' The once proud warrior fell to his knees and tore at his hair as he wept uncontrollably.

Kasyapa turned to him, his eyes blazing with a feverish light, and he spoke in a deep voice that Nura had never heard before.

'The gods have punished me for going against them. They have taken from me what I valued most of all, my sons. But fear not Nura, the promise I made will stand good. One day a prince from one of these tribes will unite the sons of Aditi and he will sow the seeds of an empire that will rule the world.'

The words of the Arya had a calming effect on Nura, but he had one more question.

'What of Asura, your other son?'

Kasyapa's eyes took on a terrible glint.

'It is against his children that the four tribes will unite. They will pay a heavy price for their father's betrayal.'

Nura watched as the Arya turned and walked away towards the mountains to the east, never to be seen again.

Mitra opened his eyes as he came awake with a start. His mind was in a whirl with a million thoughts. The origins of their tribes had always been shrouded in mystery. Now he realised why. He tried to sit up and that's when exhaustion overtook every fibre of his being. He fell back on his bed in a deep sleep. For days he locked himself in his hut and did not see anybody while he recovered his strength. Then one day, he left the settlement quietly and made his way to the mountains in the north.

On Indra's eighteenth birthday, Mahisi announced a huge feast to which she invited all the prominent families of Aryavarta. She and her army of women slaved long and hard over the preparations. The feast was like no other Aryavarta had witnessed; the festivities and wine flowed long through the day and well into the night.

The highlight of the evening was a musical recital by Sachi. She had sat with the bards and composed a ballad on the slaying of Baldar. She strummed on a harp and as she sang, her melodious voice transported her listeners to the scene in the great swamp. So great was the impact of her recital that, for a full minute after it was over, there was dead silence in the hall. Then the audience broke into rapturous applause. They hailed the bravery of Indra and praised his father for the gift of such an heir.

Once the guests had left, Indra and the boys made their way to their living quarters. All of them, with the exception of Soma, were a little drunk from the wine. Agni suggested they continue the revelry at Nira's Tavern. Both Varuna and Vayu received his suggestion enthusiastically; only Indra and Soma were hesitant.

Nira's Tavern was located in the slave quarters and had started as a place for the slaves to unwind after a hard day's work. It provided alcohol, women and a fair amount of discretion at a price. While it was forbidden for members of the tribe to patronise this establishment, the authorities usually turned a blind eye to indiscretions.

The establishment was run by its namesake, an Egyptian slave once renowned for her beauty. Nira was a tough-as-nails woman who had only two rules: spend money availing of the services, and take whatever disagreements one had outside the establishment. Non-adherence to these rules usually resulted in a rapid eviction from the premises.

The boys were escorted to a room and the women were presented to them. Agni, Vayu and Varuna wasted no time making their choices. Indra opted for a quart of their finest liquor, while Soma politely declined both liquor and women. The dancing and revelry went on well into the night and soon the crowing of the roosters brought them back to reality. Soma was the first to wake and he called out to the others. Indra had spent most part of the night asleep. He shook himself awake as they paid up and prepared to leave.

The boys were still in a buoyant mood as they made their way out of the slave quarters. Vayu and Agni sang one of the bawdy songs from the tavern and ignored Soma's pleas for silence. They turned a corner around one of the shacks and ran full tilt into a night patrol led by Atreya.

One of those in the patrol was Khara, still smarting from his defeat in the Spardha four years back. He was an ardent supporter of Pusan and now saw an opportunity for revenge. He and the guards outnumbered Indra and his friends two to one. The Falcons were also unarmed and this lulled Khara into a sense of false security.

'Well, well, well! What have we here? It is our champion, Indra. Come out to do a bit of whoring, have you? Do you think he would be ready for a fight? Perhaps not! It is likely that the whores of Nira have blunted his spear.'

Varuna felt his friend's temper rise and he grabbed Indra by the arm. 'It's not worth it, my friend. One must choose one's battles. Come, let's walk away.'

Indra nodded; he shut his eyes and took a deep breath as Mitra had taught him. Feeling more in control, he and his friends made their way past the patrol towards Mahisi's.

Their inaction seemed to encourage Khara. He called out to them loudly. 'What do you think Sachi would say when she finds out about this?'

As if on cue one of the guards quipped. 'Finds out about what, my lord?'

'When she finds out that her future husband is a whore chaser.'

Indra stopped and turned around. His companions did not notice the darkness that clouded his eyes. They did not restrain him because they expected him only to rebut Khara's remark.

But Khara was not finished.

'A whore chaser just like his father.'

Indra looked around and spotted a stone that lay on the ground. Before the others could stop him, he had picked it up and flung it at Khara. The missile was the size of an orange and thrown with unerring accuracy. It struck Khara bang in the middle of his forehead and he hit the ground with a thud. There was a moment of stunned silence. Soma was the first to react, shouting, 'Run!'

The Falcons raced away, making towards the woods to the south of the settlement. They did not stop until they had put a few miles between the patrol and themselves. They sat down under a pine tree and tried to come to terms with what had just happened. Their situation was dire, to say the least. Indra was well-versed with the laws of the tribe; he had killed one of the night guards on duty. The penalty for that was death without a trial. His current standing would have no bearing in this matter; the rule was the same for nobility and commoner alike. He turned to his friends.

'This is not your problem. Go back home and leave me to take care of this.'

'We have sworn to serve you to the death if need be,' Varuna said, speaking for everyone. 'Would you have us go back on that vow? Whatever happens we are in this together.'

Indra smiled. 'With you'll by my side, what need do I have for a tribe or an army. We have no time to lose: Soma and Agni, hurry back and bring our horses and weapons. Varuna, Vayu and I will backtrack and cover our trail. Meet us at the dead tree on the south road as soon as you can.'

It was noon by the time they finally spotted Agni and Soma. They came at a rapid pace and, as they drew near, Indra saw the reason for their urgency. Twenty horsemen led by Pusan and Atreya were in hot pursuit. The three of them mounted their horses in full flight as arrows whizzed by their heads.

'Make for the swamps,' Indra said as he took the lead. The Falcons rode like the wind and soon the reed beds of the great swamp were in sight.

'Let us stay and fight. Those boys seem to have forgotten the hiding we gave them in the Spardha,' said Vayu.

'No. To kill anyone else will only make it worse for us. Follow me in a single file, and whatever you do, do not step off the trail.'

Indra led them into the marshy wetland and the reeds soon swallowed them up.

Behind them, Pusan had brought his horse to a halt at the edge of the swamp. 'Let them go,' he called out. 'Just make sure they do not track back into our lands again. Spread the word to all the farms in the area—anyone found aiding the outlaw Indra will share his fate. They will not survive one night in that swamp.'

Leaving Atreya in charge of patrolling the area, Pusan made his way back to Aryavarta.

Indra's knowledge of the swamp was the only thing the Falcons had going for them in that hostile terrain. He led them through a narrow path among the reed beds, carefully avoiding the shallow pools of water that teemed with giant crocodiles.

It was almost dusk by the time they came to the spot under the tree that was once the lair of Baldar. A few bleached bones of his prey were the only signs left of the great beast. Indra thought it would be a safe place to spend the night. Soma made good use of his skill with the throwing stick and brought down a few quail. They roasted them over a fire and spent their first night as outlaws under the starry sky.

It was three whole days before the Falcons reached the end of the wetlands. They had followed the upstream course of the river Mittani which cut through the swamp on its way west. As they stepped out of the reeds, the panoramic view that unfolded before their eyes took their breath away. As far as the eye could see was a lush green meadow full of beautiful wild flowers of various hues.

Herds of ibex and antelope grazed, completely unfazed by the appearance of men on horseback. Indra and his friends leapt off their horses, stripped away their clothes and jumped into the river. Without the black mud and dead vegetation, the waters of the Mittani were a clear icy blue here.

They did not say a word to each other as they washed off all traces of the swamp from their bodies. Then they swam around to get the circulation back into their limbs before hunger drove them reluctantly out of the water.

Too exhausted to hunt, they fed the horses and tethered them close to the fire. Then after eating their rations of dried meat, they used their saddlebags as pillows and stretched out on the open plain, staring up into the star-filled sky.

7

It was two months before Mitra returned to Aryavarta. Almost immediately, he realised something was amiss. He made his way to Mahisi's farm, where a relieved Paras met him. Mitra listened in silence as Paras narrated the series of events that had occurred since his departure. The gravity of Indra's predicament did not escape the seer. He requested Paras to ride ahead and inform Vasu that he would like an audience. Mitra then went to the river to wash the dust of the trail off his body and to contemplate his future course of action.

It was dark by the time Mitra reached the Sabha for his meeting with the regent. As he approached the hall, he saw the Lions in full battle regalia assembled outside the building. Atreya, who avoided Mitra's gaze as he entered the hall, led them.

As Vasu rose to greet him, Mitra noticed that the old warrior was unsteady on his feet and his eyes betrayed his intoxicated state.

'Greetings Master! My heart is gladdened by your return to Aryavarta.'

Mitra's reply was curt. 'Greetings, my lord regent. I wish I could tell you the feeling was mutual, but I'm saddened to hear what has befallen Prince Indra.'

Before Vasu could reply, another voice was heard.

'The person you call a prince is a fugitive from justice. He has killed a member of the night guard on duty. The punishment is death under Deva law—something you might be unfamiliar with as you are not of our clan.'

It was Pusan, sitting amongst the younger members of the Sabha. Mitra looked around the hall. A few of the older members were conspicuous by their absence. Vasu sighed and sank back in his chair wearily.

Mitra cocked an eyebrow in surprise.

'I am familiar with the laws of your tribe. Perhaps it is you who needs to familiarise yourself with the law, Pusan. For you seem to be unaware that it is forbidden to speak out of turn in the Sabha.'

He turned to Vasu.

'I had requested an audience with the regent. It was him alone that I was addressing.'

'My father is indisposed; it is only out of respect for you that he is present here today. I look after his affairs now. So if you have anything to say, I suggest you say it to me.'

Mitra looked at Vasu. The old warrior shut his eyes to avoid the sage's gaze.

'What I have to say can wait till his health is better. Goodnight to you all.'

As he turned to leave, Pusan called out to him.

'Just one more thing, my lord! This Sabha no longer requires your services. In future, if we have need of your counsel, we shall request it.'

As Mitra made his way back to his hermitage, he became aware that he was being followed. He veered off the trail into the woods and the rider behind him followed at a discreet distance. As he rounded a bend, he whispered a hurried command to his mare. Then, standing on the back of the horse, he reached out and grabbed an overhanging branch and hoisted himself onto it. The mare continued ahead on the trail, and a few moments later, the horse and rider on his tail appeared. Mitra crouched low on the branch and sprang on top of the rider.

The man was completely unprepared for the attack from above and was thrown off his horse with Mitra on top of him. The seer jabbed his forearm into the man's throat and spoke in a whisper. 'Who are you? Why are you following me? Answer quickly or die.'

The man gasped for breath and said, 'Forgive me, my lord. It is I, Atreya. I must speak with you on a matter of great importance.'

Mitra released the pressure on the young man's throat. He got to his feet and dusted his robes. 'You will get yourself killed, skulking about like this in the dark. Come with me, this is hardly the place for us to talk.'

Paras, waiting at the hermitage, was surprised to see Atreya ride alongside the sage. He did not say anything though, but busied himself in tending their horses.

Mitra offered the young man a seat.

'Now tell me. What is it that you have to say that could not wait till morning?'

Atreya bowed respectfully.

'My lord, I was part of the night patrol that intercepted Indra and his friends. We were instructed by Pusan to keep quiet at the inquiry.'

Mitra stared at the young warrior with interest.

'What are you trying to say? Speak plainly.'

Paras had just come in and he listened now with interest as Atreya continued.

'Khara provoked the attack—he insulted Indra's father.'

Mitra was thoughtful.

'Are you willing to testify if there is a trial?'

'Yes, my lord. On my honour as a soldier, I will testify.'

Mitra studied the young man's face carefully. 'You have done well by coming to me. Now go and do not speak to anyone else about this.'

As Atreya turned to leave, Paras could no longer contain himself.

'Why should we trust you? You, who are willing to betray your own dal?'

Atreya ignored Paras and looked at Mitra as he spoke. 'I am a Deva warrior first, before I am a Lion, and I believe no one is better suited to rule our tribe than Indra. Goodnight, my lord.'

Mitra watched the young warrior leave.

'Be prepared to leave at first light, Paras. We must find Indra before he gets himself into anymore trouble.'

Varuna and Soma offered to make camp while Vayu, Agni and Indra set off after a herd of antelope. The animals saw them approach and began to take flight. Indra pointed to a frisky young stag; Vayu and Agni nodded and flanked out in either direction.

With a short burst of speed, Agni cut their quarry off from the rest of the herd. The stag was beautiful and strong; in his prime. He still did not consider these strange animals a threat. He started to pick up the pace as he led them on a chase with giant, springing strides. The three hunters let him run, careful to maintain a steady distance between them and their quarry. Then soon enough the stag began to tire and the hunters started to increase their pace as they unslung their bows.

The stag sensed them draw near and prepared for one last burst of speed. He sprang into the air and suddenly his body stopped mid-stride. Arrows smashed into his ribcage from three different directions. The stag was dead even before it hit the ground.

Indra was the first off his horse. Knife in hand he approached the kill. He knelt down, turned the carcass over and made a deep incision in its chest. He spread the skin apart and looked at the heart of the stag. All three arrows had pierced it; he looked up at the other two with a smile and shrugged his shoulders.

'It's a tie.'

The three of them quickly got to work as they skinned and butchered the carcass. It was nearly sunset by the time they reached their makeshift camp near the river. Varuna and Soma had made a perimeter with the thorny bushes that grew abundantly at the edge of the swamp. It would keep lions and wolves away. Soma had found some wild potatoes, which he cleaned and put into the fire with the meat. The Falcons had a delicious meal of grilled venison and potatoes and settled down for the evening.

Well into the night, Indra sat by the fire, lost in thought. Around him his companions lay fast asleep. He had lost count of the days they had spent on the endless southern plains. He knew that their flight from Aryavarta had not been the best solution to the problem. They could not live like this forever: his companions were homesick, it was only their love for him that had kept them going through these monotonously long days.

He sighed as he looked at the beautiful night sky. Indra decided that the time had come for him to return to Aryavarta and bear the consequences of his actions. He had no regrets for what he had done. He had not cared about the insults against himself; but no man could insult the memory of his father and live to tell the tale. He added a little more wood to the fire, then lay down and shut his eyes. They had long given up keeping watch at night, relying on the fire to keep predators at bay.

The next morning, Indra announced his decision. It evoked mixed reactions among his companions. Agni, as was his wont, was the first to react.

'Well it's about time. I'm looking forward to meeting with Pusan and his Lions again.'

'I say we surrender ourselves to the judgment of the Sabha,' Soma said after a little thought. 'You killed a man who insulted your father. Surely they will see the justice in that.'

'Not if the Sabha is in the control of Pusan and his cronies,' Varuna pointed out pessimistically. 'And it may very well be so.'

Vayu had his own ideas about their next course of action.

'There are enough people in Aryavarta who support us. I say we raise an army and take the settlement by force.'

Indra had heard enough.

'I will not raise my sword against our own people. Come, let us head back to Aryavarta. As long as Vasu is regent, I will be assured of a fair trial.'

The Falcons followed the upstream course of the river Mittani as it snaked its way towards the northeast. Its waters were deep and fast flowing here and it took them nearly a day to find a place to ford it. Indra was the first across and soon all of them stood on the opposite bank in front of an imposing forest of cedar trees. Indra drew a map on the ground with a stick and indicated which way they must travel.

'Let us make camp here for the night. Tomorrow, if we make our way due northwest through this forest, we will be a day's hard ride from the eastern border of our land.'

Paras stoked the fire and cast his eyes uneasily about; his nerves were on edge, his mind consumed by disturbing thoughts. The night sky above was clear with a bright moon, yet the earth seemed to give off a gentle mist that rose to the sky like smoke. The light from his fire cast strange-shaped shadows and enhanced the eeriness of his surroundings.

This was their second night in the wetlands of the river Mittani; they had no idea how far the swamp extended. Next to him Mitra lay fast asleep. His breathing was gentle. Paras could not believe that the master could sleep so well in this terrible place. The two of them had left Aryavarta separately a few days ago, so as not to arouse any suspicion, and met near an oak tree at the edge of the swamp. They had not spoken much since then. The swamp, with its treacherous trails, had not afforded them the luxury of conversation.

Paras had watched in disbelief as Mitra had tracked Indra and his companions through that shifty terrain following their now month-old trail. Whenever there was no physical evidence of their presence, the seer had used his intuition. As they had made camp that evening, what little misgiving Paras had of his mentor's tracking abilities soon disappeared. He found one of Soma's abandoned throwing sticks at the edge of the path.

Mitra's voice brought him back to reality.

'Sleep now, Paras, we must break camp at dawn.'

'But it is still my watch, my lord, and you need your rest,' Paras protested.

'But your mind is not on the task at hand. I don't want to end up in the belly of some beast just because you were lost in your thoughts.'

Paras bowed his head in shame.

'Forgive me, my lord. But please let me sit with you awhile for I cannot sleep.'

The seer brushed aside the apology.

'There is nothing to forgive, my young friend. Tell me, what is it that troubles you?'

Paras thought long and hard as he tried to frame his question.

'My lord, I do not think it is wise to bring Indra back to Aryavarta on the basis of Atreya's word. He could be leading us into a trap.'

'It is for Indra to decide whether or not Atreya's word is trustworthy. After all, it is his fate that hangs in the balance. He has faced Atreya on the floor of the Spardha and he will know better than us if his honour as a soldier means enough to Atreya to betray his mentor and his dal.'

Mitra added a few sticks to the fire and sat down to keep watch. Paras, unable to argue in the face of such logic, settled down near the fire and soon fell asleep.

It was well after daybreak when Paras awoke. Mitra was nowhere to be seen. Assuming that the master had gone ahead to scout the trail, the young warrior went down to the water's edge to wash his face. He waded through the thick mud to get to the clearer water in the middle of the pool.

Just then he heard a shout. He looked up to see Mitra in the distance waving his arms. Just then a black shape leapt out of the water and a pair of giant jaws closed with clap-like thunder only inches from Paras' head. The soldier was quick to react and ran towards the bank. The thick mud made it difficult for him to move fast, while behind him, the giant crocodile cut through the water towards him.

Up ahead, Mitra picked up Paras' spear and turned towards the man and the monster.

Paras was a couple of steps from the bank when he felt the creature's jaws get hold of his leg. He reached forward, grabbed hold of the reeds growing at the edge and tried to pull himself to the shore, but the crocodile had got a good grip and it began dragging him back. The creature began its death roll. The young warrior realised that any resistance would mean the loss of his limb, so he rolled along with the beast and tried to force open its great jaws with his hands.

Mitra watched his companion and the giant crocodile thrash about in the water. He stayed low on one knee as he held the weapon ready and looked for an opening. The crocodile stopped its roll for a moment to readjust its grip. The seer wasted no time; he took aim and cast the spear. The weapon flew flat and straight and struck the crocodile in the eye. With a roar of pain, the beast opened its jaws. Paras pulled his foot free and made a run for dry land while the crocodile retreated into the depths of the pool.

Paras fell to the ground, exhausted from his efforts. Mitra knelt beside him and examined the leg. He noticed that the young man had been very lucky; the leather thongs of his sandals had prevented the creature's vicious teeth from inflicting any serious injury. But for a few minor scratches, he was all right. Mitra reached into his bag for a jar of antiseptic salve and smeared it on the injured ankle. Then he got to his feet with a smile and said, 'By my estimation we will be out of the swamp well before nightfall, so if you have finished clowning about, we can prepare to move on.'

Indra was the first to wake. It was still dark, the early morning sun hidden behind the tall cedar trees. There was something strange about this forest. The sounds of the birds and animals that usually heralded a new day were completely absent. Perplexed, he went to see to the horses but was surprised to discover them missing. Indra immediately woke his companions and apprised them of the situation. Soma, who had tethered the horses in the evening, was shocked to discover their loss. Their saddles and weapons had also been taken. The only weapons they had were their short bronze swords, which they always kept close at hand.

Indra was furious with himself for not having appointed night watches. Their peaceful, monotonous routine on the southern plains had made them careless, and now they had paid the price. Their situation was precarious to say the least; they were in the middle of nowhere with no horses or armour.

'These people could not have gone far. They were clever enough to conceal their tracks around camp, but they would not have wasted time doing it for long. I'm sure we will be able to pick up their spoor in the forest.'

They split up and made their way into the forest looking for any signs of the thieves. Indra tried hard to calm himself; he needed all his senses under control. He wished Mitra were around: he could have done with his advice. Next to him, Soma, who was deep in thought, suddenly remembered something.

'Paras' brother was killed near this forest; he told me that it was forbidden for our tribe to enter it. Maybe these lands belong to a hostile tribe and we are trespassing.'

Indra was not in the mood to be governed by rules.

'I don't care. It does not give anybody cause to steal our horses. The people who did this are going to die slowly and in great pain.'

He stopped as the trail widened ahead. In front of him was a pile of horse dung. He examined it and discovered it was not more than a few hours old. Ahead of him on the path, Soma called to him excitedly. He had found the tracks of their horses.

As Indra knelt to examine them, something else caught his attention. Next to the horse tracks, he found rather strange-looking sets of footprints. They looked human, except for the toes that seemed to extend into sharp claws. Soma also examined the tracks with interest.

'Nothing human could have made these.'

Indra looked up at him.

'They might not be human, but they are intelligent. They sneaked into our camp and made off with our weapons and horses—that cannot be the work of a wild animal. Call the others and catch up with me. I'll go ahead and check out these tracks.'

Indra moved on and was swallowed by the forest. Soma mimicked the cry of a falcon and the others soon joined him. He quickly told them what they had discovered. They drew their swords and hurried down the trail after Indra; the hunt was on.

As he made his way through the jungle, Indra was amazed at how quickly and efficiently these creatures had moved through the darkness. They seemed to have been about eight to ten of them. Most likely they were a hunting party that had chanced upon their camp, but there were a lot of things he could not explain. How had they managed to keep the horses quiet? Deva horses were trained only to recognise one master; to have led them quietly away in the night like sheep . . . it was unexplainable.

He saw a dip ahead on the path where the forest sloped away into a steep valley. When he looked down from the rim of the slope, he was amazed by what he saw. The mist rose like plumes of smoke from the depths of the valley, enshrouding the dark green foliage in a thick white cloud. Indra looked down and realised that the task at hand might not be as easy as he had initially thought. Most of the descent into the valley would have to be in near zero visibility.

And then he heard a deep, sinister voice—as if someone were speaking in his head. 'Leave now or die.'

As Indra stared down into the slope, he heard Soma and the others come up behind him. He turned and motioned for them to be silent. As they stealthily approached, he whispered to them, 'Whatever we are chasing is down there, waiting for us.'

Even as he spoke, he saw the foliage behind his companions part, and a branch whipped through it. Indra screamed, 'Look out! It's a trap,' and threw himself to the ground.

The branch had been bent backwards and released; it moved with the speed of a whiplash and struck his companions in the square of their backs. They toppled headfirst into the valley. Without a moment's hesitation, Indra drew his sword and plunged down the slope after them.

The young warriors tucked their heads into their knees and rolled down the slope, a technique that they had learnt in training to break their fall. The slope levelled out into a broad ledge that stopped their descent. As each of them reached the ledge, they got to their feet and drew their swords. Soma, the lightest, was the last to arrive. As he got up, Vayu saw something drop from the trees onto his friend's back.

'Soma! Watch out!' he called.

But the Pisacha had already landed on Soma's back, its fangs going for his jugular. Soma turned his head and the creature's huge fangs caught and ripped off the top of his ear. Soma screamed in pain.

Indra saw the shape of the creature as it prepared to bite into Soma's neck a second time.

'Soma! Duck!' Indra yelled and, raising his sword, launched himself into the air.

As Soma bent his head, he felt the bronze blade pass millimetres above him. It struck the creature on its neck and severed its head clear off.

Indra wiped the blade on his tunic as he got to his feet and called to the others. 'Chakra!'

The other three immediately moved into formation with him and formed a defensive circle around the wounded Soma, as Pisachas sprang from the treetops and came at them from all directions. The creatures ran into a wall of bronze blades, the Falcons, with a stunning display of swordplay, cut them to pieces. Yet, wave after wave continued to come. Within the protection of the chakra formation, Soma bound a rag around his head to protect his torn ear and called out that he was ready again for battle. Indra barked out a sharp order. 'Forward!'

The chakra slowly changed from a defensive to an offensive formation as they moved forward to finish the enemy once and for all. Indra watched one of the creatures re-attach its severed limb and attack him. He swung his blade and decapitated it.

'Take their heads! That's the only way to kill them.'

With the element of surprise now lost, the Pisachas were no match for the superior strength and skill of the Deva warriors. Before long, twenty-five Pisacha heads rolled on the jungle floor.

Indra motioned for the others to be quiet and listen. They could hear the faint rustle of branches, but the sound was travelling away from them, below, into the valley. The Pisachas had posted a lookout; others would know what had happened to their hunting party.

The Falcons looked along the ledge for a way down and soon found a narrow path cut into the slope that doglegged its way to the bottom of the valley.

The Pisacha lookout watched as Indra instructed his companions to spread out on the valley floor. They split up and moved silently through the trees. The lookout was forced to change its position frequently to keep an eye on all of them, playing right into Indra's hands. As soon as the creature moved, the rustle of branches gave it away. Two fist-sized rocks thrown by Varuna and Agni struck it in the chest and knocked it down from its perch. The creature hit the ground and was up and running almost instantly, hotly pursued by Agni and Varuna.

The others started to converge on the creature from all directions, but it was too fast for all of them. It carved its way through the thick fog, clambered up a steep mountain trail and disappeared into a cave. As they stood near the cave and contemplated their next course of action, Soma arrived with good news. Their horses were alive and were corralled with good food and water.

A quick search of the area revealed their saddlebags and weapons; they had been hidden in a little burrow near the horses. Armed and well supplied, they readied themselves to take on the cave.

'Torches and swords, boys! And for Surya's sake, try not to kill each other in there,' Indra called out, as he lit his torch and led the way into the cave.

The light from the torches threw spooky shadows on the walls of the cave as the Falcons made their way through it. They took each step with caution as they waited for the Pisacha attack to come. The cave narrowed and slowly began to snake its way upwards into the mountain. Varuna shone his torch against the sides of the cave and saw that there were many handholds carved into the rock. He wondered what they were for as he whispered to Indra, 'I don't like this; what're they waiting for? They should have attacked by now.'

Agni laughed. 'After their little ambush failed, they must be skulking in their holes, afraid to step out.'

'Shhhh! Listen,' Indra said as he strained his ears.

The sound started to get louder. Varuna was the first to react; he suddenly realised what the handholds were for.

'It's water! Hold on to the sides.'

The five of them had just about made it to the sides of the cave when a wall of water hit them. They were swept off their feet and were barely able to cling on to the walls. The flood lasted only for a few minutes, but their torches had been swept away or ruined beyond repair. They were now wet, cold and, without their torches, blind. The Falcons cast away their robes; their weight now they were wet would only hamper them in battle. Clad only in their loincloths, swords in hand, they continued up the passage into the pitch-blackness.

They climbed in silence, Indra setting a comfortable pace; he wanted to conserve their strength. He had a strong feeling that they would need every ounce of it. At long last he saw a glow ahead. They quickened their pace as they reached the end of the passage and soon all five of them stood at the entrance of a giant cavern. The walls and ceiling were covered with phosphorescent algae that glowed in the dark. Its stunning beauty took their breath away.

Agni was the first to break the silence. 'All right, I know this is beautiful. But I'm wet, cold and a little hungry. So can we move on, kill these wild men and get out of here?'

Vayu rubbed his belly. 'I'm with you on that one, especially the hungry bit.'

Indra was the first to look down and notice the floor of the cavern.

'Well, before that, we might have to get wet again. Look!'

His friends looked down to see that the floor of the cavern was not a floor at all. They were faced with a large pool of water, still, dark and deep.

Agni did not waste any time; he sheathed his sword and plunged into the pool. The others followed suit. They swam quietly so as to not disturb the water; they were not sure what lurked within its depths.

Indra crossed the length first and trod water a few feet away from the opposite bank of the pool. The walls had several large bare patches with algae missing. On closer inspection, he realised that they were tunnels leading out of the cavern. The others arrived and for a moment they huddled together in the freezing water as Indra struggled with his choice of which exit they should swim for.

The Pisachas took the decision out of his hands as they chose that very moment to attack. The Falcons felt a rain of stones hit them. Though small, the stones were unerringly accurate. One struck Indra on his forehead and he shouted for them to split up and swim for the shore. His vision was blurred as blood flowed from the cut on his forehead into his eyes. He saw a small sandy beach leading up to a tunnel. He took a lungful of air, dove under the surface of the water and swam for it.

Indra clambered onto the beach and drew his sword and dagger. Several pairs of red eyes watched him as they moved forward to attack. Indra did not wait—he let out a blood-curdling yell and ran at the Pisacha line.

Varuna was an expert swimmer. As the shower of stones began, he took a deep breath and made for one of the tunnels furthest away at the extreme end of the cavern. He was sure none of the others would attempt to swim under water that far. Not that he did not appreciate their company, but right now he just wanted room to swing his sword and kill some more of those beasts. He relished the thought of more combat. No rules, no wooden sword, this was life or death. This was the real deal.

He broke surface near a rocky shelf at the mouth of the tunnel. A few of the Pisacha had gathered here in wait. A blood-curdling yell from Indra momentarily distracted them. Varuna leapt on to the shelf and echoed the yell. Before the creatures could recover from their surprise, he drew his sword and dagger and rushed at them.

Varuna hacked and slashed his way to the entrance of the tunnel and the Pisachas fell in huge numbers to his blade. After a while his arms began to tire, but the attack showed no signs of letting up. He carved a path across the shelf through to the entrance of the tunnel. The creatures came at him from three sides and started to push him into it. Varuna immediately realised that he had chosen the wrong exit. With his back to it, he staved off the relentless attack.

Just as he felt his arms were going to tear from their sockets, it was over. He dispatched the last of them, a female that had bitten a huge chunk of flesh from his thigh. As he staggered back he slipped on the blood of one of his victims and fell backwards. He tumbled and slid on the loose gravel into the tunnel, which sloped downwards before it fell into a sheer vertical drop. Varuna tried to cling to the edges but only succeeded in dislodging a huge rock that fell into the deep pit after him.

As Varuna hit the bottom, the rock fell on him and pinned the lower half of his body to the ground. He struggled to break free, but the rock was lodged too tight. Even as he thought his predicament could not get any worse, he felt a trickle of water against his face. Varuna pushed the rock with all his strength, but it would not budge.

The water level continued to steadily rise around him even as his struggles to break free intensified. As the water rose above his head, the brave Falcon continued to pit his strength against the rock, but it was to no avail. Slowly Varuna's struggle ceased and his body became still.

Agni found himself forced through a tunnel by a throng of the creatures. In the dark he had lost count of the number of heads he had taken. Yet they continued to pour in and fall on his sword, to be chopped to pieces. Then as suddenly as it had begun, the attack ended. Agni continued to swing his sword wildly a few times before he realised there were no more of the enemy left to slay.

He leaned on his weapon and caught his breath. Barring a few superficial wounds, he was relatively unscathed. He started to make his way further up the tunnel when suddenly something fell on his head. It was a Pisacha, a juvenile.

What it lacked in size the little creature made up for in sheer ferocity. It wrapped its hind legs around Agni's neck in a vice-like grip as it tore at his scalp. He grabbed it with his free hand and tried to prise it off his neck. Just then one of its claws went right into his eyeball and ripped it out of its socket. The intense pain gave Agni superhuman strength. He screamed as he pulled the creature off his back by the hair on its head. Then he held it at an arm's length, spat into its face and sliced off its head.

Agni struggled to stay on his feet. He reached for the side of the tunnel to brace himself, but felt only thin air. Just then a body crashed into him and he toppled into space. He hit the ground and found himself tumbling through a shaft along with one of the Pisacha. He hit the bottom with a resounding thud.

Momentarily winded, he struggled to his feet. He found that

he was in another tunnel. The air in there felt thick and moist and had a particularly unpleasant smell. As he felt the walls on either side he found they were scalding hot. He needed to get out of there quick. He groped around the floor and found his sword. Finally something was going right for him. He smiled at the thought and listened for any sound that might betray the position of his enemy.

He heard the scratch of claws against stone; it was on his blind side. Agni's smile widened as he swung the sword with all his might in the direction of the sound. The bronze blade struck an overhanging rock and threw out a flurry of sparks. Agni's one eye widened in terror as the very air around him exploded into flames.

The tunnel Vayu chose was the nearest, but the most inaccessible. It was high above the water level and required him to scale a steep rock face. He'd seen creatures pour out of this tunnel and spread themselves across the cavern walls as they prepared to repel the Falcons' attack. Their speed and agility on the slippery rock face was amazing to behold. Vayu held his sword between his teeth and started the steep ascent. He used the strength of his upper body to good avail and made use of the numerous footholds to make quick progress up the rock face.

Vayu was already half-way up to the tunnel when the Pisachas spotted him. There was mild panic in their ranks as they turned and headed back towards the entrance of the tunnel to cut him off. Vayu quickened his pace and was there a moment before them. He waited now, sword in one hand, dagger in the other. The creatures began to screech in alarm and tried to stop him from getting into the tunnel. Vayu just stood there and hacked them to pieces. Somewhere in the distance he heard Indra's battle cry. He screamed his response at the top of his voice, momentarily frightening the creatures. As he waited, the next attack came at him from within the tunnel. Three Pisachas jumped onto his back and struggled to knock him off his feet.

As Vayu shook them off, more creatures rushed to the entrance of the tunnel from behind and tried to drive Vayu back. The precariousness of his position only served to spur Vayu on: he chopped and hacked his way into the depths of the tunnel. The creatures were no match for his ferocity and they fell in large numbers before his sword.

The tunnel opened out into a small cave. As Vayu entered it, panic set in among the Pisachas. They began to pile up their dead in his path to obstruct him but soon it was all over. Vayu felt around the floor of the cave with his feet and discovered a pile of dry wood. Using a few pieces of flint from the cave, he made a fire, fashioned a makeshift torch and took a look around. He was shocked to see that a majority of the creatures he had killed in the cave had been females and juveniles. He pushed aside the pile of corpses and looked to see what the creatures were so desperately trying to protect.

In the light of the torch, he saw what looked like a stone altar built against one of the walls. On it, neatly arranged, were bowls of clay, a stone axe, a flint spearhead and a variety of primitive tools. He realised that these creatures had been human once and they had zealously preserved the last vestiges of their humanity in this little shrine.

Vayu was saddened by what he saw; he could not believe that so many females and young had died to protect what seemed like worthless old implements to him. Their actions made them more human than he could have ever imagined. He was filled with remorse at his own ruthlessness. He took a deep breath and sank down to his knees as he surveyed the carnage around him.

A slight sound made him turn in that direction and he saw something that filled his heart with pity. A young Pisacha was squeezing its way out through the corpses. Vayu lay down his sword and offered his hand, and the creature hesitantly took it. As it neared him, it tightened its grip on his hand and leapt for his neck. Before Vayu had an inkling of what had happened, the young Pisacha's razor-sharp teeth locked in his throat. He tried to scream but no sound came out.

Vayu grabbed the creature by its neck and tried to pull it away, but the Pisacha tightened its grip around his throat and severed his windpipe. Vayu tried to breathe, but the air would not reach his lungs. He coughed as warm blood began to fill into his chest cavity. He opened his eyes and saw the creature's face next to his own. Its malevolent red eyes were fixed on him as it waited for him to die. Vayu's grip around its neck slackened. As he struggled for breath, the little creature bent its head and eagerly began to feed.

Soma was the last of them to make it out of the pool. The loss of blood from his torn ear had weakened him considerably. His vision was blurred and he floundered about in the pool as he looked for a tunnel to swim to. Just then, he heard Indra's battle cry. It was very close, and reassured, he swam in that direction.

As he dragged himself onto the beach, Soma found it hard to even stand straight. He used his sword to prop himself up and staggered to his knees. As he looked up, he saw a group of Pisacha advance towards him menacingly. Soma waited; he saw their red eyes stare down at him. Two of the creatures stepped forward, crouching as they readied to pounce. He focused on a point a span's length below the line of their eyes and tightened his grip on the sword.

As the two creatures sprang, he swung the sword. The blow had all his weight behind it and was on target as it cleanly cut through the neck of first one and then the other. The two Pisacha were dead before they hit the ground.

Soma fell to one side with the effort. The force of the blow had wrenched the sword from his grasp and it now lay in the sand close by. The other creatures were more circumspect now as they fanned out in a semi-circle and approached him. As he drew his dagger and waited, Soma was sure he would not survive the next attack. He promised himself that he would take as many of them with him as he could.

The attack did not materialise. A surprised Soma watched the group of Pisachas turn away from him at the last minute and rush off. As he looked up with relief to see where the creatures were going, he saw Indra. The Deva prince was standing on a flat rock as scores of the creatures attacked him from all directions. His sword was a blur in his hand as he swung, pirouetted and danced his way through the throng, dealing death and destruction. Soma suddenly felt blackness descend over him and he dropped to the sand, unconsciousness.

When he came to his senses, he saw Indra still on the rock, sword in hand. Around him lay piled the bodies of the dead Pisacha. Soma was so weak he could barely raise his head; he called out to his friend in a weak voice.

Indra woke as if from a trance as he heard a faint voice call his name. He made his way through the pile of corpses and found Soma lying close to the water. He rushed to him and took his head in his lap; it was sticky and wet—and still. Indra saw that the pale sand around him was dark with blood. His friend had bled to death.

Indra held Soma's body close to him and wept. He called out to the others, but there was no reply. He had a sinking feeling that they had suffered the same fate. He could not believe how grossly he had underestimated the Pisacha. He had assumed they were dealing with mindless, savage beasts, and the Pisachas had been anything but that. They had worked like an organised army led by an astute general.

They had learnt quickly from their first defeat and planned their next ambush to perfection. Their second attack had split the Falcons, thus preventing them from functioning as a unit. Once they were alone, the creatures had used their superior numbers to good effect and picked them off one by one. Yet through the battle, Indra had seen no sign of their leader.

Just then, he heard a voice in his head. It was the same one from the forest that had initially warned them to keep away.

'Greetings, lord of the Devas. You have won a hard-fought victory. Now step forward and collect your prize.'

He understood now—the Pisacha leader had used telepathy to communicate with his troops, much the same way he was communicating with Indra now.

Indra spoke softly, but there was no mistaking the deadly intent in his voice. 'Do not mock me, man, beast or whatever else you may be. The only prize I want now is your head and I'm coming to get it.'

Indra stood up; the battle with the Pisachas had taken a toll on his body. The flesh on his shoulders and back had been ripped to the bone in many places. The pain however, did not distract him; it only fuelled his rage as he ran for the tunnel.

Uruk, lord of the Pisachas, sat on a huge rock, his eyes closed in deep meditation. The cavern in which he sat was made up entirely of quartz. Moonlight entered it from a hole in its ceiling and fell on him. His pale body shone and the light from it reflected off the crystal walls and ceiling and gave the whole chamber an eerie glow.

Indra entered the crystal cavern after a long and arduous climb through the tunnel. His mind and body had been pushed way beyond the limits of their endurance. Only one thought drove him now, the desire for revenge. He raised his sword and advanced towards Uruk.

The lord of the Pisachas stood up and folded his hands in supplication. 'I, Uruk, chief of the Pisacha tribe, thank you, my lord, on behalf of my people for freeing them from this vile existence. I regret that I cannot give you the pleasure of taking my life, for I wronged a power far greater than you or I. It is to that power I must now submit myself.'

He spread his arms wide and raised his head to the light. Just then, a shadow passed over the moon and threw the room in darkness. Then, as Indra watched astounded, a bright yellow light entered the cavern and fell on the rock.

Uruk's body burst into flames and was entirely consumed within moments. Indra saw that not even ashes remained of his adversary. The beam of light now moved slowly across the floor towards him.

Indra stood still, sword in hand. He had no idea how he was going to fight this mysterious force, but he was not going to turn tail and run. If this was to be his end, he was ready to face it. The beam of light hit him and Indra felt a gentle warmth envelop his body. The pain that had been coursing through his body was gone, replaced by a sense of calm. His eyelids grew heavy with sleep. He shut his eyes and felt himself being lifted out of the cavern, through the beam of light, before he lost consciousness.

As he came to his senses, Indra felt himself being transported through a vortex at a speed way beyond what his senses could comprehend. Vivid images flashed before his eyes: he saw two giant landmasses collide with each other and the earth begin to fold upwards towards the heavens, towards him. Indra watched in amazement as, from the giant fold that had formed across the land, molten lava began to ooze. He was witnessing the birth of a mountain range, the most magnificent the world had ever seen. Then snow began to fall, and he saw it cover the peaks of the mountains. The images began to speed around him and soon they were moving at a hypersonic pace. He began to lose consciousness again.

When he awoke, he found himself suspended in space, among the stars. He looked around and saw his companions naked as the day they were born. Soma was there, his ear intact, his face as beautiful and radiant as ever. They all seemed to be staring upwards in a deep state of trance. Indra looked at his own body, astounded. His wounds, even old scars, had all disappeared. It was as if he had been reborn.

He tried to sit up and found he could do so easily. It was then that he noticed that they were all slowly circling a giant pillar of light, brighter than a thousand suns. As he looked up and down, it did not seem to have a beginning or an end. For all its brightness, it seemed to give off only a warm, comforting glow that made their bodies shine like gold.

Then from the pillar, right before his eyes, creatures began to emerge, human in shape, but with no physical form. They seemed to be made up entirely of light. As one of them approached Indra, he noticed the face; it wore a gentle, benevolent expression. Within its body, Indra could see tubes of light in multiple hues crisscross through it like veins and arteries. As he gazed into the creature's deep, dark eyes, he felt all his fears and misgivings disappear. A great sense of calm engulfed Indra and he surrendered to it.

The creature reached out its hand towards him and touched him in the centre of his forehead, between his eyes, with its index finger. Indra felt an incredible surge of energy through his body, he heard himself cry out like a newborn child, and then there was nothing.

Mitra shivered as a cold draught of wind hit him, almost putting out the campfire. There was a dull ache in his head, something he had not experienced in years. It was their third night in the vast southern plains. Mitra had spent the last couple of them awake, casting his awareness out into the vast openness. He'd tried to pick up traces of the auras of his boys, but had found none. The exercise had weakened his body and mind considerably, which explained the headache.

Mitra knew the only remedy was rest and meditation, but he had time for neither. The situation had started to worry him. Where could they have disappeared? He had stayed close to the river, as he knew Indra would have done the same. But had

Indra been in a position to make that choice? It baffled Mitra, how they had just disappeared. He decided to relax and make another attempt before dawn. It would make the coming day very hard on his body, but he did not care.

Paras woke up at daybreak to the sound of laughter. He was amazed to see the sage chuckling away to himself. Looking out into the rising sun, Mitra said, 'I have found them.'

Indra opened his eyes and found himself beside a pool of water. The walls of the cavern he was in were covered with a green glow. He looked around and saw that the others were awake. Like him, they had no idea how they had got there. The only way out was a dark tunnel behind them. They gathered their weapons and torches and made their way out.

The Falcons walked in silence, unable to find the words for what they had all experienced. Of one thing they were sure: it had not been a dream. Indra could sense a certain vibration in the pit of his stomach, a low rumble that he could feel but not hear. Suddenly Soma's voice broke the abnormally long silence.

'Can you'll feel that thing in your stomach?'

One by one all of them admitted to it. Any further discussion on the matter was curtailed as Indra, who was leading the way, spotted daylight ahead. With a huge sigh of relief they increased their pace.

They stepped out of the cave and stood in the light of the early morning sun that was breaking through the thick fog around them. In unison, they looked up to the heavens. They felt the vibration become stronger. Then it started to move upwards through their body. Through the abdomen, chest and throat, into their heads. They felt it burst out through the top of their heads like a volcano. The fog began to lift and bright sunshine hit the floor of the valley for the first time. Their horses saw them and whinnied with joy. On the floor of the valley, bright little flowers started to bloom, their faces turned towards the sun. Butterflies appeared, and bees and dragonflies. It was as if the forest had started to come alive again.

As they made their way through the forest, they suddenly saw a dark cloud in the sky; it seemed to descend towards them at great speed. As it neared them, they realised what it was. Thousands of birds were returning to roost in the Forest of Cedars. Soon the canopy was filled with birdsong.

They camped that night in the forest and by mid-day found themselves on the eastern border of Aryavarta. There they found Mitra and Paras waiting for them. The two had ridden day and night to rendezvous with them. The reunion with their teacher was a warm and joyous one for the Falcons.

As Paras brought them up-to-date with the situation in Aryavarta, the sage studied his boys, amazed to see the change in them, particularly Indra. There was a calm and self-assured way about him now. The boy he had left behind a couple of months ago was now a man.

Indra listened to everything they had to say, and then laid down his future course of action.

8

Paras rode ahead and arrived at the settlement well before noon. It was the day of the weekly market and the square outside the Sabha bustled with activity. Paras stood on the steps of the hall and called out in a loud, clear voice.

'Citizens of Aryavarta, I bring to you a message from Indra, son of Daeyus. He is on his way to claim his birthright, the throne of Aryavarta. Any citizen who has an objection will be given a chance to state his case today. Let the Sabha be convened.'

Paras was pleased to note the great cheer and enthusiasm with which his words were received. The months of absence had in no way diminished Indra's popularity among the common folk. He slipped away in the ensuing confusion and awaited the arrival of his new king.

As he rode towards the Sabha, Indra was delighted to see the citizens of Aryavarta gathered in the streets to greet him and follow him to the hall. The members of the Sabha had assembled outside in full strength, eagerly awaiting his arrival. Mitra was pleased to note that the regent was genuinely happy to see the prince safe and well.

As he alighted at the steps of the hall, Indra heard a sharp voice cry out, 'Seize him! He is a murderer and an outlaw.'

He turned to see Pusan and his Lion Dal, armed to the teeth, make their way towards him. Atreya was conspicuous by his absence. The Falcons drew their swords and formed a protective circle around their leader.

Vasu was quick to spot the imminent danger and he called out in his authoritarian voice, 'Stand down, Pusan. Prince Indra has to be given a chance to prove his innocence. I order you'll to surrender your weapons and submit to the authority of this Sabha.'

At a quick nod from Indra, the Falcons relinquished their weapons. A furious Pusan and his cohorts did the same.

Though Vasu was happy to give Indra the floor of the house to present his defence, he was sceptical as to how successful the young man would be. His companions were co-accused, so their statements would not be admissible.

Indra stood in the well of the house and the members leaned in, eager to hear what he had to say.

'My dear citizens, I, Indra, son of Daeyus, stand before you accused of murder. I have only this to say in my defence: the man I killed insulted the memory of my dead father. I only did my duty as a son to restore his honour.'

Pusan stood up.

'Bold words, but worthless, without any proof. You and your companions were found near Nira's Tavern. Fearing arrest, you killed one of the guards while he tried to discharge his duty. The other guards can substantiate this charge. Do you and the co-accused have anybody who can speak for you?'

Indra bowed respectfully to Pusan.

'Yes, I have a witness who will corroborate my statement. He was present when the event occurred and he does not stand accused. I call on Atreya of the Lion Dal.'

There was a gasp around the hall at this totally unexpected

turn of events. Pusan watched in shock as Atreya, dressed as a common citizen, took the floor. The brave young Lion looked straight at a livid Pusan as he gave his statement as to the events that occurred that fateful morning. Atreya's testimony was enough to convince the members of Indra's innocence. Vasu wasted no time in delivering the verdict: 'Not guilty!'

The news was greeted with roars of approval outside where the entire populace of the settlement, citizens and slaves, had gathered in the square, anxious to hear what the verdict of the Sabha would be.

Indra now stood up to address the Sabha.

'My lord regent and members of the Sabha, I, Indra, son of Daeyus, am here to claim my birthright to lead the Devas as their rightful king. If anybody has just cause to object, let them do so now.'

He looked towards Pusan with a smile. A furious Pusan faced Indra squarely as he spoke. 'I, Pusan, son of Vasu and Madri, challenge your right to lead our tribe. We who carry the bloodline of the Arya Kasyapa cannot allow ourselves to be ruled by the illegitimate son of a demon.'

A hush fell on the audience; to question the legitimacy of a man of noble birth was an insult that could only be avenged with blood. All eyes were on Indra as they awaited his next move.

Indra pretended to be shocked at Pusan's statement. 'My lord! I am dismayed by your allegation. You leave me no choice but to challenge you . . .'

Pusan could not hide his smugness; he did not even wait for Indra to finish. He thought he had him exactly where he wanted him. After all, he was older, stronger and definitely more experienced in the art of combat.

'I accept. Choose your weapon and the time. I will teach you a lesson you will not forget.'

Mitra watched Indra carefully; although his ward's face did not betray his emotions, he caught a triumphant glint in those blue eyes. Suddenly he was not sure who had trapped whom into this duel.

Indra bowed slightly to Pusan. 'With your permission, I was hoping we could settle this the old-fashioned way.'

Vasu noted how he paused for dramatic effect. Indra had grown up in the short time that he'd been away. He already carried himself like a king. Everyone in the Sabha leaned in, eager to hear what Indra would say next. His words were spoken loud and clear:

'I challenge you to a Dvanda.'

A hush greeted these words, followed by cries of protest from those who fully grasped its meaning. Vasu and a few of the older soldiers were out of their seats as they made their disapproval very clear. Pusan's smile faded a little. He suddenly found himself questioning Indra's sanity. Pusan knew what a Dvanda was; to agree to it against a mad man would be suicidal.

Mitra was dismayed at Indra's announcement. He could not fathom the reasoning behind his decision. The Dvanda was an ancient, barbaric way the northern tribes had used to settle disputes. It was a knife fight to the death. One hand of an adversary would be tied to the hand of his opponent with a rope made of horsehair. The length of rope between them would be exactly three feet. They were then given short daggers of identical shape and size. The rules were simple: the two men would hack and stab at each other till only one of them was left standing.

One of the primary reasons the Dvanda had been banned was because more often than not it descended into a bloody scrap from which neither opponent walked away alive. It was cruel and barbaric, even by the Devas' standards. Vasu called for silence, but in vain. Finally he shouted over the din. 'The Sabha will not allow a Dvanda to take place. It requests Prince Indra to reconsider his challenge.'

Indra bowed to the regent.

'I beg your pardon, my lord, but the laws clearly state that a Dvanda can be used to decide the right to kingship. Provided both the opponents are in agreement. Unless I'm mistaken, this is a duel that will decide who will eventually lead our tribe. So unless Pusan has an objection, the Sabha cannot interfere.'

A helpless Vasu tried a softer approach.

'My boy, I promised your brave father that I would look after you. Allow me to honour my raja's last wishes. You are like a son to me. Please! Desist from this madness.'

'You loved my father, my lord. Surely you understand my need to avenge an insult to his memory. If I'm like your son, do not fear, at the end of this duel, you will still have one son you can be proud of.'

Pusan watched Indra closely; there was something different about him. And these were not the words of a mad man, but of someone with supreme confidence in his own ability. Pusan quickly dispensed the thought from his mind. He was at least half a head taller than his opponent, with a significantly longer reach. This was going to be easy.

'I have no objection, let's get this over with,' he said.

Indra bowed, first to Vasu and the other members and then to Pusan.

'Good, then our business here is concluded. We will meet at the square outside tomorrow, at first light.'

He nodded to the others and they left.

Sachi's heart had filled with joy when she heard of Indra's return, but her celebrations were rudely cut short by the news from the Sabha. Madri tried in vain to offer her some kind of solace, but there was nothing really that she could say to console her daughter.

Sachi walked out of the house down towards the Mara River, to her favourite spot, a rock that jutted out over the water's edge. It was a perfect place to be alone, hidden from view by the overhanging branches. It was only when she was there that she allowed her tears to flow. By tomorrow night, only one of the two men she loved more than her own life would be alive.

On one hand there was her brother, whom she had loved from the day she was born. Whatever differences of opinion she had with him, he had been a kind, generous and protective sibling.

She looked down into the clear blue waters of the Mara; it reminded her of the eyes of her beloved. Ever since she had been a little girl, she had grown up with the knowledge that Indra would be her husband. It would be impossible for another man to take his place.

Just then, she heard her father's voice call out to her. She ran to him with a loud cry. 'Father, you were there! How could you let this happen?'

Vasu took his beloved daughter in his arms.

'I am sorry, my child. I tried to talk to Indra but he would not listen. Neither to order nor to plea.'

Sachi untangled herself from his arms and wiped her tears.

'Then I will go to him. He claims to love me more than anything else in this world, let me see how he can deny me this request.'

Vasu held his daughter back; the old warrior had tears in his eyes as he spoke.

'I would gladly let you go if I thought there was even the slightest chance he might accede to your request. I have looked into his eyes; this is not the boy you and I once knew. This is a man who has made his decision, even the gods cannot make him change it.'

Her father's words only confirmed what she already feared. Still, she was not willing to let it go.

'What of your son? Why didn't you stop him?'

'Stop him from what? Having ambition? Wanting something that he truly deserves? I am bound by my vow to Daeyus, he isn't. I know this is as difficult a time for you as it is for me. I will scour the earth and find you a better husband than this mad, headstrong fool. Now go back into the house and pray for your brother's victory.'

Sachi looked at her father. There was a hardness to his voice that she had never heard before. She turned and ran back into the house.

Mitra finished his evening prayers and stepped out of his hut. A worried Paras informed him that Indra had not shown up for training or taken any food and drink that day. The man in question sat a little distance away, under a tree. His eyes were focused in the direction of the setting sun. He was lost in his thoughts and did not appear to notice the two of them. The seer asked Paras to leave them and he went and sat next to his pupil.

Indra continued to look ahead, and then he said, 'I had to do it. It was the only way out.'

'I understand your need to challenge and defeat him. But the Dvanda—was that really necessary? I fear you underestimate

Pusan. He is a great warrior. Surely you can see the advantage that he will have in this contest.'

'He has the advantage of height and physical strength. But it was you who said that it is not size and strength that makes a great warrior. It is the heart. I do not think he has the heart.'

'If you are wrong, it will cost you your life. Listen to me, my boy. All is not lost. I will speak to the regent. Let this be decided by a duel with training swords as is the norm.'

Indra turned to his master, his eyes blazing with a determination and confidence that Mitra had never seen before.

'This world is not big enough for the two of us. If I lose the duel with him, I cannot be king, and if I cannot be king, I have no desire to live anyway. That is why I chose a fight to the death.'

The citizens of Aryavarta gathered in the square well before sunrise. Both warriors were extremely popular, and the crowd was almost equally divided in its support.

The two fighters stood toe to toe in the middle of the square, not taking their eyes off each other. The rest of the Falcons, along with Mitra and Paras, had found themselves seats at the top of the stairs from where they had an uninterrupted view of the proceedings.

As the sun rose, Vasu stood up to address the crowd.

'Citizens, it gives me no pleasure to make this announcement, but I'm left with little choice. Today, two of our greatest warriors will fight against each other in a Dvanda, a fight to the death. Bring the rope.'

A soldier brought the rope of horsehair and handed it to Vasu. The regent approached the fighters. He bound Indra's left hand to Pusan's right, making sure the length of rope between them was not more than three feet. The old warrior's eyes welled up with tears as he wished them luck. He kept his voice steady, stepped back and pointed to a brass gong that hung near the stairs.

'At the sound of the gong, the fight will commence. It will end only when the victor cuts the rope off the dead hand of the vanquished. The gong will sound again to mark the end of the contest. Anyone who tries to intervene during the fight or in any way tries to influence its outcome will be put to death instantly.'

The elite guard, fully armed, placed themselves as a protective human barrier between the fighters and the crowd.

'May Surya lend strength to your arms, and may the greater warrior prevail.'

Vasu sat down and nodded for the gong to be sounded.

The two fighters circled each other warily, clutching a knife each in their free hands. Clad only in their loincloths, they presented quite a contrast in appearance. Pusan was tall, strong and well-built. His shoulders, chest and arms were massive from years of training. His legs were thick and sturdy, like tree trunks. He looked every inch his part, a Deva warrior in peak fighting condition.

In contrast, Indra was much smaller in build. His body was lean and wiry, with every muscle clearly defined. What he lacked in musculature he made up in speed. He nimbly dodged and blocked Pusan's strikes as he looked for an opening. They both used an overhand grip with the blade pointed downwards.

Suddenly Pusan gave the rope a mighty tug and knocked Indra off balance, towards him. With all his weight behind it, he brought the knife down in an overhead stabbing motion.

Indra saw the blade coming. It was aimed at the point where

his neck connected to his shoulder. If it landed, it would bring an early end to the duel. He watched the knife all the way and at the very last moment he stepped back. Indra was fast, but not fast enough; the point of the knife grazed his chest. Pusan's supporters roared their approval as their champion drew first blood. Vasu found himself unable to remain neutral any longer and joined in the applause. His son was going to win.

Vasu had spent a very troubled night, torn between the love for his son and his duty towards his fallen raja. But the father in him had prevailed. Now as he watched the fight unfurl, he was glad for Indra's choice. It could mean that his son would be the next raja of the Devas. No one could deny Pusan the right to sit on the throne after this victory. The old warrior smiled to himself. So what if he had not been able to be king, it was his bloodline that would rule the Devas.

The fight did not appear to be going well for Indra at all. He was bleeding from the numerous cuts all over his body. It was only his speed and agility that had kept him alive till now. As he watched the mismatched contest, Mitra knew it was only a matter of time before one of Pusan's strikes found its mark.

Suddenly, the sky above them began to darken. Mitra looked up and saw dark clouds start to gather. As they swirled overhead, there was a loud clap of thunder. The fight stopped for the briefest of moments.

Indra looked up to the heavens and rain began to fall on his face. Mitra cursed under his breath: as if the fight wasn't one-sided enough already. The odds were now further stacked against Indra. The rain would make the ground very slippery. Oddly enough, the Falcons did not seem perturbed at all by the way the events were unfolding in front of them.

Pusan paused for breath as he studied his opponent. All he had to do now was to wait for Indra to make a mistake. Indra changed his grip on the weapon; he now held the knife in his fingers, pointed upwards. Paras looked at Mitra, his expression saying it all: what in Surya's name was Indra doing?

The rain began to fall steadily now. Indra stood in a puddle of water that had turned bright red with his blood. It was a wonder to most people how he hadn't bled to death yet. The seasoned warriors marvelled at how his wounds hadn't slowed him down at all. Pusan, who was relatively unscathed but for a few minor cuts on his knife hand, now attacked with renewed vigour. Indra backed away cautiously as he avoided a couple of vicious strikes. Suddenly Pusan, who was holding the rope tight, let it go slack, which threw Indra off balance.

Pusan came at him with the knife held high. From his unbalanced position, Indra could not step away without losing his footing so he went the other way, sliding towards his opponent. As his legs crashed into Pusan's, he used all his strength and momentum and tugged at the rope. Pusan lost his balance. For one brief moment, he had to check his strike and use his arms to steady himself. That was all the time his opponent needed.

Indra held the knife like one would hold a pointing stick and swung his arm in a lazy, wide arc. The blow appeared to miss its mark. Indra rolled with the strike and got to his feet. The crowd was surprised to see him hang back without pressing his attack. By now Pusan had managed to steady himself. As he raised his head, a red line appeared at his throat. There was a cry of anguish from Pusan's supporters as their champion's head gently fell back. The line on his throat was now a gaping wound from which blood was starting to gush.

Mitra's jaw dropped in astonishment; Indra had not missed his mark. The knife had severed Pusan's jugular vein, windpipe and carotid artery with surgical precision. It was the perfect death strike.

Vasu let out a cry of anguish and ran towards the arena. His only son was dead; his dream, shattered.

Indra bent over his opponent's fallen body to sever the rope that bound them together. He felt no elation at the victory, only regret at the passing of a great warrior. He heard a sound behind him and turned sharply, knife in hand, to see Vasu rush towards him. Suddenly the old warrior lost his footing, tried to check his forward momentum, but fell on Indra. The dagger in Indra's hand entered his soft gut and buried itself to the hilt.

Vasu gasped in pain as he fell to the ground. Indra took him in his arms, unable to control the tears that were streaming down his face. The regent had been more than kind to him throughout his childhood. After Mitra, he was the closest thing to a father Indra had known. Vasu opened his mouth to speak.

'My boy, when your father left you and the tribe in my charge, my only regret was that I could not join him in a glorious death. I feared I would die old and lonely in my bed, with my flesh slowly wasting away. Thank you for giving me a soldier's death. I go happy in the knowledge that my life was taken by the greatest warrior this world will ever see.'

Indra tried hard to keep his voice steady, around him the rain continued to fall.

'Do not worry, my lord. It is only a scratch, the physicians will have you up and about in a few days.'

Vasu's body stiffened. He gripped Indra's shoulder and raised his head with difficulty so he could look into the boy's eyes.

'Sachi! Her only fault is that she is Pusan's sister and my daughter. But she loves you more than anything in this world. Promise me you will honour the pact and make her your wife.'

'Your daughter means the world to me, my lord. I would be lucky to have her for a wife.'

Indra felt Vasu's grip on his shoulder slacken. The old

warrior was gone. The rain stopped and the square was once again bathed in bright sunlight.

There was no celebration to mark Indra's victory, no loud cheering. While Pusan had had his fair share of detractors, Vasu had been loved and respected by all. A tearful Indra handed the regent's body to one of the guards. He severed the rope at his wrist and heard the sound of the gong announce the end of the fight. Just then, he felt a blackness surround him. From the corner of his eyes, he could see Soma and his companions run towards him. He took a couple of steps towards them and collapsed in their arms. On Mitra's instructions, they rushed him to Mahisi's house where the physicians could take a look at him.

It was dark by the time Dhanavantri, the chief physician, came out of Indra's hut. His face wore a worried expression. He had already pronounced two people dead, and he was not entirely hopeful about the third.

'I wish I had some good news for you, Master Mitra. But the truth is, by all accounts Indra should be dead. He has lost way too much blood. I have cleaned his wounds and applied a poultice. It is up to the gods now.'

Mitra put his arm around the physician and led him out of earshot of Indra's companions. He did not want the boys to worry.

'Tell me Dhanavantri, how do you explain the fact that he is still alive?'

'I cannot!'

Dhanavantri leaned in closer; his voice was now a tiny whisper.

'I felt his prana, his life force, when I examined him.'

'Is it strong?'

'Strong? It is ten, perhaps a hundred times stronger than an average healthy human being's, and that too in his weakened state! I had examined him after the Spardha; he was strong then, but this I cannot explain. Now he does not even seem human.'

Mitra's grip tightened on the physician's shoulder and the man winced. Mitra realised what he was doing and immediately relaxed his hand, but his voice was still stern.

'Speak to no one about this. Consider this an order from your new raja.'

The old physician smiled.

'Do not worry. I spoke to you only because I know you have an understanding of certain things that cannot be explained. I have no wish to talk about this to anybody and have people question my sanity. This secret is safe with me.'

As the man departed, Mitra turned to the boys who had big smiles on their faces. Mitra was not amused.

'What are the smiles for? Did I miss some joyous moment?'

Varuna spoke for them.

'Indra will not die. He will be fine as soon as Soma arrives.'

Mitra remembered something he had neglected to do when he had met them after their period of exile. He now scanned their auras and noticed now how brightly they shone. This was not normal. Clearly these boys had had some kind of divine experience. He decided to probe further.

'How do you know he will be fine? And where is Soma?'

'Indra told us himself. Soma has gone to fetch a brew that will revive him.'

'What do you mean Indra told you himself? He is lying in the hut unconscious.'

Agni had waited impatiently to get into the conversation.

'We heard Indra's voice in our heads.'

Vayu tried to explain.

'What Agni means is that we can communicate with him, using our thoughts.'

Mitra was amazed. These boys were saying that they could use telepathy, a craft that took even learned seers like himself years to perfect. Just then, Soma arrived with a little bowl and rushed into the hut. Mitra turned to the others.

'How long has this been going on? Why didn't you'll tell me anything?'

Varuna was hesitant.

'We wanted to, but we were not sure you would believe us. We could scarcely believe it ourselves. We thought it was all a dream.'

'Wait, there's Indra.'

Mitra turned as he heard Vayu's words and looked on disbelieving as Soma and Indra walked out of the hut and headed straight towards them. The prince had wrapped his body with a cloth, but otherwise he looked like he was in the pink of health. As he neared his master, Indra removed the cloth. His wounds had healed completely.

Mitra listened in amazement as the Falcons took turns bringing him up-to-date with their adventures. Indra told him about their strange encounter with the Pisachas. When they had woken up in the cave, each one had presumed that it had been a dream. They did not even speak to each other about it, fearing they would be made fun of. Only a chance remark by Soma had made them realise that they had all had a similar experience. When they had sat together and analysed what had happened, they realised that it had not been a dream at all.

Vayu and Agni then got up and began to have a fistfight. Their hands moved so fast, it was almost a blur. They ducked, weaved and swung out of the way of punches at a speed that baffled the eye. Varuna then went up to a big rock that was at least five times his own body weight. He picked it up almost effortlessly and flung it at them. Vayu and Agni moved in perfect synchronicity and turned to meet the missile with their fists. The boulder shattered into tiny fragments and showered Mitra with dust.

'As you can see, our bodies have changed. We are faster, stronger and more powerful than before.'

Mitra dusted himself as he listened to Indra.

'Well, that's putting it mildly. But wait, what about the Dvanda? You did not look very powerful there.'

'I was tempted to use my powers, but it would have served no purpose other than to spark fresh rumours about me being a demon.'

'I'm glad that along with power, you have been bestowed some wisdom. You were right in concealing your gift. But the stunt you pulled was dangerous, you could have been killed.'

Indra shook his head. 'No—he was much too slow.'

Mitra suddenly remembered Soma's wonder potion.

'What of this brew? How did you'll come by it, Soma?'

'Last night as I slept, I heard a voice in my head. It was one of the seven beings that we saw emerge from the Pillar of Light. When I opened my eyes, I was in a dark wood. A single shaft of moonlight came through the trees and illuminated a tiny plant in front of me. The voice told me to pick up the plant. Once I had done so, the moonbeam lit up another plant. Before long I had an assortment of plants and herbs with me. I made a potion with it and was instructed to give it to Indra after the challenge.'

Mitra was not sure what to say; but he was their teacher—he could not be at a loss for words.

Soma reached into his bag and pulled out an ampoule with a stopper.

'I have a little of it left if you would like to try it, Master.'

Mitra first shook his head, then his curiosity got the better of him.

'Maybe just a little.'

He put the ampoule to his lips and took a small sip. He shut his eyes as he swallowed the bitter liquid. When he opened them, he felt himself flying through a dark tunnel. Then he was cast out into what could only be described as a city of light. The structures, the beings, everything around seemed to be made of light beams that were constantly in motion. As one of the creatures approached, all the light beams crisscrossing its body began to turn a dark red. It had a grimace on its face as it raised its index finger at Mitra and wagged it in a clear gesture of denial. Then he heard Indra's voice. He opened his eyes and saw that he was clutching Indra's wrist tightly. Embarrassed, he let go.

'Are you all right?' Indra asked, concerned.

Mitra nodded, afraid to speak. He turned to Soma, who looked at him rather anxiously.

'I have still not perfected it. I have to figure out the exact proportions of all the ingredients and also reduce the concentration and improve the taste.'

Mitra gripped the boy by the shoulders.

'Listen to me carefully. This potion is meant for the five of you alone. Do you understand? Never give it to anybody else, regardless of the circumstances. Is that clear?'

'Yes, Master.'

'Good! Are there any more surprises you have in store for me?'

The Falcons looked at each other and smiled. Then Agni, Vayu and Varuna stood up and closed their eyes. They chanted a mantra under their breath; it was in a language Mitra could not understand. Then Agni opened his eyes and pointed at a dead tree, a fair distance away. A small fire started at its base. Then Vayu stepped up and blew gently. The flames rose, till soon the branches at the very top of the tree were on fire. The heat from the burning tree forced them to take a step backwards. Then Varuna opened his eyes and pointed towards a little stream. A jet of water sprang from it, high into the air. As it came down, it doused the flaming tree.

Mitra turned to Indra and raised his eyebrows.

'What about you? Don't you have a trick or two to show me?'

'I'm not sure, Master. But do you remember the little thunderstorm during the Dvanda this morning?

'Yes . . . unusual for this time of the year.'

'I think I made it happen.'

Mitra marvelled at the prowess of his pupils. Yet his pride was tinged with regret. His time as their teacher was nearing an end. His students were no longer men, but gods.

Unlike the funerals usually reserved for Deva warriors, the funeral ceremony for Vasu and Pusan was a solemn one. The manner of their passing, especially that of Vasu, had been too tragic for the customary celebration.

Mitra stood alone in a corner and mourned the passing of his friend. As they lit the funeral pyres, Madri tried to jump into the flames and join her husband. It took all of Mahisi's strength to hold her back. Sachi gently pulled her mother away and held her close as she watched the flames. Although her beautiful face was calm, a heavy cloud of grief hung over it, and this did not escape Mitra's notice. As the flames rose, her eyes met his but showed no sign of acknowledgement or recognition.

Indra sat on the bank of the Mara near the ashram, his mind occupied by thoughts of Sachi. It pained him that he couldn't be at her father's funeral—Mitra had strongly advised Indra and his companions against it. Tempers could flare up among Pusan's supporters if they saw Indra at the funeral looking hale and hearty. Maybe it was for the best that she would not see him there. What if she hated him? It would not be surprising. Even if she forgave him for killing her brother, could she ever forgive him for her father's death? Perhaps there was a way: he would be the best husband in the world to her. She would want for nothing: children, jewellery, kingdoms . . . he would lay the world at her feet. Then perhaps with the passing of time she would learn to forgive him.

'Indra, come quick! You cannot miss this.'

Soma's voice brought him back from his thoughts. He turned to his friend.

'You remember that big black bull that we used to be scared of as kids? Vayu is trying to wrestle with it.'

Before Indra could reply, something made him look up. He saw a big black mass flying across the river. It was the bull. The soft grass on the opposite bank cushioned its fall. It rolled a couple of times and got to its feet with a groan.

Indra shook his head and said, 'Maybe it's best if you'll stay away from Aryavarta for a little while.'

It was late by the time Mitra got back to the ashram. The whole day had gone in mingling with the nobility in Aryavarta. Mitra found politics tiresome, yet it was necessary. Indra's absence from Aryavarta had fuelled several rumours, including one that he had died from his wounds. The other, more dangerous rumour spread by Pusan's sympathisers, was that Vasu's death was not an accident, but murder. While no one openly questioned his right to the throne, Vasu's death had left a sour taste in the mouths of even Indra's most ardent supporters.

Now as he lay in bed, he was unable to sleep. He had not told Paras what he had learned from the boys. It was best nobody knew till the time was right. He knew now that all that was left for him to do was to teach the boys to handle their powers with responsibility. But how would he be able to hide their gifts from the citizens of Aryavarta? There was also the delicate matter of Indra's marriage: it was the only way to keep the Devas united. But would Sachi agree to marry the man who had killed her brother and was suspected of having murdered her father? Finally, his exhaustion got the better of him and he drifted into a deep sleep.

Mitra rose early, well before sunrise, and went down to the riverbank to perform his morning ablutions. As he rose from his customary dip, he heard a voice from the opposite bank.

'The air in Gandhar is heavy with the weight of your troubles, old friend.'

Mitra looked up and saw a familiar figure; in his hand was a staff with a crook. He bowed respectfully.

'Greetings, Master Bhrigu. It gladdens my heart to see you.'

Mitra watched with a smile as Bhrigu bounded across the river towards him, his feet barely causing a ripple as they skimmed over the surface of the deep, fast-flowing water. The two men embraced warmly. Mitra led him to his hut and offered him some fruit and a bowl of milk.

Mitra waited for the sage to finish his meal and then said,

'Your arrival is like a godsend to me. I am sorely in need of your counsel.'

'I'm afraid it is my own pressing need that has brought me here.'

Mitra was surprised. What need could a sage of Bhrigu's prowess have of him?

'My problem can wait. Please tell me how I may assist you.'

'Since we last met all those years ago, a great deal has changed in my life. I have a wife now and four children. I . . . I had four children, now I have three.'

His voice cracked with emotion and Mitra waited patiently for him to continue.

'I lost a son, my first-born, ten days ago. He was still a boy, seventeen years old. He was struck on the head with a wooden club. His head was cracked open like a nut . . .'

The old sage began to weep, unable to continue. Mitra put his arm on the man's shoulder in a gesture of consolation.

'Do you know where we can find the people who did it?'

The sage composed himself and nodded.

'We are a small community of a hundred people who live at the foot of Mount Mandara, five days march to the north of here. We live off the land, farming, rearing some sheep and a few cattle. Last year our peaceful existence was shattered by the arrival of another tribe. They live on the slopes of the mountain and send raiding parties to attack us. They steal our grain, livestock and women. Our men are not warriors; they possess courage but lack the skill to defend themselves. My son tried to get the men together and build an effective force against them, but he lost his life in the last raid.'

Mitra thought quickly. This could present a solution to his immediate problem. Indra had to take charge of the throne and Soma was needed to help him with his duties. But the others he could send with Bhrigu. This would suit his purpose well. Firstly, he would not have to worry about the boys' powers being discovered by the Devas. Secondly, they could only benefit from being around a man of Bhrigu's wisdom. He made up his mind.

'I have the solution to your problem, rather three solutions. How soon do you require to leave?'

'I have travelled night and day to get here. I'm ready to leave immediately, as every moment's delay only increases the danger my people are in.'

The noise outside told him the boys were awake. He excused himself and went to fetch them.

As he entered the hut of the Falcons, a loud argument greeted him. It was the usual suspects, Agni and Soma. Agni had a handful of what looked like mushrooms in his hand. He held them out towards Mitra.

'Look, Master! Bad enough he spends all morning sifting through cow dung picking these things up. But he insists on bringing this filth into our hut. I woke up this morning with the smell of shit in the air.'

'Give that back to me, you stupid oaf. Stop meddling in things that do not concern you.'

'All right that's enough, you two,' Mitra said. 'Agni, Varuna and Vayu, get your things together. You'll are going on a little trip.'

The boys jumped up in excitement.

'What trip, Master? Where are we going?'

'You'll are going to live with the sage Bhrigu at his ashram for a little while. Now hurry, it is not wise to keep the sage waiting. Where is Indra?'

'He has not returned from his bath. Is he going away as well?' Soma asked, worried he was going to be left all alone.

'No. Ask him to come to my hut when he returns. By the way, do find some other place to keep your stuff Soma, it does stink in here.'

'Yes, Master.'

Mitra went back to his hut where Bhrigu was pacing about impatiently. Mitra took the opportunity to tell him about the adventure the boys had just had. Bhrigu listened in silence, fascinated.

'These beings they saw. Did they tell you how many of them were there?'

'Indra mentioned there were seven of them.'

Bhrigu's grief-stricken eyes now shone with excitement.

'The Saptarishis! Many sages including myself have awaited their arrival for years now. What we saw all those years ago in the stars is finally coming to pass.'

Bhrigu saw Mitra's confused expression and realised that he had been mumbling to himself.

'Forgive me, my friend, and allow me to explain. The Saptarishis or the Seven Seers are creatures of light, the physical embodiments of the Supreme force, Brahman. From which the entire universe was created. It was foretold that they would arm the One who unites the sons of Aditi.'

Realisation began to dawn on Mitra. He piped in, excited as a child, 'Then it is true. Indra is the One, from the prophecy.'

Mitra suddenly realised that, in his excitement, he had interrupted Bhrigu. A conduct that was quite unbecoming of a seer.

'Forgive me, Master. Please continue.'

'Do not be troubled, my friend, the occasion demands such excitement,' Bhrigu said with a smile and continued. 'This man will be a great king. He will establish a great empire and restore the balance of power in the world. Another Arya will then appear in this world and spread the light of knowledge through it. This boy of yours will finally help accomplish what your common ancestor Kasyapa, the first Arya, was sent here to do.'

Mitra remained quiet, the pieces of the puzzle coming together in his head. Bhrigu interrupted with a warning.

'This power that they have received must be handled with care. Indiscriminate usage can deplete their prana or life force greatly enough to kill them. I will give them exercises to strengthen their bodies as well as their minds. I suggest you do the same for Indra and Soma.'

Just then Indra's voice interrupted them.

'May I enter, Master Mitra?'

When Mitra nodded, Indra walked in, first bowing to his master and then to Bhrigu.

'My companions have just informed me about their good fortune. I regret that the affairs of my people keep me from being of service to you. I would love to have come and lived with you and imbibed some of your great wisdom. But right now, I will have to be content with your blessings, great sage.'

Bhrigu studied the warrior with interest and then, laughing heartily, said, 'You already have that. I must say, Mitra, your young warrior wields words as well as he wields a sword. He will make a great king.'

Just then, excited voices could be heard outside the hut. The three walked out to see Varuna, Vayu and Agni busy saddling their horses.

'You will have no use for those animals where we are going. We will travel on foot,' Bhrigu said.

The boys groaned as they digested that piece of information. Like all good cavalrymen, they hated the prospect of travelling on foot. Bhrigu and the boys then said their goodbyes to Indra and Mitra. Just as they turned to leave, the sage remembered something.

'By the way, I saw a big black bull on the other side of the river. I think he is one of yours.'

Mitra looked at the boys in surprise. Indra, Varuna and Agni burst out laughing; Vayu could not hide his guilt.

'It is a fine breeding bull, Master. Let us take it with us. He will sire many fine calves for Master Bhrigu.'

9

Indra's coronation was a subdued affair. Much as the Sabha and his companions tried to convince him to have it otherwise, Indra would not agree. The death of Vasu still hung heavy on his conscience, and he did not want any celebrations. The Sabha was convened, and after the ceremonial dip in the river, Mitra draped around him the scarlet robe of kingship. The members of the Sabha raised their voices in unison and saluted their new raja.

After the ceremony, General Kanak addressed the gathering. The general was a legend in the tribe. He had distinguished himself during the siege of Ur. Mitra remembered him as a peerless archer who had lost his arm in that battle. The unfortunate incident had cut short his brilliant military career.

Since then he had made his name as a great weapons instructor. It was Kanak who had mentored both Vasu and Pusan to the championship in the Spardha. Although a permanent member of the Sabha, he now led a rather reclusive, retired life, not concerning himself with the administrative affairs of the land. He had been an ardent supporter of the late regent, and there were quite a few apprehensive faces amongst Indra's supporters as he now stood up to address the gathering.

'Devas, the dark clouds of sorrow have finally lifted from Aryavarta. The time has come for us to rally as one behind our new king. A lot of talk has been going around about the circumstances that led to the death of the regent. I was there and bore witness to the tragedy, as did many of you. Vasu was like a son to me, no one was more saddened by his death than I. But he broke the rules of the Dvanda and paid for it with his life. This is the way I see it. If anybody here sees it differently, let them speak now.'

The general paused; there was pin-drop silence in the hall as everyone looked around to see if any of the rumourmongers would rise up now to bell the cat. But nobody said a word.

'Good, we are all in agreement then. If I hear anymore loose talk about murder or treachery, I would like to remind everyone of you'll that I still have an arm left, and it has not forgotten how to wield a sword.'

He let the threat hang in the air for a moment. When he spoke again his tone was much softer.

'I would now like to take the liberty of being the first to pledge my loyalty to Raja Indra. I was privileged to fight alongside his father when he was about his son's age. I see Daeyus' fire and strength in him. May he live long and spread the glory of our tribe across the far corners of the world.'

He went down on one knee and bowed his head. Every man in the hall followed his example. Indra acknowledged their gesture and asked them to rise.

Mitra, though not of the tribe, was an honoured guest at the ceremony. He was delighted to see the support Indra had received from this rather unexpected quarter. The general was highly respected by even the staunchest of Pusan's allies. He had just saved Indra a lot of trouble, perhaps even a lot of unnecessary bloodshed.

One of the first things Indra did as raja was streamline the administration of the settlement. He was greatly aided by the fact that Vasu had been an extremely capable administrator; his appointees were efficient, hardworking and honest in the way they discharged their duties. Indra spoke to every one of them personally and congratulated them on their good work. These men who had been fearful of losing their posts since the arrival of the new king, now worked with renewed motivation.

With the administration under control, Indra turned to an area that his predecessor had not been very efficient in, the Sena. With the death of Daeyus and Krupa, Vasu and the other officers had essentially given up their desire to be soldiers again. The once feared warriors had turned into bureaucratic fat cats, content to bask in the lazy luxury that life in a paradise like Gandhar brought.

The indulgent father, against his better sense of judgment, had put Pusan in charge of the Sena. Pusan was a great warrior, but he had not been a good leader. Indra was surprised to learn that the once powerful Sena was now a mere police force of two hundred men. Pusan's cronies, who were more sycophants than soldiers, occupied key positions within it. Warriors of merit who did not toe the line or protested against the leadership were sent to distant border outposts or were made glorified herdsmen.

Indra commissioned the construction of a huge army barrack close to Mitra's ashram. From there he planned to build a Sena that would surpass even his father's in strength and ferocity. Only two of the old guard were retained: Atreya and Puru. With the two of them to assist him, he personally interviewed every single recruit. Only the most eligible were picked. Most of them had already distinguished themselves in the Spardha. Soon the clash of bronze began to echo around Aryavarta. It finally began to look and sound like a Deva settlement once again.

After two days and nights of travel, Bhrigu and the three young men could finally see the sage's ashram, nestled at the foot of Mount Mandara. Suddenly they noticed plumes of smoke rising up in the air, quite unusual for that time of the day. Fearing the worst, they hurried in that direction. As they approached the ashram, the boys realised that it was much bigger than they had expected. It was more like a little village, with a number of huts and crop fields. But now, some of the huts and a couple of fields had been burnt down to the ground.

The entire village had gathered outside the largest hut and the sound of wailing could be heard from within it. A worried Bhrigu rushed in. Inside, his wife and the other women were inconsolable with grief. On enquiry, they learnt that there had been a raid just that morning. While the villagers had managed to drive the raiders away, two women had been taken. One of them was Maha, Bhrigu's eldest daughter.

The warriors decided to wait for the cover of the night before they set off in pursuit. They spent the last hour of daylight trying to garner whatever information they could about the raiders. A quick examination of the battlefield told them that there had been fifteen men armed with clubs, daggers and slingshots. The villagers told them that the raiders had attacked an hour before dawn.

Luckily for the villagers, it was an auspicious day, so more than half the village had woken up early to offer prayers. They had banded together with their sickles and staves and chased off the raiders. Unfortunately, two women who had gone to draw water from the well were spotted by the retreating thugs, quickly apprehended and carried off up the mountain.

Darkness descended quickly upon the village. The three warriors took the blessings of the sage and started their trek up the mountain. The raiders evidently had no fear of being pursued—they had not bothered to cover their tracks.

Once they were out of sight of the village, Agni, Vayu and Varuna were quick to put their newly-acquired powers to the test. They leapt from rock to rock like monkeys, each one trying to outdo the other with extravagant acrobatic displays. They made rapid progress and within the hour they spotted the shadows thrown by the raiders' campfire on the mountainside.

Now they moved more cautiously. Vayu and Varuna took the flanks while Agni circumvented the camp and took up position further up the slope. They could hear the screams of a woman and the loud chatter of the men around the campfire. The language was alien to them.

From his position above the trail, Agni had the best view of the camp. He saw one of the men emerge from under an overhang, laughing loudly and adjusting his clothing. His cohorts made obscene gestures and applauded him. Agni used telepathy and asked the others to wait. A few moments later, a second man emerged. As two men got up, evidently to take their place, Agni gave the order to attack.

The Deva arrows flew true and fast. Three of the four men standing were the first to die. The fourth started to run up the trail straight towards Agni. Vayu and Varuna concentrated their attack on the men around the fire, shooting fast and with unerring accuracy. Within a few minutes it was all over. The only survivor ran up the trail and straight into Agni's fist. He lay out cold on the ground.

Agni dragged him back to the camp where Varuna and Vayu

had retrieved their arrows from the corpses. Agni went to look for the women under the overhang. One of them lay on the ground, torn and bleeding. These men had been like animals. One look at her and he knew she was beyond help.

The other woman sat with her back against a rock and glowered at him. She had gathered her tattered clothes and was holding them against her body in an effort to protect her modesty. There were marks of the men's teeth and nails on her body. Agni averted his eyes, took off his cloak and left it at her feet.

When he returned to the fire, the sole survivor was coming to his senses. Agni grabbed him and raised him to his feet. The man took a clumsy swipe at Agni, who ducked and unleashed a flurry of punches into the man's body. The Deva was in an unforgiving mood. He kicked the man in the face, breaking a couple of teeth, and the man screamed in pain. Agni then grabbed him by his thick bushy hair and drove his knee into his face, shattering his nose. Varuna and Vayu finally dragged him away; they needed the brute alive for questioning. The man, his face a bloody mess, continued to scream at them in an alien tongue.

At first the Devas did not notice the young woman emerging from the shadows. She tried to walk tall with Agni's cloak wrapped around her body. The man leered at her and made an obscene gesture. The three young warriors saw this and made a move to chastise him, but before they could, the woman picked up a burning log from the fire and drove it with all her strength into the man's groin. The man let out a loud scream of agony before he fainted. She flung the log back into the fire and returned to her place in the shadows. The three warriors could not but help admire the young woman's courage and fortitude.

The next morning they made their way back to the ashram.

The prisoner had lost all his bluster. With every step he took he screamed in pain as his thighs brushed against his burnt nether region.

They soon reached the village and the prisoner—now a fearful, whimpering wreck—stood before Bhrigu. The sage was surprised to discover that the man spoke Pakhtu. On interrogation, the man revealed that, after the death of chief Thora, there had been a battle for succession among his sons. One of his illegitimate sons, Tajak, had taken a band of followers and made their way south out of the Pakhtu lands. He intended to set up his own tribe and had taken to raiding peaceful settlements to acquire resources and women for breeding.

Bhrigu was dismayed that the son of an old friend had conducted these heinous acts against his people. He asked the man to go to his chief with a strong message that he should leave them alone in future or face the consequences.

The three warriors watched their prisoner limp away up the mountain. They did not agree with Bhrigu's decision to release him. They knew it would only serve to forewarn the enemy of their presence when they planned their next attack. But when it came, the ashram would be prepared. They would teach Tajak and his renegades a lesson they would not forget in a hurry.

Nala opened his eyes and looked around. He was lying in a field of poppies. He sat up and looked up at the clear, blue sky—it was a bright, beautiful day. He heard a rustle in the flowerbed as one of his men approached; he had in his hand a long wooden pipe. The man knelt beside Nala and from his pouch removed a tiny ball of a sticky brown substance. He placed it carefully on one end of the pipe. The other end he put in Nala's mouth. He then created a small fire and then used an ember from it to light the pipe. Nala drew long and hard on it as he took in a lungful of smoke. He then handed the pipe back to the man and lay back as he allowed the smoke to drift through his nostrils.

It had been months since he and his men had been sent here to man the last outpost on the western frontier of Aryavarta. It was a beautiful fertile land, full of fruit-bearing trees and flowers. Ahead, the river Mara flowed into the Mittani where it emerged out of the wetlands and made its way west through the distant mountains. The first month had been idyllic. Nala had kept up a strong training regimen to alleviate the boredom that life in paradise brought. Now three months had passed and there was still no sign of the patrol that was to relieve them. One day, Nala caught one of his men inebriated on sentry duty; he ordered him to be flogged.

As he watched the punishment being administered, he saw that the man took the brutal treatment meted out to him with a dreamy smile plastered on his face. The next day, the very man whose punishment he had ordered introduced a curious Nala to the dreams of the poppy.

He opened his eyes as his mind was brought back to the present. Since that day, he had chased these dreams day and night. It was the only relief he had from the boredom of his present existence. Now, as he looked up at the sky, he saw a speck that seemed to move swiftly towards him. It looked to him like an extraordinarily large bird. He looked around and found his bow and quiver near at hand. He got to his feet, notched an arrow on to his bow and took aim. As he prepared to let fly the arrow, he heard a voice clear in his head.

'Stay, brave warrior. Though your mind is enslaved by the poppy, I know I dare not doubt the trueness of your aim.'

Nala was shocked. Could that be the bird that had just spoken to him? He lowered his weapon as his intended target began to come closer to the ground. It was then Nala noticed something that made him question his sanity even further; the object was no bird at all, but a man, a winged man

The man landed and took a few steps towards the astounded Nala. As he approached, he folded his wings and right before Nala's eyes they began to change—the feathers disappeared to reveal lean, muscular arms. The man reached Nala and bowed slightly.

'Greetings. It was not my intention to startle you. I seek an audience with the king of the Devas.'

The man was tall with an aquiline face. His white blond hair was pulled back in a high ponytail. His almond-shaped eyes were the deepest green and shone like emeralds. As he looked at Nala, a hint of a smile played on his lips. He looked young, no more than a few years older than Nala, but his eyes seemed to carry the wisdom of ages in them. Nala was not sure if he could trust his senses anymore: he had just seen the man fly like a bird and now, without having moved his lips, his voice had sounded in Nala's head. He decided his best approach would be a matter-of-fact one.

'We have no king, only a regent. I will send one of my men to escort you, as I cannot leave my post.'

The stranger's face wore an incredulous smile.

'You seem less informed than me as to the affairs of your tribe, my friend. I am here to offer my services to Indra, king of the Devas.'

Nala could not believe his ears. Could this be true? If it was, it was no less a miracle than what he had just witnessed. Indra was back, and had succeeded in clearing his name. Things were starting to look up again.

'On second thoughts, I will accompany you to Aryavarta. By what name are you called?'

'Travistr,' the man replied.

Indra had just returned to his tent after a hard day's training. As king, he had decided not to build a palace, but opted to go back to living in a tent like his father before him. The royal tent had been pitched a few yards away from the barracks, so Indra could keep a close watch on the training of his troops.

Indra had heard about a few rumblings in the Sabha. Although it was an insignificant minority, there were a few members who did not see the point in Indra leading their children into battle. These men had one thing in common: they'd all got used to a life of comfort. Like their cattle, they had gotten fat and content. They had begun to forget the old ways of their tribe.

Luckily, the vast majority, which included the young men under his command, did not share this opinion. They lived for the glory and thrill of battle. It was not their desire to die in their beds of old age; they wished to live under the shadow of death and cheat it with their skill at arms.

As he washed the weariness from his face and limbs, a page informed him that General Kanak sought an audience. He wiped himself dry and prepared to meet the old warrior, a man—Indra knew—who if he could still hold the reins of a horse and a weapon could not have been stopped from riding out to battle.

The general entered and bowed respectfully. Outside, the clash of maces and that of sword against shield could be heard. The general smiled.

'I am pleased to note that Aryavarta has again started to look and sound like a Deva settlement. I am certain your father who is watching over you from the heavens will be proud of you, my king. But I urge you to not commit the same mistake he did.'

Indra raised his eyebrows. 'I do not understand, my lord general. What is it that you wish to say?'

The general cleared his throat; this was a delicate matter that the Sabha had entrusted him with, something that went quite against his soldierly demeanour.

'My lord, we at the Sabha know that the time has come for you to avenge your father and it will not be long before you lead our mighty army once again to war. But we urge you not to make the same mistake that he did. Please take a wife and give us an heir before you leave. Surya forbid, if something were to happen to you, this tribe cannot bear witness to another bloody duel for succession.'

Indra smiled. 'The concerns of the Sabha are not unfounded. I am ready to marry the woman that was chosen for me. Please request the Sabha to carry my proposal to the Lady Madri, for the hand of my betrothed, Sachi.'

As General Kanak left, Indra sat lost in thought. He loved Sachi more than anyone else in the world, yet he had not visited her since her father's tragic death. He could face a thousand warriors in battle, but he did not have the courage to face her. Indra knew more than anyone else how much she'd adored her father. He hoped she would find it in her heart to forgive him.

Mitra sat in the courtyard of Vasu's house and awaited the arrival of the Lady Madri. He had been entrusted with the task of putting forward Indra's marriage proposal. Lady Madri came out of the house and bowed respectfully. She had aged considerably in the past few weeks. Her eyes were heavy with sorrow. Mitra gently conveyed the king's message. She thought for a while and replied with all the dignity she could muster.

'I know it is my duty as a parent to decide on my daughter's marriage, but given the circumstances, I think I would like to leave the final decision to my daughter. You will find her on the banks of the river, behind the house.'

Mitra was not too happy with his current predicament. He had to convince a girl to marry the man who killed her father. He reached the banks of the Mara and called to her. As Sachi approached, Mitra studied her. Her face was calm, yet he could sense the grief buried deep in her heart where it wore away at her soul. Mitra decided to come right out with his message.

'My lady, the raja wishes for you to consider his proposal of marriage.' Even as he spoke the words, he regretted it. He had been too formal, a little too impersonal and straight to the point. This was clearly not his forte.

Sachi, with her head bowed, took her time to reply.

'Tell the king that I accept his proposal. I only have one condition.'

Mitra could scarcely contain his joy. He had not expected it to be so easy. Sachi had not let her personal grief come in the way of her duty; she would make a great queen.

'Of course! You only have to name it. The king will be prepared to fulfil any of your conditions.'

Sachi smiled; it was a smile that did not reach her eyes.

'My condition is not for the king. It is for you. I will make my request at an appropriate time.'

'Your request will be my command. Now allow me to take leave and carry this joyous news back to the raja.'

Both Indra and the Sabha greeted Sachi's decision with great delight. The wedding was fixed for a week from that day. After a long while, the population of Aryavarta was unanimous in its joy. The city wasted no time in its preparation for the grand event.

A man moved stealthily through the trees, avoiding detection by the Deva night patrol. He leapt huge distances, from branch to branch, landing silently each time. It was not long before he found himself on a giant oak that arched over the royal tent. One quick look around was all it took to see that it was unguarded. The man leapt to the ground and quickly entered the tent.

A sudden sense of imminent danger brought Indra awake. He opened his eyes and saw the intruder in his tent. As the man neared his bed, Indra leapt straight at him like a leopard going for the kill. The man was taken by surprise, but was able to move his head a fraction as Indra's fist crashed into his jaw. The little movement saved him from a broken neck, but the force of the punch was enough to knock him to the ground.

'Stop!' the man called out in an urgent whisper. 'Just because I have been away for a few days, this is no way for you to greet an old friend!'

Indra, who'd been readying to push forward his attack, now hung back with a relieved smile.

'Soma! Had I known it was you, I would not have stopped with one punch. I suppose you didn't think my coronation was an important enough event to attend?'

Soma took his friend's hand, got to his feet and embraced Indra.

'I'm sorry, I was busy working on something.'

'Well, whatever it was, it better be good, because apparently you did find time to visit Nira's whores on several occasions. They have been going around town talking about your newfound sexual prowess.'

Soma grinned sheepishly.

'They were a necessary distraction, I'm afraid. Now I must ask you to follow me, I have something of importance to share with you. Oh! Just one more thing—please try and keep up.'

He ran out of the tent and leapt nearly five times his body length onto the branch of the oak tree and began to retrace his journey. Indra groaned loudly and then proceeded to follow his friend. Oblivious to the Deva patrols below them they leapt from tree to tree and made their way deep into the forest.

They made rapid progress through the canopy and soon they were in a region of the forest that Indra had never seen. The thick undergrowth made progress on the ground impossible. In the middle of this dense jungle was a clearing in which sat a log hut. Soma jumped down from a branch in front of the building.

As Indra leapt to the ground, he felt a dull throb in his head. He had not practised the mental exercises that Mitra had given him and the unfamiliar usage of his divine powers had weakened him. He was a bit surprised to see that Soma did not seem to be affected.

'Soma, you were warned not to use your powers unless absolutely necessary. Don't you realise it can destroy you?'

Soma grinned like the cat that had just got the cream.

'Give me a moment, my friend, I think I may have the solution to that very problem.'

He entered the hut and returned shortly. In his hand, he bore a cup made of the finest crystal. As he held it up to the sky, Indra saw in its depths a pale gold liquid that shone in the moonlight. Soma chanted a mantra and offered the cup to the young raja.

'For you, my king, the elixir of the gods.'

Indra held it to his lips and drank. The liquid had a sharp taste and burned his throat a little. Then he began to feel a warmth in the pit of his abdomen. Slowly it spread to other parts of his body and it was not long before he felt his entire being pulsate with divine energy. All his fatigue disappeared. He shivered in excitement as he hugged Soma.

'I cannot wait for Agni, Varuna and Vayu to return. This is the greatest weapon that you have given us. Thanks to you and this potion, which shall henceforth be called "soma", we are not just going to be great warriors. We are going to be gods.'

Varuna stood on a newly-built guard tower and looked out into the night. From experience, Bhrigu had told them that attacks usually came an hour before dawn. Agni and Vayu were already up in the hills where they kept watch on Tajak's horde. They were two-hundred strong and holed up a few hours' march away, ready for the final assault.

The last few weeks had been a hectic scramble to put up defences for the ashram. They had shifted the entire community at least a mile away from their previous location in the shadow of the mountain. The place had been a death-trap and a nightmare to defend. Now they had built a ten-foot high wooden stockade and six guard towers around the new ashram with pine logs taken from the hillside. Every man, woman and child had worked themselves to the bone, and now they finally had a defendable position.

When the attack came, the enemy would have at least a mile of flat ground to cover before they hit the stockade wall. The three warriors had made plans to whittle down the odds considerably by then.

Quivers full of arrows, axes, clubs and hammers were passed around the camp. The villagers lined up, courage and determination writ large on their faces. Every one of them down to the smallest child knew that defeat would mean a very painful death or a lifetime of torture and slavery.

Vayu had trained the men under Shukra, the oldest surviving son of Bhrigu, in close combat. Varuna watched them now, bunched together, hands clasped tightly around their weapons. These people were strong, honest, hardworking folk, but Varuna had his doubts about their skills as warriors. It was one thing to practice weapon drills for long hours, but quite another to apply it in actual combat and kill a man. Varuna hoped the men had the stomach for it.

He and Agni had trained the women and the older children in archery; they had taken to it quite well and learned quickly to work as a team. The younger children, who could not wield bows, had been trained to ferry supplies and retrieve fallen arrows. He knew in his heart that they had done all they possibly could. With a little bit of luck they just might be able to teach Tajak's raiders a lesson they would not forget in a hurry.

The screech of a falcon pierced the still night. It was the signal he was waiting for. Varuna alighted from the guard tower and Bhrigu went to him. The sage, save for his staff, did not carry a weapon.

'It is time, Master. Call your people to arms.'

As Tajak led his men down the mountainside, he lost some of his confidence. Something about the scenario troubled him. He had expected to charge down with his men and wreak havoc on the ashram, but it had disappeared. He looked around at the fields: the crops were being tended to, which meant the sage and his people had not moved far. Then he heard the hunting call of a falcon from the slope of the mountain behind him. It added to his discomfort: the bird did not hunt at night.

Agni and Vayu followed at a safe distance as Tajak led his men forward in a tight formation through the fields of corn. The horde soon crossed the fields and came upon a patch of bare land. In front of them was a ditch covered with dry wood, leaves and grass. Tajak laughed. 'Fools,' he thought to himself as he looked at the clumsy trap and leapt over it. As he climbed a gentle rise, the wall and guard towers of the ashram came into view.

Tajak stopped in surprise. His man who had survived the previous raid had told him—before he had been decapitated— that Bhrigu and his people had help. However, Tajak had not expected to encounter fortified resistance. He ordered his men to stop while he plotted his next course of action. Ahead he saw another ditch: it was covered clumsily much the same way as the one he had passed. He heard the call of the falcon again, this time it came from within the walls.

Varuna lit up an arrowhead that was covered with an oil-soaked rag and shot it high into the air. Tajak watched the flaming arrow as it came towards them from within the walls. He stood his ground and was about to laugh when he saw that the arrow was falling short of its mark, when the enemy's plan suddenly dawned on him. He screamed, 'Run! It's a trap!'

The arrow struck the ditch in front of him and it exploded into flames. Tajak turned to see two more flaming arrows land in the ditch behind them. Vayu took a deep breath, chanted a mantra in his mind and blew gently. A gust of wind caused the flame to fan out in an arc. Agni roared in delight. He and Vayu had prepared a ring of fire: it gave Varuna and his archers a perfect kill zone.

'Archers! Ready your bows.'

Varuna stood once again on the guard tower and gave the command. The women and older children notched arrows and raised their bows.

'Shoot!'

They released their bowstrings and forty arrows flew in an arc over the wall and landed right in the middle of the enemy force. Varuna whooped in triumph.

'Archers! Shoot at will!'

He watched as the arrows fell among the panicked horde. For days and hours on end he and Agni had concentrated on training them to land their arrows on that bare patch of earth, and today the villagers did not fail them. It was like shooting fish in a barrel.

Tajak realised very quickly that to linger there would mean certain death. He ordered his men to charge forward. The men who could still move responded and followed Tajak as he leapt through the wall of fire.

Vayu and Agni ran along on either side of the fiery ring, their bows busy as they shot arrow after arrow into the savages. From his vantage point, Varuna saw what the enemy planned and ordered Shukra and his men to charge. If they could take the head of Tajak, their troubles would be over permanently. Shukra and his men opened the gate and charged at their enemy.

Tajak saw them come and looked around. About twenty of his men had been able to keep pace; the others struggled with their wounds or the flames. He himself had an arrowhead lodged in one shoulder. His face was a bloody mess from another arrow that had ripped open his cheek till it hung from a piece of skin and flapped against his chin as he ran. His hair and beard had been burnt away in patches. He looked like a demon from hell.

Shukra saw Tajak approach and his courage failed him. Tajak spat, showering him with blood. Then he let out a terrifying yell and raised his club. Shukra dropped his weapon and ran. The men who had come up behind him were taken completely by surprise by the flight of their leader. They slowed to a halt, unsure of their next move.

Varuna screamed at them to fight. His quiver was empty and he looked around desperately for an arrow. Tajak did not break his stride as he threw his club. The heavy weapon twirled through the air and struck one of the men on the head. It split his skull and scattered his blood and brains on the others next to him. That was it. The men lost their nerve and fled towards the fields, away from the action.

Tajak gave a roar of triumph and charged towards the open gates of the ashram. He and his men burst through the gates as Varuna leapt off the guard tower to challenge them. Tajak barked out instructions to his men.

'Kill the warrior first. The rest are sheep waiting to be slaughtered.'

He walked over to where the children cowered in fear.

'Look at them, like frightened deer. Perhaps they'll taste just as good. I think I will roast one of them alive.'

Before he could carry out his threat, a figure threw itself at him and landed squarely on his back. It clawed at his already mutilated face and caused him to scream in agony as he shook it off his back. It was Maha. Tajak dragged her to her feet by her hair and thrust his dagger into her side. Maha screamed in pain, but she did not let it deter her. As she twisted towards him, the knife laid open the side of her belly. Maha gritted her teeth and with her dying breath brought her hand up. In it, she held her last arrow. She called on her final reserves of strength and drove the shaft right through the soft flesh under Tajak's chin, into his brain. She went with a smile on her face, comforted by the knowledge that her enemy had died before her.

Outside the stockade, Agni had gathered the men together and finished off what remained of Tajak's raiders. Only Shukra did not participate. He sat on the ground and stared out into the distance. He knew he had failed his people. Agni looked around for Vayu, but did not find him. He called out to the men to fan out and search for him. They found him unconscious on the field and brought him into the ashram.

Bhrigu was remarkably calm as he knelt beside the corpse of his daughter. Varuna stood by in support. Thanks to Maha, their victory had been comprehensive. Only two dead and about half a dozen wounded. The enemy had been comprehensively routed, slaughtered down to the last man. Bhrigu stood up and looked at Varuna who paid his last respects to the fallen girl.

'She had the spirit of a warrior within her.'

The father looked away into the distance with a wry smile.

'I never imagined such a warrior would spring from my loins. Perhaps it is best then that she died such a glorious death. Life might not have been kind to one such as her.'

Varuna knew the sage was right. Her spirit would have never been able to live the life of servitude that was expected from women in an ashram. Just then, Agni rushed in carrying an unconscious Vayu over his shoulder. Bhrigu asked for the warrior to be brought to one of the huts where he could examine him.

It did not take long for Bhrigu to find the reason behind Vayu's mysterious condition. There was no external sign of any wound or injury on him. Yet his heartbeat was so faint, a novice might have presumed he was dead. The sage turned to the two warriors.

'Did he use his divine powers during the battle?'

'Yes, Master. It was necessary.'

Bhrigu led the two of them outside.

'These powers that have been bestowed on you are like a double-edged sword. You must train and strengthen yourselves before you use it, or you could do yourselves irreparable harm.'

Agni looked at his own muscled body and then at Varuna's and raised his eyebrows in surprise.

'But we are Devas. We are strong.'

The sage laughed.

'I have no doubt of your physical prowess, but you must strengthen yourself from within. Goodnight for now, your training begins tomorrow.'

The next day, after the dead had been cremated, the boys lined up, ready for their first lesson. Vayu had made a speedy recovery and was able to join the other two. Bhrigu found a spot for them under an old fig tree and asked them to sit down cross-legged.

'Now, for one hour I would like you to sit down and empty your mind. Remove all thoughts from it.'

The three boys closed their eyes and began what was to become the hardest exercise they had ever done in their lives.

Sachi sat by the river, bathed in the light of a magnificent full moon. Though her cheeks were wet with tears, it did nothing to diminish her great beauty. It was the eve of her wedding, and all she could do was wrestle with the biggest dilemma of her young life. Every time she thought of her lover who was soon to be her husband, it was her dead father's face she saw. Nobody understood her plight, she felt, not even her own mother, whose soul appeared to have been drawn out of her. She walked around the house, silent, a living, breathing corpse.

She looked up at the moon; other than as an object of beauty, it held no particular significance for her. Like her people, the sun was all she worshipped. Yet in the last few days, she had felt drawn to it. It seemed to offer her some kind of comfort. Even as she gazed upon the beautiful orb in its full splendour, she saw something appear in the middle of it. It was a face of a woman of exquisite beauty. The face looked at her with a benevolent smile. Sachi bowed her head as she clasped her hands in prayer. Suddenly it became very clear to her what she had to do.

The royal wedding was just the occasion the citizens of Aryavarta needed to put all the sordid occurrences of the recent past behind them. Everyone in the city had gathered outside the Sabha for the ceremony, following which there was to be a grand sacrifice and feast. Nala and Travistr arrived just in time to join the wedding celebrations.

Mitra noticed the stranger and was immediately drawn by his aura. Their eyes met and the stranger nodded courteously. As Mitra returned the gesture, he realised that the stranger was an adept of the highest order. Like him, the man did not touch the wine. This was strange, given his warrior-like appearance and the occasion. He reminded himself to question Nala about him later. As he looked around the room, his eyes went to Madri, who sat still as a statue. Her eyes were vacant as they stared ahead; she did not partake of the food or the wine.

Mahisi more than made up for her friend's indifference by taking on the duties of the hostess. She had served up the choicest food and now had brought out some fine wine that she had preserved all these years for just this occasion. The wine soon got the bards going and the hall began to resound with the old songs of valour. One of them even sang about the duel between Indra and Pusan. Pusan and Vasu were not portrayed in a very kind light in the ballad and finally Indra had to have the drunken bard escorted out from the gathering.

Through it all, Sachi conducted herself with the utmost dignity. Mitra's heart went out to her. He could sense her grief even as she maintained her poise through the celebrations. Finally it was time for the groom and the bride to retire for the night. The gathering cheered and made ribald jokes about the groom's prowess. Indra thanked them and left with his bride.

It was well past midnight when the king made his way to the bridal chamber. Sachi sat on the bed bedecked in jewellery and fine silk as she awaited her husband. The entire chamber and the bed had been decorated with beautiful, fragrant flowers. She looked up as he entered and their eyes met; her beauty took his breath away.

Indra paused to admire the vision that presented itself to him. She continued to stare at him; her face was hard, not betraying any emotion. Gone was the girl who was his childhood playmate. This woman was unrecognisable to him, and he had to admit, eminently more fascinating. He hoped she would pass some sort of cheeky, irreverent remark to break the shadow of solemnity. All he wanted was to take her in his arms and show her how much he loved her. Then he remembered how much water had passed under the bridge since they had last met. He made a vow to himself that he would, in time, with his undying love, heal the wounds that he had caused her.

He went to her and gathered her in his embrace. She buried her head in his shoulder as she tried to control the sob that escaped her lips. He hugged her as tightly as he dared and then slowly broke the embrace. She kept her gaze down so he could not see the sorrow in her eyes; it only served to enhance her fragile beauty.

As Indra looked upon the face of his bride, Sachi closed her eyes and struggled to hold back her tears. However, a drop found its way down her cheek. He held her face in his calloused hands as gently as he could. He was afraid their roughness would in some way blemish that flawless face. Then, he slowly leaned forward and kissed the teardrop away.

She opened her eyes and looked at him. He saw her pain—it stabbed at his heart like a knife. He drew her face to his and kissed her gently on the lips. Her mouth parted and her hands clutched at his shoulders. His breathing quickened as he broke away. Slowly he began to undress her, drinking in her beauty with his eyes.

Sachi lay back; she felt shivers of pleasure as his mouth and tongue moved all over her body. She grabbed his head and ran her fingers through his golden hair. Then she saw him loom over her, his perfect body shone like gold in the firelight. She felt a stab of pain as he entered her, then he gently began to move. Her breath caught and her fingernails dug into his back and drew blood. It only served to spur him on to move faster and harder. Then suddenly she woke as if from a dream. Her body stiffened; it took all her self-control to stop herself from pushing him away.

Indra's eyes were shut, his breath became ragged as he felt the muscles in his lower belly tighten and then he felt the sweet pleasure of its release. He fell on top of her and held her tightly in his arms. He felt his heart would burst from the love he felt for her at that moment. She gently pushed him off her. Indra held on to her and slowly drifted off to sleep. Sachi lay awake for a long time. The tears rolled down her face freely now and stained the pillow.

It was well into the next day when Indra stirred awake. He smiled as he recollected his nuptial night and reached across for his new bride. He felt his hand being rudely pushed away. Indra sat up in surprise; it was hardly the reaction he expected after that ethereal wedding night.

Sachi turned and looked at her husband, her eyes cold and naked with hate.

'My lord, I have done my duty as a daughter and fulfilled my father's final wish. I will bear you a son, but he will be yours in name only. He will rule this great land after your death. And I will dedicate my life to pray for that day to arrive soon.'

She pointed to the white sheepskin they had lain on in the night. In the middle of it was a bright red stain, her virginal blood.

'Show that to your subjects. Let them know that a Deva woman will always put her duties above her personal feelings. She will even give herself to the man she hates. But know this before you leave: the very thought of your touch sickens me. If you ever try to touch me again, I will kill you. I will poison you or stick a dagger into you while you sleep. I swear this on the souls of my father and brother.'

A broken-hearted Indra saw in her eyes that it would be hopeless to present any kind of argument. Sachi had made her decision. He picked up the sheepskin and walked out of the chamber. He did not look at her again so she would not see how deep were the wounds she had inflicted. Outside, the crowd broke into a cheer, which progressed to thunderous applause when he hung the bloodstained sheepskin on the fence. Indra walked away towards his tent amidst the cries of joy.

That evening, Mitra was surprised to learn that the new queen had summoned him. When he arrived at her quarters, a stranger greeted him at the door. A tall, thin man dressed in the white and gold robes of a priest. The man bowed low as he addressed Mitra. There was something vaguely familiar about his appearance.

'Greetings, oh most learned one! I am Makara, the new priest of the royal household. It will be my honour to escort you to Her Majesty's presence.'

As he stood before the new queen, Mitra could not shake off a sense of foreboding. Sachi's face was impassive as she spoke.

'Master Mitra, I need you to do something for me.'

'You only have to say the words, my lady. Your wish is my command.'

Sachi's beautiful face now wore a smug smile.

'It is my wish that you gather your belongings and leave Aryavarta this very moment. Speak to no one—just leave, and never return.'

Mitra could not believe what he was hearing. She read the unspoken question in his eyes.

'You are the closest thing that the king knows to a father. I wish from today that he should know what it feels like to lose a father, especially at the hands of one you love. For I shall be sure that he is informed that it is I who banished you.'

The thought of departure from Aryavarta did not trouble the seer. It had been in his thoughts ever since Indra had been crowned king. But to see such hate spring from the heart of the one person Indra truly loved saddened the old master. He bowed courteously and left.

Ishtar gazed into the depths of a crystal ball and watched Mitra walk away from Aryavarta. For the first time in ages, she laughed. She had spent the last many years locked away in her chambers on top of the ziggurat. The rigorous practice of meditation had increased her spiritual powers tremendously. She knew that it would not be long before her powers would be put to the ultimate test.

Fate had dealt her a stroke of good fortune by delivering Sachi to her. It had been child's play for Ishtar to gain control and influence her tormented mind. In one masterstroke, the goddess had removed Mitra from Indra's side and broken his heart. Now all that was needed from Sachi was to have Indra delivered to her. Their battle would be at a time and place of her choosing, and this time she would win.

10

Indra and Sachi carried on the charade of being the perfect couple in love. Not even Mahisi or Paras could tell there was anything amiss. True to her word, Sachi had told Indra why Mitra had left, but the populace of Aryavarta did not see the seer's sudden departure as anything unusual. They presumed he was off on another spiritual quest.

The king seemed a bit quiet and aloof on the few occasions he was seen in public, but his subjects and his soldiers assumed it was the maturity that had come with added responsibility. Indra spent all his spare time training alone on the banks of the river. He tried in vain to exhaust himself physically so he could fall asleep at the end of the day. The nights were unbearable, as he lay beside the woman he loved, unable to even reach out and touch her.

Finally, the day arrived when Sachi missed her first moon. Although the royal family tried to keep it quiet, the news spread like wildfire around Aryavarta. A grand sacrifice was planned to thank the gods for this gift.

On the appointed day, the royal couple made a rare public appearance together. The two of them held hands through the ceremony. The priests finished the rituals with a prayer for the good health and long life of the heir.

Then Indra stood up to address the gathering. He thanked them all for their blessings. He then informed the surprised citizens that he had taken a vow of celibacy. Until he avenged his father's death, he would not lie with his wife again. Sachi pretended to unhappy about the announcement, although every word that Indra had spoken was at her behest.

Weeks passed and Indra hid himself in his tent, drank copious amounts of wine and tried to come to terms with his grief. Sachi's face haunted him in his sleep and waking hours. Her cold words still rang in his ears. Nothing seemed to interest him anymore. Even Mitra's departure had not upset him; he drowned himself in wine, somehow convinced it would take away his pain.

Early one morning, after a heavy night of drinking, he heard his name being called. He did not even look up from where he lay.

'Go away, Soma! Leave me alone.'

'I'm sorry, my lord. It is I, Nala. There is something you should see.'

Indra sat up; his head throbbed as he forced himself to open his eyes. He remembered he had meant to recall Nala from his frontier posting and then completely forgotten about it. He was glad to note that the great archer was well and back in Aryavarta. Something about his tone and expression now made Indra take notice. When he finally stepped out of the tent, what he saw took his breath away. Standing before him was Travistr on a magnificent war chariot.

'Greetings, Raja Indra! I have travelled long and far to offer my services to you.'

Indra gazed at the chariot: it was made from bronze and wood and the craftsmanship was exquisite. He had to tear his eyes away from it to look at the man, but when he did, he immediately sensed from his aura that this was no ordinary mortal.

'Who are you?'

The man smiled, and Indra heard his voice clearly in his head.

'I am as much a mortal as you are, my king.'

Aloud, he said, 'I'm Travistr. Weapons are my trade.' He gestured to the chariot. 'Please join me.'

After weeks, Indra was not assailed with thoughts of Sachi. He circled the chariot, studying it closely. It could accommodate a rider and a warrior on the footplate. He climbed in and Travistr took off. The chariot flew across the meadow, the two horses working perfectly in tandem as Travistr pulled off a series of sharp turns and manoeuvres.

Indra was stunned by the chariot's performance. He picked up one of the bows lying in the chariot and let fly a few arrows. The vehicle was fast, yet stable enough to give him more mobility and accuracy than if he were on a horse. As they got back to where Nala and Soma waited, he noticed the arsenal that the chariot carried: there were javelins, extra quivers of arrows and an assortment of other weapons. That was it; all his sorrows and heartache from the recent past were forgotten. His voice shook with the excitement of a child being presented with his favourite toy.

'Can you make me a thousand of these?'

Travistr nodded.

'Give me fifty of your best craftsmen, and I will have them ready by spring.'

Indra got down from the chariot and walked around it, still admiring the workmanship.

'You shall have a hundred, and whatever else you require. Soma, see to it at once. Now if there is nothing else, I would like to drive this chariot.'

'One more thing, my lord.'

Travistr had a sword strapped to his back, a practice not favoured by the Devas, who preferred to wear their blades on the hip. He now unstrapped it and presented it to the king.

Indra looked at the finely worked scabbard. It was made of black leather with silver trims. The hilt of the sword was simple, with a soft black leather cord wound around the handle and a giant crystal at its end. As he held it in his hands, he realised that it was at least five times heavier than his own blade. But for his divine strength, he would have found it hard to wield it.

He unsheathed the blade and saw that it was black and straight with twin edges that had been honed to razor sharpness. As he swung the weapon in a few practice strokes, he was pleased to note that in spite of its weight, its balance was perfect. This was a sword fit for a god. Indra was sure there was no other weapon of its kind in the world. Eager to test it, he asked Nala and Soma to attack, and the two warriors drew their swords and readily obliged.

Two bronze swords came at him from opposite sides, aimed at his neck. Indra stepped back and swept the sword upwards in an overhead block. The black blade cut through their weapons like they were a pair of sticks. The broken blades fell at Indra's feet.

The awe in Indra's voice was unmistakable.

'It is a formidable weapon. But it belongs to you.'

Travistr shook his head and laughed.

'I only made the sword, my lord, but I'm not worthy enough to wield it. It is only the greatest warriors in the world who have had the privilege to carry this sword into battle. On the death of its owner, the sword returns to me. Till it finds a new master.'

Indra was curious.

'Are you telling me the sword finds its own master?'

'Yes, my lord. Look at the blade again.'

Indra examined the shiny black surface of the blade; just above the hilt, emblazoned in letters of gold, was the word, 'INDRA'.

'Does it have a name?'

'Kadaag. That was what it was named, in a long forgotten tongue.'

'What does it mean?'

'Unstoppable.'

'It is well named,' said Indra as he turned his attention back to the man.

'Why do you come to me with such wondrous gifts? What is it that you seek?'

A flicker of emotion entered Travistr's eyes for one brief moment and then he was back to his inscrutable self as he replied.

'I am to aid you in the fulfilment of your destiny. I seek no favours or reward for this. It is my karma.'

'Then I am indeed fortunate. Thank you, my lord.'

Indra sheathed the blade and tied the scabbard around his waist. He leapt into the chariot and drove away with a wave of his hand.

The next few months went by quickly and the first few chariots arrived. The Deva warriors, adept horsemen that they were, quickly adapted to their new method of warfare. Soma, in particular, excelled in the art of driving the chariot. He assumed charge of training the horses and took his place as Indra's charioteer.

Travistr was true to his word. As the winter-frost melted over the meadows of Gandhar, a thousand Deva chariots were ready to march to war.

On the night before the eve of their departure, Indra lay in his tent, unable to sleep. The time had come for him to avenge the death of his father and reassert the might of the Devas across the plains of Central Asia. King Shalla and the city of Susa would soon feel the might of his black sword.

The troops had been called to muster at dawn, and the men were glad to get the chance to say goodbye to their families. Indra had appointed Paras as regent in his place. He now bid the warrior farewell. To Mahisi, he entrusted the care of Sachi and the child that would soon be born to them. He hoped the time away would heal her wounds and she would one day forgive him and truly be his wife.

The whole of Aryavarta gathered at dawn to bid farewell to the raja and his army as they began the long march westward. Indra marched at the head of the column, his shining armour and flowing locks of gold making him look every inch a god. As he acknowledged the blessings and good wishes of his subjects, his eyes searched the crowd in the hope that he would see Sachi, but he was disappointed.

The column started to pick up pace as they left the city. It was the largest army that the tribe had ever mustered. Indra had split them into four divisions of two hundred and fifty chariots each. While one of the divisions was under his direct command, Nala, Atreya and Puru led the other three. The mood was buoyant as the bards who marched along began to sing their songs. Every soldier's face shone with pride and excitement in the anticipation of the glory that awaited him.

Their progress was swift and soon the army found itself on the western border of their land at the confluence of the Mara and the Mittani. Travistr and his team of craftsmen had left earlier and been extremely busy. As a testimony to their efforts, the army found a dock ready with fifteen giant barges tethered there. They wasted no time in getting the chariots and horses on board and soon the little flotilla began to make its way west.

The river basin at the confluence was full of water from the winter ice melts and the swift-flowing current greatly aided them in their progress. The journey was largely uneventful, barring a few swift rapids. In some places they had to disembark, dismantle the barges and carry them overland till the river became navigable again. For the soldiers who had never seen a life outside the paradise of Gandhar, this was an adventure of a lifetime.

It was with some sense of relief that they finally emerged out of the mountains on to the vast plains of Central Asia. As they disembarked, Indra gave the order to burn the boats. The men knew that there was no going back now. Indra took his place once again at the head of the column and raised the black sword in the air.

'To Susa!'

The cry was echoed by over two thousand enthusiastic voices.

Timon, chief of Shalla's espionage network, paced nervously outside the royal chamber. It was well past midnight, certainly not a good time to wake the king. But such the circumstances—he had no choice. The huge doors were thrown open and Shalla stepped out in all his naked glory.

Drowsily, he asked, 'Timon? Your face at this time of the night can only mean the news is not good.'

Timon knew his master well: it was best to come straight to the point where bad news was concerned.

'Your eastern and southern garrisons have been destroyed, my lord.'

Shalla was now wide awake; he could not believe his ears.

'Destroyed! What do you mean, destroyed? We are talking about two thousand soldiers.'

'Slaughtered, my lord. Down to the last man. Both camps were attacked simultaneously. No one was left alive.'

Shalla sat down and racked his alcohol-addled brain. Only Sargon the Asura would have both the gall and the potential to send an army out against him. But his kingdom lay to the west, and Shalla had his spies all over Sumer monitoring the Asura king's every move. This could not be Sargon—but then who? The whole thing did not make sense to him.

'Did you see the men who did this?'

Timon nodded gravely.

'They move swiftly on horse-drawn vehicles and are faster than any cavalry I have ever seen. Their present camp is a day's march from these walls. I have my men watching them. If they march at dawn, they will be here before the sun sets tomorrow.'

Shalla struggled to keep calm as he turned to one of his guards.

'Awaken General Druma. Ask him to summon the War Council.'

Indra and his commanders sat around the fire at the Deva camp, their mood a bit forlorn. Atreya, who had led a team of scouts to reconnoitre the fort, had just returned and finished his report. Indra was the first to break the silence.

'Hmm, forty foot walls of sandstone. Anyone have any ideas?'

'What about the gates?' Soma asked.

Atreya turned to him. He had bribed some nomadic shepherds who lived around the city and managed to extract some information from them.

'Good question! The Moon Gates of Susa are made of oak at least three feet thick and reinforced with bronze plates. They need twenty bullocks working in two teams to open and close them every day. There are at least three hundred archers and spearmen in the parapet above the gates. To take a battering ram to it will not be easy without a sizable infantry battalion.'

Travistr stepped out of the darkness into the firelight. He addressed Indra, speaking with quiet determination.

'Make camp and wait for me within sight of the gates. I will get your chariots into the city.'

He melted back into the darkness.

Later that night, when he and Indra were alone, Soma could not help but express his reservations about Travistr.

'Who is this man? He comes and goes as he pleases. Builds wonderful things that we have never seen before or imagined. Is he a god or a demon?'

Indra laughed heartily.

'What are we, Soma? I must confess I did not feel very god-like when we slaughtered that garrison. High on your brew, all I felt was the surge of energy in my body and a thirst for more blood.'

'Well perhaps we are demons, after all. What did you do when you felt this way?'

Indra laughed and thumped his friend on the back.

'I lopped off a few more heads and felt a lot better.'

Shalla stood on the ramparts of his mighty city walls and stared out at the horizon. He could see in the distance an approaching cloud of dust. General Druma informed him of Timon's arrival.

'What news do you have for me?'

'I have just been to see one of the survivors from the southern garrison, my lord. The man was delirious, half-crazed with fear.'

'What did he say?'

The king's tone warned Timon that it would be best to tell the truth, yet he hesitated before he spoke.

'He said that the army was led by a demon with eyes that shone like a wild beast in the night. His men called him Indra. The man swears that this Indra was stronger, faster and more skilled than any warrior he has ever seen.'

Shalla tried not to show the effect Timon's words had on him. He recalled the name and within his chest, his heart skipped a beat. Could it be the demon from the prophecy—the son of Daeyus?

'Demon or human, I don't care. He and his army will be crushed beneath these walls. Pass the word around. The man who brings me this Indra's head in battle will get five years' wages as a reward.'

Timon raised his eyebrows in surprise as he made a quick calculation of what five years of his wages would be. It was a small fortune, and Shalla was usually not one to part with even a single coin if he could avoid it.

It was dusk by the time Indra and his men arrived within sight of the magnificent city. They camped on a little ridge with a clear view of the Moon Gates. As the last rays of the sun fell on Susa's mighty walls, he gazed at them and suddenly felt anxious.

He could think of no possible weapon that would make a dent on those massive blocks of sandstone. The wide ramparts and numerous towers teemed with archers and spearmen. To get near those walls would be suicidal. That ruled out the use of grappling hooks and ladders. Neither did he have the strength in numbers nor the resources to lay siege to the city.

Any way he looked at it, the problem seemed insurmountable. He called out to the others to make camp and rest for the night. The walls would still be there tomorrow.

The next day, Indra sent Atreya and Nala with two teams of scouts around the walls to check for any weakness in the city's defences. The troops spent a restless day polishing their weapons and tending to their horses. Towards the end of the day, the scouts returned. There was a reason why Susa had never been conquered before. Her defences were impregnable.

The young king walked towards the city in the fading light. The lamps in each guard tower were being lit. On any other day, this would have been a beautiful spectacle. The watch had just changed and Indra saw the mass of troops on the ramparts. He felt a shiver run through his body as a cold wind began to blow in from the desert. Where was Travistr, he wondered. In his hands lay the fate of his army of two thousand. Just because his men were ready to die for him, he could not send them on a suicide mission.

'Prepare to enter the city by first light tomorrow.'

Travistr's voice sounded in his head, the calmness of it dispensing all doubt from Indra's mind. He wore a big smile as he walked back to the camp. He called out to his commanders, 'Get some sleep. We will take the city at dawn.'

Later that night, Soma woke Indra from his sleep.

'You have to see this.'

As he walked with Soma towards the ridge, he saw streaks of

fire fall from the heavens. Right before his eyes, he saw one of them strike a guard tower and explode into a giant ball of flame. He saw burning bodies throw themselves off the tower, screaming in fright. Indra roared with delight.

'The gods of the sky are with us. Prepare for battle, my men. The time has come to avenge our fathers.'

A great cheer of enthusiasm went around as the Devas began to thump their swords against their shields.

Shalla watched in dismay from the ramparts of his great wall as the first fireball struck the ground a few yards in front of the gates, illuminating the beautiful structure. Soon the heavens were filled with flaming missiles that began to rain all around his city, setting its trees and the roofs of its buildings on fire.

Just then, one of the guard towers a few paces from where he stood was struck. He gave instructions to Druma to organise enough men to put out the fires and retreated to the safety of his palace. For the first time in his life, Shalla feared for his city and his empire.

From her vantage point high above the city, Ishtar saw that the attack was not an act of the gods. Across the distance, before her eyes, small hooded figures scurried about operating several giant catapults. She was surprised when she recognised them. They were Yakshas, celestial beings whose greed for gold made them abandon their forest homes and eke out a life within the bowels of the earth. They never interfered with the affairs of humans; she could not understand how or why they had come to Indra's aid.

Then she sensed another presence, a familiar one. It was the one she knew as the Alchemist. Now it made sense to her: gold was the only religion those greedy little creatures knew. To them, the Alchemist was a god. Ishtar sighed as she realised how heavily the odds were stacked against her and her city. She was in above her head with one hell of a fight on her hands.

Travistr felt the compelling presence of Ishtar as he looked towards the burning city. He wondered why she hadn't played her hand yet. She, not the warriors or the walls, would be Indra's real test. The flames started to spread; it made the city shine like a jewel against the night. He called to the leader of his siege engineers.

'Kubera, direct your fire towards the gates.'

One of the hooded figures bowed his head and shouted instructions to the others, who briskly went about doing his bidding.

A few hundred yards ahead, Indra watched the fiery projectiles crash into the Moon Gates of Susa. Slowly, they began to catch fire. It was almost dawn. Indra sent two divisions under Atreya and Nala to attack the parapets and ramparts near the gates.

The soldiers and populace of Susa made a valiant effort to put out the flames, but the Yakshas' catapults had done their damage. Now Nala and Atreya attacked, making little skirmishing runs towards the walls. Their accurate shower of arrows took its toll and made rescue efforts even more difficult for the Elamites. The flames continued to burn high and scorched the soldiers on the parapets, forcing them to back off.

Meanwhile, Kubera and his men stood before Travistr with their heads bowed. Their war machines had been packed away into wagons.

'Thank you, my brave little brothers. You have done me a great service today.'

Travistr watched Kubera step forward, his beady little eyes shining within the darkness of the hood.

'It is our pleasure to serve you, learned master. Your blessings are all we crave for.'

As Travistr watched them leave, he knew they would extract their pound of flesh for this favour one day.

As the first rays of the sun hit the walls, Soma held up the crystal chalice filled with the potion soma. Indra emptied the contents down his throat, blew his conch and led the charge. The line of chariots flew towards the city like a tidal wave, gathering speed before it crashed to the shore. As they approached the burning gates, without breaking a stride the formation changed into the classic arrowhead with Indra at the point.

As the chariots of the Devas burst through the burning gates into the city, they left the Elamite front line in total disarray. The men had spent the whole night putting out the fires that threatened to consume their city. Now they tried in vain to stand their ground as the chariots swept over them. The ones that did not fall to Deva arrows and spears found themselves crushed under the wheels of their chariots.

Indra's eyes blazed with a manic intensity and his arms worked tirelessly. Arrows poured out of his bow into the Elamite ranks. The enemy broke their line and fled in panic before him. They raced down the broad avenue, the Devas in hot pursuit, and arrived at the central plaza. Around this big square were the royal palace and the temple.

As Indra led the chariots into the square, the Elamites began to push boulders and logs into their path. Soma and the other drivers were forced to slow down and manoeuvre around the obstacles. As soon as the chariots lost their momentum, the Elamite soldiers poured out of the numerous streets around the plaza and surrounded them. Indra threw aside his bow, picked up Kadaag and leapt into the mass of enemy soldiers.

From the balcony of the royal palace, General Druma watched his king scream orders to his men. It had been Druma's plan to lure the Devas into the plaza and then surround and immobilise the chariots. Now that the plan had worked, Shalla was there to take the credit.

'Kill their horses but spare the chariots, for we will have use for them!'

The Elamite soldiers pressed forward to do his bidding. Indra heard the screams of his dying horses and roared with rage. His black sword went through shield and armour, cutting enemy soldiers in half. Somewhere close by, he could hear the thump of Soma's mace as it struck flesh and broke bone.

The battle raged on through the day, and by evening, of the five hundred men in Indra's division, only a handful remained. They had fought themselves into a defendable niche between two buildings. Around them lay piles of dead Elamite soldiers. The enemy still came though, climbing over the bodies of their own dead. Indra and Soma had no idea how the rest of the troops had fared; they now made their way to the roof of a building to take a look.

The battle raged on in two areas. Puru's division had followed Indra into the city and were hemmed in on a narrow street. Outnumbered and trapped, they doggedly fought for their lives.

Atreya and Nala had fought their way up the walls and gained control of the ramparts. They now held their positions even as they inflicted huge losses on the enemy who were coming at them from all sides.

As the sky grew dark, beams of pure white light emerged from the top of the temple, illuminating the Deva positions. It was Ishtar. The Elamite archers and spearmen moved in from the shadows and began to attack. The light gave them easy targets to aim at while keeping their own positions hidden from the Devas.

Indra knew he had to do something quickly; the tide was turning swiftly in favour of the enemy. Soma offered him the crystal chalice. He quickly downed its contents. As the brew went down his throat, his tiredness vanished. He looked up at the lights and remembered something.

'Witchcraft! Mitra had warned me about the witch of Susa. I will make for the temple and kill her. You take the men and head for the palace. We must end this quickly if we are to be victorious.'

He leapt off the roof into the enemy throng and fought his way towards the temple.

In a cave on Mount Kailash, a distraught Mitra stood before a naked hermit. The holy man's hair was matted and hung to his knees in clumps. He stood on one leg with his hands joined above his head. His eyes were half closed in deep meditation.

Mitra did not move a muscle. Facing him, its massive hood only inches from his face, was the biggest snake he had ever seen. He looked into the lidless black eyes of the king cobra and saw the excruciatingly painful death that lingered there.

'That's enough, Vasuki.'

The serpent flicked its tongue at Mitra; it brushed lightly against his cheek. Then it relaxed its hood and slithered away into the dark recesses of the cave. The hermit studied Mitra, an amused expression on his face.

'How do you hope to find what you seek if you constantly allow these worldly attachments to distract you?'

Mitra bowed low; he did not dare look into the face of the Master. He focused on the blue mark at his throat when he spoke.

'Indra is the hope of my people. He is the one who will unite my warring kinsmen under one great nation. How can I be selfish and seek moksha when the fate of my people is in jeopardy? He is still young and does not know of the peril he is in. He thinks he is going into a battle of his choosing, but Ishtar will destroy him, or worse, turn him into her slave.'

The hermit laughed heartily.

'Your concern for your people is noted, but you forgot to mention that this Indra has become like a son to you. Go Mitra! Go back to your tapas.'

Indra, charged on the soma, ran up the steep stairs of the ziggurat. He made swift progress, taking several steps at a time. The temple guards tried in vain to challenge him. The black sword whirled in the air and their bodies toppled down the stairs into the bloody plaza. He entered the main temple, his eyes searching frantically for her. The priests fled at the sight of him. Only the high priest, a wizened old man, pointed his staff at him and started to utter a curse. Indra drove the black sword through the man's chest, cutting off the words in his throat. He did not even break his stride as he leapt over the dead body of Braega and continued to make his way up the stairs to the very top of the monument.

Ishtar watched the handsome demon come to her with a smile. It was time for her to play her hand in this battle. Indra entered the private chambers of the goddess of Susa. There was an alluring fragrance of jasmine blossoms in the air. As Indra took a deep breath, his rage and blood lust from the fierce battle left him. He stopped and took a look around. The chamber was made up of the whitest marble that glistened like a pearl in the moonlight. He dropped his sword and took in the sublime setting. Then he saw her and his heart leapt in his chest.

It was Sachi, dressed in her wedding finery. This time her smile was warm and inviting. Indra stood transfixed by her beauty. She came close to him, her face near his. Her warm breath in his ear drove him wild with desire as she whispered, 'Come, husband! You must be tired. Let me take care of you.'

She took off his armour and tunic and led him naked to a tub filled with warm, aromatic water. Indra sank into its depth, welcoming its warmth. Her eyes hungrily devoured his naked body as she stood in front of him and slowly disrobed. Indra's throat went dry and the breath caught in his throat at the sight of her. She climbed in with him and began to gently cleanse his wounds with a soft washcloth. Under her breath she began to hum one of his favourite songs. Indra closed his eyes and threw his head back. Her hands caressed his body all over, removing all the tiredness and pain. Then they slowly moved between his legs. Indra felt a stab of desire unlike anything he had felt before. He grabbed her and pulled her towards him.

Ishtar laughed with delight as Indra carried her in his arms and rose from the tub. She wrapped her legs tightly around his waist. This was going to be a lot easier than she'd thought. When he placed her down on the bed, she spread her legs and allowed him to enter her. She felt the divine energy that pulsated through him and moaned with desire. Soon she would draw it out of him along with his seed.

Ishtar had long ceased to enjoy the sexual act. For her, it had become a potent weapon that she had mastered. She enjoyed the entrapment and the subsequent destruction of her adversaries through sex, more than the act itself. Yet, this time it was different. As she looked at the beautiful man who lay on top of her, she felt a desire rise within her quite unlike anything she had felt before. She shut her eyes and began to cry out in pleasure. Indra quickened his rhythm; his breathing grew ragged as he neared his sweet release. She cupped her hands around his buttocks and pushed her hips up to meet his thrusts.

Suddenly she became aware of another presence. She opened her eyes and looked out of the window up at the moon. A shadow began to creep over it. The cool breeze had stopped. The fragrance in the air was gone, replaced by the revolting smell of burnt flesh and rotten carcasses. Then she heard a voice in her head, gruff, and filled with rage.

'Your time is up, you old crone. No more will you lure innocent young men to their destruction. Come! It is time for you and me to play.'

She shivered in fear as she recognised the voice.

Bhairav! What was he doing here? Her eyes darted about the room, and then she saw him, leaning against one of the pillars. He was a fearsome sight. Matted locks hung down to his feet. His beard was long and unkempt. His naked, muscular body was dark and shone like anthracite. A necklace of severed human heads hung against his chest. In one hand he held a fearsome-looking sickle, and in the other, he carried a bowl fashioned from the top of a human skull. She tried not to look at his huge, engorged phallus, but her eyes were automatically drawn to it. He laughed and stuck his tongue out at her. It was bright red and dripped with fresh blood.

Ishtar suddenly felt Indra's lips on hers; he kissed her gently, yet passionately. All his love for Sachi went into that kiss. For a brief second she closed her eyes, swayed by the intensity of his emotions. Then she felt his hands on her shoulder as he roughly pushed her down and thrust violently into her. She opened her eyes and looked into Indra's eyes. They had turned a deep black. Ishtar saw her own terror reflected in them. His thrusts grew harder and more violent. She felt he was going to tear her apart and tried to resist but to no avail. As a Tantric, she knew she had no equal, but the being that opposed her now was Tantra itself. She tried hard to regain control, to bring her mind back to face the dire peril she was in, but found herself unable to do anything but surrender to the pleasure. She screamed with every thrust as she approached an orgasm.

Ishtar shuddered violently, her mouth frozen in a brilliant smile. She was in the throes of ecstasy when Bhairav bested her at her own game and drew out her prana through his phallus. He then left Indra's body in a blaze of light. The impact of his departure threw Indra across the chamber, against the wall. He got to his feet, shaken. Sachi was gone; where she had lain was another woman. Then right before his eyes, the strange woman began to change. She started to age, her flesh began to melt away and her hair began to fall out in clumps. The skin on her face withered and fell away, revealing a skull that began to crumble. Soon all that was left of the patron goddess of Susa was a pile of ash.

A dazed Indra donned his clothing and armour, gathered his sword and left the temple. He was not sure what had happened, but he knew he had been in way over his head and was lucky to come out of that encounter alive. He looked down and saw that the Devas had taken the city. The Elamite army had been slaughtered down to the last man. As he reached the palace, the dead had been removed and the civilian population herded into the square. They cowered in fear when they saw him. They were like cattle, he thought to himself. He would sacrifice them to his ancestors and the gods.

Nala and Atreya brought a visibly shaken Shalla before him. The Elamite king still could not come to terms with his loss. He tried to bribe Indra with treasure, he offered him his daughters. He continued to bargain for his life even as Indra swung the black sword. Shalla's severed head rolled down the steps and fell at the feet of his frightened people.

Indra had done his duty as a son and avenged his father. Yet the act gave him no satisfaction. There was a tiny vestige of Bhairav still left in his body and it gave him an insatiable thirst for blood. He contemplated wading into the crowd with his sword and taking off their heads. His men stood around, their weapons drawn as they eagerly awaited his orders to do the same.

Just then Soma entered with a prisoner. Indra noticed that his friend treated the man with respect, something he did not do very often. The man was dressed like a bard who had long seen better days. In his hand was an old harp that looked in far better condition than its master. He had the vacant gaze of a blind man.

'I found him on a street corner, he was singing through the battle.'

Indra gave a sigh of exasperation.

'So why didn't you just slit his throat? Why do you bring him to me?'

Soma lowered his voice as he approached him.

'The song he was singing. I think you should listen to it.'

Indra shrugged. 'After what this victory has cost us, I could use some distraction. And these people might enjoy a song before they die. You may begin, old man.'

The bard stepped forward and began to strum on his harp and sing. He had a beautiful, clear voice and he sang of a great battle within the confines of a mountain pass. As the song progressed, tears ran down the faces of Indra and his Devas. The lyrics exalted the bravery of Raja Daeyus and his army of sixty. The bard was none other than Captain Nehat, the officer who had first led the Elamite cavalry into the pass. He had given up his life as a soldier and lived all these years as a street bard. He had composed this ballad in honour of a brave enemy.

The entire square was silent as his song ended. Indra looked at his men. There were many among them who had lost a parent or relative in the battle at the Pass of the Wolves. No one had known what exactly transpired there. To now hear such a glowing account of the bravery of their fathers moved them beyond measure. Indra wiped away his tears and addressed the old man.

'You have pleased me beyond my expectations, old man. Ask of me what you wish.'

'Spare my city and its people, oh king!'

It was a bold request to make, but Indra did not hesitate to comply.

'Granted! Ransack the palace and the temple. Take all their weapons and horses. But spare the people and the city.'

Soma waited for the others to leave before he turned to Indra.

'How can you spare the city? Our men will want their share of the spoils.'

'Divide the treasure of the palace and the temple among them.'

'But those belong to you by right.'

Indra laughed.

'What use are these baubles to me now, Soma! I am a god.'

11

The west wind blew across from the vast open wilderness of Central Asia. Indra stood alone on the ramparts of Susa, lost in thought. The cold wind did nothing to quell the feverish intensity that coursed through his body. He longed for a drink of soma, but just the idea of making his way back to the palace for it was exhausting. The last two weeks had been lost to the pleasures of Shalla's extensive harem. The young wives and daughters of the erstwhile king had eagerly opened their arms to their handsome, young conquerors. It had taken all Indra's willpower to lure himself away from those beautiful women and Soma's brew.

He looked at the land through which his ancestors had fought and plundered their way from their distant homeland in the north. He had grown up on the songs of their journey through the land of the two great rivers, Tigris and Euphrates. Now he knew they watched over him from the heavens.

The sound of footsteps brought him back to the present. Two of his men arrived leading a prisoner between them. They threw the man at Indra's feet.

'We found a tunnel going under the walls and kept a watch on it. He was found trying to sneak out of the city. He says he has useful information for you, my lord.'

Indra looked down. The man grovelling at his feet did not seem like someone from the city.

'Why do you try to sneak off like a thief at night when I have spared your city and your miserable lives?'

The man did not lift his head. His voice shook with terror as he spoke.

'My lord, this city is not safe anymore. The Asura General Bhadra marches towards us from the west with an army of five thousand warriors.'

'Who are you? How do you have this information?'

The man looked up with a smile. He had a keen instinct for self-preservation, and it told him that everything was now going to be all right.

'I am Timon of Ashkavan. I have more information about what goes on in these lands than any man in this city.'

'Your life will depend on the truth of your claim. Take him away and question him thoroughly. By tomorrow I want to know everything there is to know about this army that marches against us.'

The thought of another battle filled Indra with excitement. But he would not fight it cowering within these walls. It would be fought on the open plain; the earth would soon run red with Asura blood. He now needed some soma more than ever. He hurried off in the direction of the palace.

General Bhadra watched in amusement as the two officers of Susa were presented to him. One of them, a pompous barrel-chested soldier, was the first to speak.

'Greetings, General! We are the commanders of the western and northern garrisons of Susa. Our city has fallen and our king is dead.'

General Bhadra raised his eyebrows in astonishment. He of all people knew how formidable a task it was to take the city of Susa. He had been planning it for years. He now stood up to his full height. Even among the Asuras, who were a big-made people, Bhadra was something of a giant. He stood eight feet tall, and his enormous body was covered with hair. He studied the two men, who had stepped back in awe at the sight of his imposing bulk.

'Who did this?'

'A demon! He goes by the name Indra. We would like to offer our services in your battle against him. We have two thousand men at our command.'

General Bhadra reached forward and grabbed the pompous man by the throat and lifted him. He seized the top of the man's head and twisted it clean off like one would twist open the stopper of a wine flask. Blood spurted out of the neck; the general took some of it in his mouth, gargled and spat it at the other man.

'His blood reeks of cowardice. What about yours?'

The commander soiled himself in terror and ran out of the tent screaming. The general curled his nose in disgust as he turned to one of his men.

'Prepare the men for some sport.'

Indra and his commanders prepared to defend the city against the approaching army. The breached gates of the city presented a huge problem. Defending a walled city was not the Devas' forte. With only about a thousand men, it would be impossible to defend the ramparts and the gateway. Only five hundred chariots had survived the battle, so even challenging the army outside the city walls would not be a wise decision. The Asuras, according to Timon, relied on their numbers, brute strength and individual skills as warriors. They could engage his chariot divisions and still have enough men to take the city. The only good news he had received that day had been that the two garrisons of Susa did not pose a threat anymore. Bhadra and his legions had decimated them.

A guard walked into the hall and bowed low.

'There is an Asura emissary at the gates, my lord.'

'Send him in.'

Indra and his men had never seen an Asura warrior before, so there was a great deal of curiosity as the emissary entered the court. The Devas were by no means a short-statured people, yet the Asura stood at least half a head higher than the tallest of them. His long hair was braided, as was his long bushy beard. His dark eyes were fierce and hawk-like; he fixed his gaze on Indra as he spoke.

'Greetings, oh conqueror of Susa. My master Bhadra congratulates you on your great victory. As a warrior he appreciates the effort and cost you might have incurred. My master is a fair man; he knows you have neither the manpower nor the strength to now defend the city. He sees no honour in defeating a valiant but weakened enemy.'

The emissary paused dramatically to let his words sink in.

'So he challenges you to a duel unto death. The winner will get the city of Susa, and all its plunder.'

Indra could not believe his ears; the gods were indeed on his side. His enemy had just presented him a way out of a potentially tough predicament.

'Tell your master I accept his most gracious offer.'

The messenger smiled, almost with a sense of relief, and bowed to Indra.

'Very well, my lord! General Bhadra will await you outside the walls at dawn.'

As the messenger left, Indra and his commanders rejoiced at the turn of events. They could not have planned it better themselves. The only one in the hall who was not cheerful was Timon. The Asura general's offer did not make sense to him. Bhadra was a bloodthirsty monster; nothing gave him more pleasure than slaughtering an army. Why would a man like that want to avoid bloodshed? Besides whatever his reasons, there was no doubt in Timon's mind about General Bhadra's prowess as a warrior. He did not relish the thought that, come tomorrow, he might have the Asura as his master.

At the Asura camp, the messenger finished his report to Bhadra and left. The general was a relieved man. The situation had drastically changed since he had slaughtered the garrisons of Susa. He had received word that there had been a rebellion in the Sumerian city of Abash. The troops stationed there had been killed and the Asura commander hung from its gates.

Bhadra knew he had to hurry back and put down the rebellion before it spread to the other cities of Sumer. Yet Susa and all its riches lay within his grasp. Fighting duels to avoid wars had been a time-honoured tradition in his land. He made the decision to avoid a long drawn-out conflict through the hostile streets of the city. Bhadra's plan was clear, by morning tomorrow he would have this little Deva puppy's head and the city of Susa. He could then leave a small force to hold the city and hurry back to quell the rebellion. The city of Abash would pay dearly for denying him the pleasure of plundering Susa.

The first rays of the sun saw the Devas and a substantial number of the local population gather on the ramparts of Susa.

They had all been witness to Indra's skills as a warrior, so there was an optimistic buzz around. Then Bhadra came into view. Clad in heavy bronze armour, he was as big as a house. In one hand he carried a wide-bladed scimitar, and in the other a wooden club that was as thick as a tree trunk. A hush fell on the crowd as he got closer and they were actually able to see how big he really was.

Bhadra bent his head and picked up the pace, his horned war helmet gave him the appearance of a giant bull in full charge. Soma stood by Indra and watched the Asura unperturbed.

'He seems in an awful hurry. Play with him for a while. Put on a show. It'll only improve your image with this lot.'

Indra nodded as he handed the crystal chalice back to Soma. His eyes shone with deadly intent as he watched Bhadra approach.

'Have another drink ready for me when I return, my friend.'

Indra set off. He wore no armour, only a white loincloth. In his right hand he carried his black sword. He ran swiftly in a zigzag pattern towards the enemy.

Bhadra watched him come and stopped. His opponent was swifter than any man he had seen. He tightened the grip on his weapons and waited. For all the Deva's speed, even a glancing blow from either weapon would kill him or set him up for the coup de grace.

Indra ran towards his adversary, sword in hand. As he neared him, Bhadra swung the scimitar, looking to cut his opponent in half. Indra did not check his run; he dropped to his knees and bent backwards allowing the thick curved blade to pass inches above him. There was a cry of anguish in the crowd as they watched their hero narrowly miss decapitation. His momentum started to carry Indra past the giant. As he slid across the coarse sand, he reversed the grip on his sword and slashed the back of Bhadra's thigh.

The cut had been executed with surgical precision; it cut through layers of thick-corded muscle and nicked the hamstring of the Asura general. Bhadra felt his right leg stiffen; he turned slowly on his other leg to face his slippery opponent. Indra was already on his feet and in motion. As Bhadra raised his blade to attack, he left his right side open for one brief second and Indra was quick to pounce on the opportunity. Bhadra felt a sharp pain under his armpit just above the protection of his armour. His entire right side went numb, his fingers opened and the scimitar fell to the ground. The stab had once again been delivered with pinpoint accuracy. It crippled one of the marmas or nerve centers of the giant warrior. As Indra danced out of reach, Bhadra's eyes widened in shock. He was not just being bested, he was being systematically taken apart.

Indra now dropped his guard and waited for his adversary to come to him. The giant warrior moved slowly as he dragged the crippled right side of his body. The Asura commanders were puzzled at his ungainly movement; up until now they had not seen Indra make any serious contact with their general.

Bhadra raised his club and advanced menacingly. Indra stood his ground, waiting. The giant put all his weight behind the club as he swung it.

As he watched the contest, Soma for one brief moment was a little worried. Indra was in too close. Even if Bhadra missed the blow, his huge girth would smother his friend.

Indra watched the giant come and, at the last minute, flung himself forward flat on the ground. He slid through the legs of Bhadra and as he came up behind him, he swung the sword. The slash was aimed low at the heel and it found its mark as it severed the Asura general's left Achilles tendon.

His left leg now rendered useless, Bhadra turned slowly on his already injured right leg, using his club as a crutch. His great bulk that had served him well in so many battles now became his enemy. He swayed like a giant old tree in a storm and then fell to the ground with an earth-shaking impact.

The crowd was silent for a moment, unsure of what exactly had happened. The duels they normally witnessed were usually bloody, brutal affairs where the participants hacked away at each other till one of them dropped dead. Here there had hardly been any contact.

Then a roar went up on the ramparts and Indra looked up to see the people of Susa chanting his name. He realised that it was not their love for him, but their fear of Bhadra that gave them so much joy. He would give them something to remember and fear, he thought to himself, as he stood over the giant warrior.

Bhadra looked up at his death in the garb of a handsome young warrior. The blue eyes that stared at him were cold and hard and shone like a pair of diamonds. His opponent bent down and ripped his armour off his chest. Bhadra felt nothing as the black sword cut a hole in his chest. He continued to stare into that angelic face with a morbid fascination.

Indra looked down at the open chest of his enemy and saw his beating heart. A cry of horror ensued from the crowd as he knelt down, reached into the cavity and ripped out the heart of the Asura general. He stood up, one foot on the body of Bhadra and offered the still pumping organ to the crowd. Then he held it up high, threw back his head and squeezed the blood from it into his open mouth.

There were a few horrified looks on the faces of the Devas, but not so on Soma's. He grinned to himself as he watched the macabre ceremony; his friend had indeed put on a show nobody would forget in a hurry. The people of Susa and the Asuras would carry this tale all across the wide plains. What better way than this for a conqueror to announce his arrival.

Indra and Timon stood atop a hill and surveyed the land ahead. They were dressed in the garb of the desert nomads. The spy had offered his services to the Devas and in a short time made himself an integral member of Indra's war council. It had been a few months since Indra had embarked on his conquest of the Asura lands. He was under no illusions about the difficulty of the task ahead of him. Timon pointed to the southwest where, in the distant horizon, he saw the telltale puff of dust.

Sargon the Grey Wolf had under his command fifty thousand soldiers—by far the largest army in the known world. Luckily for Indra, that huge army was spread out all across his vast empire putting down various insurgencies and rebellions. For months now, the Devas had been like a little barb in his flesh. They had attacked his garrisons, looted his supply lines and generally been busy whittling down the numbers of his legions.

In his magnificent court at Assur, the emperor listened to the reports of the governors from the various provinces of his vast empire. He grew weary with the news from Sumer. The conquest of that land had brought him nothing but trouble with the constant uprisings and rebellions in its many city-states. No one man in history had ever ruled such a vast territory as he, and Sargon was beginning to see the reason why. He was in the twilight of his existence and he could not remember the last time he had known peace in his empire. His grey brow knitted in a frown as he heard of the slaying of Bhadra and of the transgressions made by Indra in Sumer and his eastern provinces. He raised his hand to stop the messenger.

'This demon that you call Indra has slain my bravest general, attacked my garrisons and nobody thought it fit to inform me.'

The messenger was an old hand; he was not fooled by the calmness of the emperor's tone. He bowed low as he chose his words carefully.

'Hiranya, Bhadra's brother, had the rebellion of Abash to take care of. He has vowed to bring you Indra's head at the end of his spear once he has put down the rebellion.'

'The rebellion shows no sign of being quelled. Perhaps it is time for me to take matters into my own hands.'

Mahisha, one of his generals, was quick to respond.

'My lord, this man is a mere fly and not worthy of your consideration. Allow me to go and squash him.'

The messenger did not want another Asura general taking this problem lightly.

'My lord Mahisha, this fly has wings, he moves with a fleet of horse-drawn vehicles. It will be hard for you to catch him in the expanse of the vast plains.'

The Asuras had not yet mastered the horse; they found it hard to get their bulk onto the back of the animal. They still preferred to fight on foot. Sargon scratched his grey beard and thought for a long while before he replied.

'I think I know of a way to clip the fly's wings. Summon the Ikshvaaku princes. It is time for them to repay the debt of their people.'

Muka, the young Asura captain, watched as a carrier pigeon flew down and alighted on top of the barracks. He hoped there would be some good news, maybe a transfer to the frontline for him. The cook went to collect the message. He looked around at the men who lounged around in the shade; they were bored veterans who had done their time in the army and were now counting the days to their retirement.

Muka had grown up in a life of luxury as the only son of a wealthy nobleman from Assur. He had looked forward to his first commission to escape the boredom of his opulent existence. He had hoped to cut his teeth in the campaign in Sumer, but unknown to him his indulgent and protective father had pulled a few strings and got him posted to this remote northern outpost. Muka could not believe the cards fate had dealt him. It had traded one boring existence for another.

The cook returned with the message, Muka noticed that the man's hand shook with fear as he held it out. The message was wrapped in red and gold, the royal colours of Assur. Muka's heart leapt with excitement as he opened it. It was brief and to the point. Summon the Ikshvaaku princes to the royal court.

Muka read the message out loud to his inquisitive audience; a few groans escaped the lips of his men. The soldiers informed the young officer that the tribe lived in the inhospitable mountains of Talurkan in the northwest. The mountains were a fortnight's march through some of the most treacherous terrain in the area.

The old cook had fought a famous battle in one of its valleys. He had been part of Sargon's legions when the emperor was but a young man. Four thousand Asuras, led by the Grey Wolf, had attacked a Hittite settlement there. It had been a massacre, as twelve thousand of the enemy fell in what came to be called the Valley of Twelve Thousand Souls.

Once the battle was over, the old cook recalled, the Asuras had found themselves standing waist-deep in Hittite corpses. The once fertile valley was red with blood, its many streams and watering holes poisoned by the rotting corpses of the enemy.

The land had then turned into a vile, desolate place shunned by even the most courageous of travellers. It was said that the souls of the dead Hittites still roamed those mountains looking for bodies to possess.

Muka was one of the few Asuras who had mastered the

horse, and he knew for certain that he was the only man at the outpost who could ride with any degree of proficiency. To the great relief of the others, he volunteered to go alone on the mission.

As he set out on the lonely road, his thoughts went to the mysterious people he was going to contact. His soldiers, once they'd realised they would not have to accompany him, had been quite forthcoming with whatever little knowledge they had of the Ikshvaaku. According to them, it was a tribe that practiced an ancient and powerful witchcraft. Their ways were not known to the outside world, but they were feared and respected by the fierce northern tribes who knew them.

The cook had been present as a member of the Royal Guard when the Ikshvaaku requested a treaty with the Asuras. Their chief had ridden to the parley mounted on a huge tiger. Sargon was impressed and decided that they were more useful to him alive than dead. He granted their request for permission to make their home in the Talurkan Mountains.

After a six-day gruelling march through the dry and arid wasteland, both Muka and his horse were nearly at the end of their reserves when they came upon the huge, dark shape of the Talurkan Mountains that broke the flat horizon.

The exhausted Asura warrior led his mount up one of the numerous trails. He had no idea where he was going and he had met no other travellers on the road. They now passed through a thick forest of pines. Muka was thankful for the shade. He stopped for a while and allowed his tired horse to feed on the sparse vegetation. He found some succulent cacti, removed its thorns and crushed the pulp into his parched mouth.

Barely had his thirst been satiated when a slight sound alerted him. He saw a dark shape move quickly through the trees, then another. His horse neighed out loud, turned and bolted back down the trail. Muka drew his sword and prepared to face the threat. Ahead of him, something stepped out through the trees. It was a giant timber wolf. The animal gave a low growl and from the corners of his eyes Muka saw more wolves emerge through the trees. Within moments, the animals had him surrounded. Muka knew he didn't stand much of a chance, but he was an Asura warrior and he would sell his life very dearly to this pack. He kept his eyes on the beast in front of him, the alpha male. Suddenly, it crouched low and prepared to spring.

Muka tightened the grip on his weapon. He knew the attack would come from several directions at once. As a warrior he did not fear death, he just regretted that it would be on this lonely mountainside, unheralded and unsung. Just then a sharp cry rang out behind him and the big wolf stopped almost in midspring. It let out a series of low angry growls and slowly started to back off. Muka turned his head in surprise and curiosity. He saw a young boy walk towards him; in his arms he carried an injured fawn. His beautiful, emerald green eyes were locked into those of the wolf. The alpha turned and ran; in moments, the rest of the pack melted into the trees.

The boy laid the fawn gently on the floor and took its injured leg in his hands. Muka noticed that the leg was badly broken. The boy gently stroked the limb with his hand as he shut his eyes and muttered something under his breath. The fawn slowly got to his feet and hobbled around for a moment before it ran off up the mountain, showing no signs of injury. The boy turned to face the warrior, dwarfed by his bulk. He had a twinkle in his eyes. Muka could not believe what he had just witnessed. The boy gestured for him to follow as he made his way up the mountain.

Muka trudged along behind his young guide, almost dizzy with exhaustion as he made his way through a narrow path between two hills. It was some of the most difficult terrain he had ever encountered. It did not help that the wind through the pine trees produced a sound like the wails of dying men. The thick canopy blotted out the sun and mist rolled down from the top of the mountain. It only added to the eerie atmosphere. The boy stopped occasionally and looked around to see if the young warrior was all right. Muka struggled to keep focus—one slip would mean a long plunge into the ravine.

Muka did not know for how long he had dragged his exhausted body along that treacherous path, but he was on the verge of collapse when the boy called to him. The warrior looked up. The boy was on top of a slope, pointing downwards excitedly. Muka made his way up and peered over the ledge. All his exhaustion disappeared as he looked down at one of the most spectacular views he had ever seen.

He guessed this was the valley the cook had told him about, where Sargon had won his great, blood-stained victory. Only it was nothing like the old man's morbid description. In front of him lay a pristine paradise. The desolate land he had been told about had been replaced by green meadows interspersed with thick woods filled with a variety of fruit-bearing trees. Streams crisscrossed the landscape before they emptied themselves into the azure blue waters of a mountain lake.

They quickly made their way down into the valley and Muka drank from the crystal waters of the stream. The boy went to a tree, put his right hand to its trunk and chanted a few words. An astonished Muka watched a branch of the tree, laden with fruit, bend downwards towards the outstretched hands of the child. The boy picked a couple of fruit and handed one to the Asura. It was by far the sweetest fruit Muka had ever tasted. His strength returned to him as he kept pace with the boy down a path that led through a bed of wild flowers of every conceivable hue. Their heady fragrance intoxicated his mind and removed all fear and misgivings from it.

As they neared the settlement, Muka saw men and women go about their chores, tending to their crops or flocks. They greeted the Asura with big smiles on their faces. Their livestock grazed in the meadows along with deer and antelope. One of the fawns ran to the boy and playfully nuzzled against him.

Muka noticed that the roof and walls of their huts were made of living plants and creepers. This tribe lived in complete harmony with their surroundings, he thought. The child stopped in front of one of the huts and greeted the man who stepped out. The man exchanged a few words with the child before he turned to Muka.

'I am Vivasvat, chief of the Ikshvaaku. Tell me how I may be of service to you.'

Muka was surprised to note that the chief's appearance and dwelling was no different from that of the other members of his tribe. He bowed low and conveyed the message of his sovereign.

The chief did not hesitate with his reply.

'Tell the Asura king that my sons will be at his service by the new moon.'

Somewhere in the vast open plains of Sumer, Indra and Soma watched the members of the caravan put up a spirited resistance, but they were no match for the superior strength and skill of the Devas. Within a few moments, it was all over. The portly head merchant of the caravan threw up his arms and fell to his knees in a gesture of surrender. But it was an action that came a little too late: his armed escort had all been slaughtered. Indra soon got tired of hearing his cries for mercy; his attention was drawn to the rear of the caravan where an abandoned palanquin lay. He went to it and ripped aside the curtains.

In it was a beautiful young woman unlike any he had ever seen before. Her skin was the colour of wild honey and shone with the kiss of good health. Her hair, the colour of a raven's wing, was straight and long and framed the high cheekbones of her face. Her eyes were big and dark; she had no fear in them as she beheld him, only a sense of curiosity. Her breasts were firm with dark perky nipples. She wore only a skirt of beads but showed no sense of shame at her nakedness.

Indra felt strangely uncomfortable under her scrutiny. He grabbed her by the arm and dragged her out to where the survivors of the raid had been bunched together. As he threw her down, she said something to him in an alien tongue. The head merchant rebuked her and slapped her hard across the face.

'Forgive me, my lord. She is a witch who has brought us nothing but misfortune. Allow me to cut her insolent tongue out.'

Indra looked at her as she continued to stare at him. Her lips were cut from the blow and she licked the blood off them with a lascivious smile.

'What did she say?'

The merchant hesitated as he figured out how best to translate her words.

'She asks that you give her one hour alone with yourself, you will never want another woman again. She is evil, my lord, I would have cut her to pieces and thrown her to the wolves if I did not fear her future master.'

Indra cocked his eyebrow in surprise.

'Who is the unfortunate man who must tame this savage?'

'Hiranya, the Asura governor of Sumer.'

Timon came up to Indra and whispered in his ear. 'Bhadra's brother! He has vowed to mount your head at the end of his spear and send it to Sargon as a trophy.'

Indra laughed.

'Well then, let us give him a little more incentive to take my head. We'll take her with us. Let me see if she will make good her promise.'

Valli finished her bath by the stream shielded from the camp by a cluster of rocks. It had been weeks since she had been held prisoner. Once her captors had noticed her aversion to the horses, they had let her move freely through the camp. They were in the middle of nowhere, and there was really no place she could escape to on foot.

As she returned to the camp, she saw their king in conference with his scouts. She stared at him unabashedly. She had made her desire for him apparent, but he seemed immune to her charms. His fascination for her was like what one might have for an exotic animal. He glanced in her direction and quickly looked away as she made an obscene gesture with her tongue. She laughed and made a promise to herself that she would have him one day.

The scouts were informing Indra about a herd of wild horses that were a day's march away from the camp. They were headed straight towards them. Indra could not contain his excitement. He asked them to keep a close watch on the animals. They would be a welcome addition to his vastly depleted herd.

By dusk that day, the herd was within sight of the camp. It

was a large one—Indra counted over one hundred and fifty animals. But there was something strange about them. They moved in perfect order, like a cavalry formation. Indra looked for the lead stallion, but could not find him. The herd stopped a short distance away and snorted indignantly as they smelt the camp. Then the wind stopped and changed direction. It began to blow towards the camp.

Indra suddenly sensed unrest among his own horses. As the wild ones inched closer, he noticed something extremely strange—they were all mares. He knew wild mares did not behave in this fashion and he watched closely as they approached the paddock. This was some kind of sorcery that Indra was unfamiliar with. The mares turned together, the wind carrying the smell of their oestrus to the nostrils of the Deva stallions. Indra realised what was going on and shouted out to the grooms, 'Secure the stallions!'

But one hundred and fifty mares on heat were too much even for the well-trained Deva stallions to resist. They gave way to their primal mating urge, broke through the paddock and rushed after the wild horses. The mares and the younger fillies also followed. Within a matter of moments, Indra's army had lost nearly all their horses.

Out of sight of the Deva camp, two men sat up on their mares and smiled at each other. They were identical in looks, height and build. One of them whistled shrilly, and the mares began to split into smaller groups and spread out across the plains. The Deva horses followed and were soon lost in the vast expanse.

As night fell, the Deva think-tank gathered to plan their next course of action. Just then, Timon approached with news. Indra walked away with him into the darkness. The news, as Indra had suspected, was not good. Hiranya's scouts had picked up their trail and were only two days' march away.

Usually, this would have meant nothing more than a routine shift of camp. But now, without horses, it was a completely different situation. The army that pursued them was used to long hard marches on foot, something that could not be said of the Devas. It was rumoured that the Asuras could march almost twice the distance of a regular army in a single day. On this open landscape, it would not take them long to catch up. Indra did not want to face an Asura army on foot. He turned to Timon, who looked extremely worried.

'We cannot hope to outrun them without horses, my lord!'

'And I cannot risk any more men in a battle which clearly favours the enemy.'

Timon hurriedly drew a map of the territory in the dirt.

'We can head north and make for the city of Ur. I have friends there in the resistance who will hide us. But it is also the first place they will look for us. The alternative is to head west and cross the river at the town of Umra. If we are then able to destroy the bridge, we can lose them in the forests of Aranya. I must warn you though, my lord—the forest is fraught with enough dangers of its own.'

Indra thought for a moment before he made his decision.

'I do not wish to die trapped within the walls of Ur like a rat. We will take our chances in the forests of Aranya.'

Indra issued quick orders to the men to dismantle the chariots and bury them in the loose sand. The Devas worked through the night and by dawn they were ready to march. On Timon's advice they decided to march north first and let the enemy think they were headed for Ur. They would veer off to the west later in the direction of Umra. Indra hoped the ruse would give them enough time to get to the bridge.

Miles to the southwest, in a green valley, two riders herded a bunch of horses into a box canyon. There was plenty of water and fresh grazing there for the animals—both for the mares and the Devas' warhorses that had followed them into the canyon.

The scout stood over the spot where the Deva camp had been a day ago. His face wore a puzzled expression. Behind him Hiranya, mace in hand, paced up and down impatiently.

'I cannot understand it, my lord. The horses left the camp first and scattered across the plains. It does not appear as if they were bearing any riders. The men seem to have left many hours later; they are headed north towards Ur.'

Hiranya roared with joy.

'Their horses have bolted. By some miracle they are on foot on the plains. I will flay them alive and hang their skins to dry from the walls of Ur.'

The Asura army set off in pursuit. Soon the tracks disappeared altogether and the scout stopped again. Something about this did not seem right to him. At first he blamed it on the wind blowing in from the southern desert, but his instinct told him otherwise. He and Hiranya, who hovered impatiently around him, climbed a hillock to get a lay of the land ahead.

From that high vantage point, the country opened out in front of them for miles. As they looked to the north, they realised that they were chasing ghosts. There was no sign of the Deva army. Hiranya screamed in frustration, grabbed the scout by his throat and was about to throw him off the hill, when a puff of dust in the distance to the west caught his attention. He let out a cry of triumph.

'They're making for the town of Umra. I have them now.'

Indra and his men had marched for two days and nights without rest and now the town of Umra was within sight. The men were exhausted and at the end of their tether. In the distance behind them they could see the dust cloud raised by the rapid approach of Hiranya's army. It was going to be touch and go. Just then, Timon arrived from his clandestine expedition into the town.

'The garrison has about a hundred men, but they do not seem very vigilant and will be vulnerable to a quick assault. The bridge has only a few guards to monitor passage.'

Indra turned to Soma.

'How many horses do we have?'

'A few more than twenty.'

'Pick twenty of the best men to ride with you and me. We will keep the garrison engaged while Atreya and Nala take care of the guards and lead the rest of the men across the bridge. Hurry!'

As Soma rushed to do his king's bidding, Indra turned to Timon.

'Hiranya and his men should be here by mid-day. Go with Atreya and Nala. I cannot ask any of the others to do this, but in case we are not at the bridge by noon, make sure you destroy it.'

Timon's eyes welled with emotion; he had served many masters in his time, but never one who always put himself on the frontline in battle. He grimly nodded his acceptance.

The garrison at Umra was a quiet border post that rarely saw any action. The hundred-odd men posted there were a ragtag bunch of rogues and scoundrels from the various legions of the Asura army. They were given to drinking, gambling and fighting each other to while away their long days of boredom.

It was one such dull evening within the walls. A bare-knuckle boxing match was in progress when Indra and his men killed the sentries and crashed through the gates. The Asuras quickly recovered from their initial shock at the surprise assault and went for their weapons. The Devas fought their way to the centre of the compound. Indra ordered them to adopt a defensive formation called the Lotus. Spears and shields on the outside, archers on the inside.

The enemy came at them from all directions. Indra could not help but admire the Asura strength and resilience. No matter how many fell to spear and arrow, they just kept on coming. Soon their superior numbers began to tell. Indra was forced to abandon the formation and let every man fight for himself. This was the style favoured by the enemy, and soon things started to go badly for Indra and his men. Then the situation worsened: they heard the roars of Hiranya's army as they entered the town. This gave heart to the garrison and they fought with renewed vigour.

Just then Indra heard a sound that was like the sweetest music to his ears. It was the hunting horn of Timon: the Devas had successfully made the crossing. Indra ordered his men to fall back to the bridge. It was almost noon.

Only five of them made it out of the garrison walls alive, and Indra was glad to see Soma among them. Outside the garrison they almost ran full tilt into the vanguard of Hiranya's army. They fought for their lives as they fell back through the narrow alleys of the town towards the bridge.

Hiranya spotted the handsome figure of Indra at the bridge, keeping the Asura frontline at bay. His black sword flashed in the sunlight and dispatched Asura after Asura into the river where bloodthirsty crocodiles awaited them. Hiranya screamed in frustration as the throng of his own men kept him away from his enemy.

The bridge was made of rope and wood and it was quite narrow—only three men standing abreast could cross it at a time. Indra had sent his companions across, giving Soma instructions to cut the ropes once he was on the other side.

Indra heard the call of the falcon above the din of battle; it was the signal for him to fall back. The enemy still poured onto the bridge causing it to lurch dangerously. Indra sheathed Kadaag, turned and ran for the sanctuary of the other bank. Just as the ropes creaked and parted way, Indra flung himself into the air. From the far bank, his anxious men watched in disbelief. Their king had to cover about forty feet to safety. Indra pumped his arms and legs in the air as he propelled himself across the chasm. For one brief moment he thought he had not made it; then he felt his friend's firm grip on his forearm as he hit the edge. Behind him, the Asuras on the bridge plunged into the river; into the waiting mouths of the giant crocodiles.

Soma, still holding on to Indra's arm, grinned and whispered in his friend's ear, 'There are limits, even if one is a god.'

12

They trudged for days, making slow progress as they hacked and slashed their way through the dense forest. After several days, they were confronted with a river, the waters of which were black, thick with silt and dead vegetation. Beyond the vast expanse of it, as far as the eye could see, was a marsh. Timon turned to Indra with a sigh.

'I do not know what lies beyond this river. I have been told that it is an endless wetland. It is the delta of the Tigris and Euphrates rivers.'

Indra weighed his options carefully. What lay beyond the wetlands or how far they really stretched was anybody's guess. The forest of Aranya on the other hand, though dangerous, offered them plenty of food and water. He decided they would rest there that night, and then make their way north through the forest till he found a place where they could lay low for a while. He would then find a way to obtain some horses and rebuild his army.

Though the days in the forest had been hard enough, filled with venomous serpents and ferocious wild beasts at every turn, this one night proved to be even tougher. The men were attacked by countless mosquitoes and kept awake the whole night. Indra was forced to seek higher ground away from the river just to rid themselves of these pests.

Soon the mosquitoes proved a far greater threat than they had initially perceived. A fever broke out in the Deva camp, the likes of which their physicians had never seen before. The men woke up in the night with their skin burning. Even in the thick humidity of the forest, they shivered with chills that ran through their body. Their joints began to ache, and soon they became too weak to march anymore. They camped on top of a hill well away from the river and reviewed the situation. Indra and Soma were amongst the few Devas who had not succumbed to the fever.

In the middle of this crisis, the guards came to him with the news that the slave Valli had escaped from the camp. Indra, who had just received word that his commander Atreya was in a serious condition, paid little heed to the news. In a little tent that served as a makeshift infirmary, the Deva physicians struggled to save their brave commander.

Indra went into the tent to see how his commander was doing and found that Atreya had wet his bed copiously. The physician Dhanavantri saw the dark stain spread across the sheet; the soldier's urine was black in colour. The physician looked at Indra and shook his head regretfully. Atreya looked into the eyes of his king and gripped his arm tightly. His face was gaunt and his body had wasted away. Indra could see the desperate plea in his eyes; this was not the way for a warrior to die. Finally Indra felt the grip on his wrist slacken as weakness and exhaustion overcame the warrior and he drifted off to sleep. The physician informed Indra that it was unlikely that Atreya would survive the night.

Indra walked away from the camp, lost in thought, troubled by his own helplessness and inability to save his friend. A rustle among the trees brought him back to reality—he realised that he had wandered a good way away from the camp. He reached for his dagger and saw that he was not carrying one. Whatever it was amongst those trees began to come closer. He braced himself, ready to thwart an attack or take evasive action, when Valli stepped into the clearing. In her hands she carried what looked to him like the dried bark of a tree. She held it out to him and, to his great surprise, spoke to him in his own tongue.

'Take this. It will cure the fever.'

The desperate physicians followed Valli's instructions and boiled the bark in spring water. The bitter mixture was administered to the sick men. Dhanavantri and his team of physicians did not trust the woman entirely, so only the hopeless cases were treated first. But their fears were unfounded: by the next morning, the fever in many of the sick men had broken, and in two days, much to Indra's delight, Atreya was able to get up and walk around.

Valli's popularity now increased by leaps and bounds within the camp. She, on her part, was not at all comfortable with the excess attention, and started to cover herself with a white linen cloak. Indra caught himself staring at her on a couple of occasions. She was nothing like any of the women who usually appealed to him, yet there was something about her that was strangely fascinating. Over the next week, thanks to Valli's medicine, the death toll from the fever was kept under twenty. She had single-handedly saved the Deva army.

A lot of meat was required for the recuperating men, so Indra and Soma took on the responsibility of hunting. They went ahead alone so they were free to use their powers to travel across the treetops. The rest of the hunting expedition followed on the ground. There was plenty of game available, although it had scattered all across the forest since their arrival. The two men took this opportunity to explore the terrain. Indra decided to use the forest as his base for a while, till he could broker a deal with the Sumerian rebels for horses. Timon had already been dispatched for the task.

One day, in pursuit of a particularly swift stag, Indra was separated from his friend. He found himself alone in a previously unexplored part of the forest. As he retrieved his arrow from the body of the dead animal he realised that the chase had led him well away from the camp and he had no idea where he was. He slung the carcass of the deer over his shoulder and tried to retrace his steps back to camp.

He walked for a long while; the soma that coursed through his veins gave him plenty of endurance to bear the weight of the animal across the long distance. Soon he started to recognise signs that indicated he was close to the camp. He heard the sound of a waterfall and decided to quench his thirst. As he approached, he heard a beautiful female voice singing. Though he could not understand the words, the melody of it touched him. He dropped his burden and climbed a tree to take a closer look.

As he peered out of the canopy, he saw a waterfall that emptied itself into a deep, still rock pool. On one of the rocks, Valli basked in the sun. Her body, still wet from her dip in the pool, shone in the evening light. She spotted him then and beckoned him down. A sheepish Indra came down and stood before her, thoroughly embarrassed.

'I did not mean to intrude. But your song, I have never heard anything so beautiful.'

Valli turned on her side to face him. She made no move to cover her nudity.

'It is a song that my mother used to sing to me as a child. It is the only memory I have of her.'

Her eyes ran all over him. She had never felt this kind of desire towards anybody. He was the most beautiful man she had ever seen. Even as she stared at him, he averted his gaze. Indra could not understand his exact feelings for her. There was curiosity—she was unlike any woman he had ever known—but it was more than that. He found it hard to keep his eyes off her. His throat had turned dry; he tried to make his voice sound normal as he spoke.

'How is it that you speak our tongue?'

'It was taught to me as part of my training in Harappa. Among other things.'

'Other things? What other things?'

She smiled as she stood up.

'You cannot expect a girl to reveal all her secrets at once. Come, let me show you.'

He went to her as if in a spell. She leapt off the rock into his arms and wrapped her long, shapely legs around him. He lost his balance and, laughing, they tumbled into the rock pool. The cold water did nothing to dim their passion as their bodies entwined and their mouths found each other. Night fell, but the two of them did not realise it as they made love under the light of a bright moon. When they finally tired, they lay naked on the rock and talked. They had so much to say to each other.

Valli told him about the land of her birth under the shelter of the mighty Vindhya Mountains. She had been the daughter of the queen of the Vahini, a tribe of women warriors. The women of her tribe were greatly priced as priestesses in the great city of Harappa. It was believed that they carried the spirit of Raksha in them. Raksha was the mother goddess, the presiding deity of the Harappa.

Slave traders had captured her in a raid on her village just a year before her first moon. She was taken into the temple where she was trained to serve the goddess. She told Indra of Harappa's unparalleled wealth and power. How people from all over the world travelled there for trade and to marvel at the city's riches and beauty. Indra listened and found that it distracted him momentarily from his troubles. When she finished her tale, they continued to make love until the first light of the morning sun began to filter in through the canopy.

Indra arrived at the camp the next morning with an enormous appetite. He had to endure a few jibes from Soma. While he had been occupied, scavengers had taken his deer in the night and it was the first time he had returned from a hunt empty-handed. But he did not care; at least his secret was safe.

Over the next few weeks, the two lovers met in secret whenever Indra could slip away from his duties. The denizens of the forest were mute witnesses to their amorous escapades. They talked for long hours and shared each other's dreams and aspirations. Indra was amazed at Valli's erudition and skill. She was a healer with an astounding knowledge of herbs and potions, a linguist, an expert in political affairs and a fabulous lover. His curiosity was piqued: how had a woman so young acquired so much knowledge?

Valli told him about how she along with the most promising girls from among the initiates was handpicked by Anga, high priestess of Harappa, to join her personal order. These girls were trained in various disciplines with particular attention given to the art of pleasing men. Some of these women then found a place in the hearts and homes of the rich and powerful nobility of Harappa, sometimes as wives or more often as concubines. The most beautiful and talented, like Valli, were sent to grace the courts of other powerful rulers of the known world.

These women, whose loyalties lay only with Anga and the goddess, passed on vital information and state secrets to their mistress and enabled the high priestess to become one of the most powerful people in the world. Indra was amazed to hear her story.

'If this Anga is as powerful as you say she is, why did you betray her secret?'

'I already betrayed her when I saw you for the first time.'

She saw his confused look and smiled. Tears welled up in her beautiful dark eyes.

'While we can readily give our bodies to our male masters, it is forbidden for us to love anyone save the Divine Mother. I betrayed my mistress the moment I gave my heart to you.'

Indra felt his heart swell with love for her as he gathered her in a tight embrace.

Indra's idyllic existence was shattered when, one day, fifteen men from a Deva hunting party did not return. They had last been seen near the wetlands, about a couple of days' march north of the camp. Ordering the rest of the hunting party to keep the situation a secret so the rest of the men would not be alarmed, Indra and Soma left to investigate the mystery.

They were able to pick up the trail of the missing hunters quite easily as the soft ground near the wetlands left tracks even a blind man could follow. Then suddenly, in a grove of tall trees, the tracks abruptly vanished. The two warriors searched the ground ahead for any sign of their comrades, but there were none. They were puzzled; it was as if the men had vanished into thin air.

Indra scanned the canopy above: the dark green foliage was

thick and impenetrable. Somehow, he could not shake off the feeling that they were being observed. He communicated telepathically with Soma and asked him to be alert. No sooner had Soma nodded his understanding than two nooses fell from the canopy above and tightened around their arms and chests. The ropes were made of plant fibre and were strong, but they would have presented no problem to the divine strength of the two warriors. Indra cautioned Soma to not resist capture though; if it was possible, he wished to get to the bottom of the mystery without the use of violence.

As they were dragged up into the trees, they saw that the treetops were filled with archers ready to discharge their arrows into the two prisoners. The men were dressed in green and brown, perfectly camouflaged in their environment. They looked fierce with their hawk-like eyes, long dark hair and beards.

One of them, a handsome young man, stepped forward. An arrow was still notched to his bow ready to pierce their hearts if they showed any sign of resistance. Indra felt that there was something vaguely familiar about him. Like the rest of his men, he wore leather armour, not unlike the ones favoured by the Devas.

'Who are you? How dare you trespass on our lands?'

Indra and his men had long traded their armour for robes worn by the Sumerian peasants. Indra decided it would be unwise to reveal his true identity.

'I am Asgar of Ur. We were defeated and chased out of our homes by Sargon's forces and compelled to take refuge in the forests of Aranya. Fifteen of my men are lost somewhere in these lands—we came to find them.'

Their young captor studied them for a while. When he spoke, his tone was distinctly softer.

'If what you say is true, then you have nothing to fear from us.'

He turned to his men.

'Take them to their comrades. We will let my father decide their fate.'

Black hoods were pulled over the heads of the two Deva warriors and to their amazement they were led along a path built into the forest canopy by inter-woven branches high above the forest floor. When their hoods were removed, Indra and Soma found themselves in a wooden cage, which was then lowered down below the canopy. Around them they saw their lost comrades suspended in similar cages. Below them the forest floor was a wet bog filled with crocodiles, giant monitor lizards and venomous snakes.

Soma had run out of patience by now. He reached into his pouch and pulled out two vials of soma.

'These fools think they can hold us in these oversized birdcages. Come, let's get out of here and teach them a lesson.'

Indra declined the drink.

'No, let's stay. I would like to meet their king. Something tells me these men are not too friendly with the Asuras, and we could most certainly use an ally.'

The next morning, Indra and Soma were taken to the royal court. As they walked through the trees, they marvelled at the beauty of the arboreal city. Roads and houses had been built using creepers and the living branches of trees. Indra was amazed at the skill exhibited by the architects. The city was invisible from the forest floor and extended deep into the wetlands. He noticed that the people were in a constant state of preparedness. There were armed men everywhere, and he heard the clash of metal and other sounds associated with soldiers in training. Indra noticed that the women were beautiful; they looked and dressed very much like the Deva women.

He thought of Sachi and felt a stab of regret. Perhaps he should have worked a little harder at winning back her love. He hurriedly dismissed her from his mind. As they neared the royal abode, the path was filled with creepers laden with fragrant, beautiful flowers.

In the court, the young warrior stood before his father; he looked exasperated. The king was engrossed in his meal. His ample girth showed that he took his food very seriously. He meticulously picked off the remains of a boar as he spoke.

'You wish for me to ally with a bunch of peasants from Sumer. Have we come so far to stoop so low? These men who once grovelled at our feet, begged for their lives when we ransacked their cities, you wish for me to align with them? Treat them as our equals? Our ancestors will deny us our place in the heavens.'

The young man was aghast at his father's attitude. He looked towards the other man present in the room. He wore the white robes of priesthood, his head was shaven and his young face was grave. He gave the young warrior a sympathetic smile.

'But Father, will it not shame our ancestors that we have left our home on the vast plains where their cattle once grew fat to live in this swamp like rodents. I say we find what allies we can and take the fight to these oppressors. We can push Sargon once and for all out of these lands.'

The king threw down the piece of meat in his hand. The young warrior looked worried—perhaps he had gone too far.

'That's enough, Aryaman! Don't get ahead of yourself or I will forget that you are my son. I, Savitra, am still king here.'

The court announcer announced the arrival of Asgar of Ur at that moment and Indra and Soma entered the court. The guards asked them to kneel, and while Soma complied, Indra refused. All eyes turned to the king. One word from him and the guards were ready to end the life of the insolent Sumerian. Savitra shook with anger and the rolls of fat on him jiggled as he stood up in rage. Before he could give the order, the young priest spoke out in a clear, strong voice.

'Wait! This man is not who he claims to be. Maybe it is time for you to reveal yourself, stranger.'

The priest's tone was respectful. Savitra did not speak but sat down with a huff. Indra looked at the young priest. His aura was bright for someone his age. Indra saw in his eyes that he was already aware of their true identity.

'I am Indra, this is Soma, we are of the Deva tribe. Where are we?'

'You are in Aranyapura, in the presence of Savitra, king of the Aditya tribe. That is Aryaman, our military commander. I am Brihaspati.'

Indra and Soma could scarcely believe what they had heard. They were among Mitra's people!

Brihaspati continued. 'We were expecting you. Mitra came to me in a vision telling me of your arrival. It could not have come at a more opportune time. Come, let us dine. We have urgent matters to discuss.'

He indicated to Aryaman to follow. The four of them acknowledged Savitra and left. The befuddled king went back to his meat and wine.

After a hearty meal in Brihaspati's austere quarters, they walked out into a leafy bower to assess their current situation.

Aryaman informed them that the very existence of his tribe was under threat. The Asuras had defeated the river pirates who controlled the mouth of the delta. In a fortnight, the monsoon would hit this region and transform the muddy bog into navigable rivulets and streams. His spies had informed him that Hiranya was already ready with his army at the newly-captured docks to move into Aranya along with the rains. Although the river pirates did not know the exact location of their arboreal city, they could bring the Asura army uncomfortably close. Aryaman then excused himself and left to check on some of his men.

Brihaspati, Indra and Soma then talked long into the night. Indra learnt of the misfortune that had befallen Mitra's tribe since his departure. His brother Savitra was no warrior and had been ill advised in matters of state. They were defeated by the Asuras and had to abandon their cattle and horses and flee. They had bribed the river pirates who helped them get away and seek refuge in these swamps.

Brihaspati apologised for the lukewarm reception the king had given Indra. Savitra still resented the fact that his brother had abandoned his people in their hour of need, so he had not warmed up to Mitra's pupils.

Indra agreed to join forces with the Adityas against their common enemy. He and his men then left for their camp to prepare for what was to come.

True to Brihaspati's word, within the first week of the rains, the Asura vanguard arrived on the northern banks of Aranya. Three thousand warriors led by Hiranya started to scour the forest in search of Indra. That was not the only news that Aryaman came to deliver. He brought with him the head of Timon. Hiranya had sent it to Savitra, warning him that this was the fate that awaited all who helped Indra.

Indra was furious at the death of Timon. The spy had been a

valuable asset in his campaign against the Asuras. With his death, Indra's chances of getting new horses were remote. Also, a helpless Aryaman had been unable to convince his father to join in the battle. The Devas were on their own. Even if they managed to defeat the vanguard and Hiranya, they would still have to contend with the main force of seven thousand warriors that were on their way, commanded by Sargon's son, Naraka.

Hiranya had spread his forces out in a wide line and was prepared to search every tree and bush in Aranya.

Indra realised their best chance would be to break into smaller units to avoid detection. He divided his forces into four units of about two hundred men each. Their orders were to split up and keep a close watch on the enemy. Two units would then engage the Asuras and provide the necessary distraction. At the opportune moment, the other two would try and break through the enemy line unseen. They would then head north and rendezvous at the docks. With a bit of luck they might be able to hijack a couple of the river pirates' boats and head west. They could find a safe spot to hide in the many rivulets of the delta before the main force under Naraka arrived.

It was a plan where a lot of things could go wrong, but it was the best they had. Indra wished his men luck and sent them on their way. Valli went with Nala and his troops. Indra was glad; he did not want her close to him when the fighting began. Her presence would only serve as a distraction.

Indra and Soma decided to attack the middle of the enemy line where it would be the thickest. They hoped it would give Atreya and Nala a chance to slip through the flanks unnoticed and capture the docks.

The Devas had one big advantage—their numerous hunting expeditions through these lands had given them a good knowledge of the terrain. Now, Soma and a small band of men met the Asura frontline in a small clearing in the forest. They made it appear as if they had chanced upon them by accident and fled from there. The enemy took the bait and came after them. The Asuras, with their heavy armour and bulk, found the going extremely tough. Soma and his men used their arrows and slingshots to harrow them further. They led them into a thick grove of trees where Indra and his men waited, perched high in the trees, their bows at the ready. The thick vegetation slowed the Asuras even further and they were easy targets. The Deva archers moved like shadows through the trees and extracted a heavy toll on the enemy.

On the eastern flank, Atreya successfully led the enemy into the bog. Soon the Asuras found themselves floundering in an enormous pit of quicksand. Their great bulk and armour made them sink very quickly into the treacherous mud.

On the other flank, Valli used her skills as a huntress to lay out a series of traps in the jungle. The unsuspecting enemy walked right into them. There was pandemonium in the Asura lines as spikes flew out of the trees and impaled them, or the jungle floor gave way under their feet and they fell to their deaths onto a bed of sharp wooden stakes.

In the commotion that ensued, the Devas under Nala managed to slip past the enemy lines unseen. But soon their luck ran out and they ran full tilt into an enemy patrol. Fierce fighting broke out. At close quarters, the Asura army was a fearsome war machine and took a heavy toll on Nala's men but both Valli and Nala, along with a small band of warriors, managed to fight their way out of trouble.

Valli used her knowledge of the jungle and led their pursuers deeper and deeper into the green maze. After losing them in the dense vegetation, they made their way to the docks to discover that Atreya had already secured it. But the Asura boats were all gone. The river pirates had betrayed their new masters and left the Asuras to their own devices.

Bitterly disappointed, they flopped down on the banks of the river. They had gambled and lost. Trapped between the Asuras on one side and the river on the other, they had nowhere to go. Soma arrived at great speed. He informed them that Indra and his men had broken through the enemy lines and were on their way with the majority of Hiranya's army in pursuit. When he heard about the missing boats, he went straight back to the frontline to inform his king.

Indra did not know what to do next as he and his men fell back towards the dock. They were trapped. Even if they went north along the river, there was every chance they would run into Naraka and his army. The docks were now in sight; somewhere behind them they could hear Hiranya's roars as he urged his battered army to hurry.

On the banks of the river stood a frustrated Valli. She threw rocks into the water in an effort to calm herself. Then suddenly, round a bend in the river, she saw a boat appear, then there was another, soon a small flotilla of boats arrived at the docks. The captain of the lead boat leaned across and shouted.

'I am Riktim, sent by Aryaman to get you out of here.'

Valli ran back and shouted to the men to fall back towards the docks. She could see the tall figure of Hiranya outlined against the trees. The Asura saw her and his rage increased. Indra screamed for the men to get on the boats even as he showered arrows into the Asura frontline. Indra was one of the last men to climb on board before they cast off.

As they started to move down the river, Hiranya arrived at its banks. The boats were already well out of range of the archers, but Hiranya called for his war bow and notched an arrow. He used all his strength to bend the bow till it creaked from the effort. Then he let fly the arrow.

Indra, who was engrossed in navigation, did not see the missile head towards him. Valli looked up and saw the arrow arc towards their boat. She used all her strength and pushed Indra out of the way, only to stumble into the path of the deadly shaft. The arrow struck her in the chest and knocked her off the boat into the water. Indra screamed in rage and helplessness as her body disappeared under the surface of the murky water. The boat rounded a bend and Hiranya and the Asura army disappeared from sight.

Riktim was the youngest clan leader among the river pirates. Like Aryaman, he prized freedom above everything else. Although the other members of the pirate council had thrown in their lot with the Asuras, Riktim had refused to toe their line. He had been only too happy to help Indra against the oppressive Asuras. He planned to drop the Devas off at the western end of the river delta, far away from the pursuing enemy force. His family and clan members were meant to join him there. He hoped to re-establish his operations on the south-western banks of the Euphrates where the Asura influence was still weak.

They made their way through the maze of rivulets, taking shelter on the numerous little uninhabited islands of the delta. On the bow of the lead boat, a worried Indra took stock of the situation. It would be suicidal to face the Asuras in an open plain—they had no horses or armour. Much as he detested it, flight had again been the only option left to them. He had to find a safe place to regroup and rebuild his vastly depleted army. By antagonising Sargon, he had grabbed the tiger by its tail. Now he must ride it to the end.

Riktim was the most cheerful member of the party; he knew these waters like the back of his hand and did not expect any pursuit. The Asuras preferred fighting with the earth under their feet; Riktim did not think they would follow them through these treacherous waters. To be on the safe side though, he had left men with small fast boats at strategic points along the river to keep watch on the enemy forces.

One of these men soon arrived with the most terrible of tidings. The pirate captain had grossly underestimated the determination and drive of Hiranya and his men. A horrified Riktim heard that Hiranya had slaughtered his entire clan, along with all his family members. The Asura general had then commandeered all the available pirate boats and was now after them with a heavily armed force of two thousand men.

Indra, who was mourning the loss of Valli, could only imagine the grief of the young pirate captain. Riktim sat alone for a while, and then went up to Indra to say that he sought no reward for his services except the head of the man who had killed his family. He vowed that he would not rest till he had driven the Asuras from these lands.

For the rest of the journey, Riktim ensured that the men were kept in good morale and fighting condition by making sure there was plenty of clean water and game for them at every pit stop. As they neared their destination, Indra was optimistic that they could lose the Asura army in the vast expanse that lay west of the Euphrates delta.

When they finally arrived at a village on the west bank, a man showed up on the shore and made a signal to Riktim. It was a sign that there was danger. They dropped anchor in the middle of the river and waited for nightfall. Indra and Riktim then took one of the smaller boats and docked at the village wharf. Riktim's man was there to receive them. He seemed high-strung and nervous.

'An army came out of the west a few days ago. They are camped in the reed beds to the south of the village. They do not look like Asuras, they are smaller in stature and carry big round shields with the head of a lion emblazoned on them.'

Riktim was puzzled; his knowledge did not extend very far beyond the banks of the river. He looked towards Indra, who thought for a while before he spoke.

'They sound like Yavanas. But it does not make sense. What are they doing this far east? To my knowledge there is no treaty between them and the Asuras.'

A nervous Riktim did not like the situation one bit.

'I hope there isn't one, there is really no place else for us to go.'

The man suddenly remembered something.

'Some of them have visited the tavern and they spoke with the owner.'

The tavern owner was a one-eyed old man who had briefly been part of Riktim's father's crew. He greeted them warmly, served them some terrible wine and invited them to stay for dinner. The food was even worse than the wine, but the old man had interesting news. The Yavana commander had told him they were in search of a man called Indra.

Outside the tavern, Riktim was of the opinion that they take to the boats and find another place to dock further downstream. Indra, however, was confident that there was no love lost between the Yavanas and Asuras; he would have nothing to fear from them. He convinced the pirate to take a walk with him, and much to Riktim's dismay, made his way to the Yavana camp.

As the two of them walked through the tall reeds, they could hear songs being sung. Indra smiled to himself; they were not unlike his own tribe in their ways. As they neared the campfires, they were accosted by a patrol of sentries. Indra introduced himself and said he was there to see their commander.

The sentries were unsure if they should believe the words of this peasant who claimed to be the king of the Devas, but the strength in his voice and his warrior-like demeanour convinced them that this was no ordinary peasant. They ushered him into the camp.

As they walked through the rows of campfires, Indra noticed that the Yavanas were the shortest among the northern tribes, but they were built like bulls, with enormous shoulders and arms and thick, strong legs. Unlike the other tribes, they wore their dark hair and beards short and preferred to fight on foot.

When Indra was brought into the presence of the Yavana commander, he was surprised to discover that the man was young—about the same age as he. Like Indra, he was clean-shaven and handsome. He greeted the Deva king respectfully and informed him that he and his army were at his disposal. A grateful and pleasantly surprised Indra could not but help ask the reason for this good fortune. The young commander bowed slightly as he spoke.

'It was on the last day of the harvest festival that the Oracle of the sun spoke to my father, the king. She named you as the warrior who would unite the northern clans. She instructed him to send an army to your aid. I am Yadu, crown prince of the Yavana tribe. I have a thousand spears at your service, my lord.'

It was nearly sundown by the time the Asura army reached the west bank of the river. A furious Hiranya was not going to wait for daylight to extract his vengeance. He ordered his men to destroy the village. As the first lot of Asura troops reached the village, flaming arrows from the Deva bows began to rain down on the huts, setting the thatch roofs on fire. The light from the fires gave Indra's archers a clear sight of their targets and soon death began to rain down on the enemy.

The Asuras' formation, to their credit, stayed firm and charged towards the archers. As they went down the narrow village street, the Yavana warriors—clad head to toe in bronze armour—stepped forward in a tight line. The Yavana warriors were a sight to behold, their red plumes of horsehair fluttering in the evening breeze, their giant shields creating an impregnable wall of bronze. They screamed out a challenge as they advanced and as they met the Asura frontline, they brought their heavy spears to bear. The sands soon began to run red with the blood of the Asuras, as slowly but steadily they were pushed back to the river.

Hiranya could not believe his eyes as he saw his men being forced to retreat by the wall of bronze. From his elevated position on the bow of the boat, he saw that the flanks of the Yavana line were vulnerable to a surprise attack. He hastily barked orders to his men and a few boats started to head up the river while he led the other boats downstream.

Indra was quick to spot the movement along the river. He asked Atreya and Nala to take their men and neutralise the threat. He and his archers began to move forward; they picked off the enemy's central column as the Asuras floundered clumsily in the water.

The Asuras who headed upstream immediately ran into trouble. Riktim had made a couple of fireboats and launched it at the enemy. As the burning boats floated towards them, the lead boats of the enemy veered off course to save themselves, and the ones coming behind rammed straight into them and burst into flames. Atreya and his archers made use of the time Riktim bought them and secured a position on the beach from where they rained arrows at the enemy with devastating accuracy.

On the other flank, Nala and his men were not so fortunate. By the time they got there, Hiranya had already secured the beach. The Asuras charged towards Nala and his men and gave them no chance to use their bows. With no armour or shields, Nala and his men had the odds hopelessly stacked against them, but they gamely drew their swords and prepared to face the enemy.

In the burning village, Indra and the Yavana warriors had made short work of the enemy. They turned their attention to their right flank where Hiranya had decimated Nala's division. The Yavanas now broke their line and went in to finish the enemy. Indra was amazed to see how they used their shields as an offensive weapon. They put all their weight behind it, swung them at the Asuras and broke their skulls and bones. They even used the edge to decapitate fallen victims.

Indra scanned the battlefield, cutting and slashing his way through the enemy as he looked for Hiranya. He found him close to the river as he stood over a fallen Nala, poised to cut off his head. Indra screamed out a challenge even as he flew across the sand towards the giant figure of the Asura general.

As Hiranya turned, he saw Indra in full flight fire one arrow after another at him. Two arrows struck him in the chest and knocked him back a couple of paces. His mouth opened in surprise at the speed of the attack. Before he could close his mouth, Indra was upon him. He thrust the black sword into the open mouth of the Asura till it emerged from the back of his skull. Indra twisted the blade hard. Hiranya's head separated from his neck and his heavy body fell to the ground with a thud that shook the battlefield.

Indra screamed in triumph as he raised the head of the Asura general high in the air. The battle stopped, and the few of the enemy that had survived fled into the darkness beyond the village.

From his boat, Riktim screamed at them.

'Run, you dogs! Run to your master! Tell the Grey Wolf that the people of this land will not lie down and take it up the arse anymore.'

The victors spent the next couple of days tending to the wounded and helping the villagers rebuild their burnt homes. Indra and Yadu made sure that the dead were cremated as per the rites of their respective tribes. Just as the funeral pyres were lit, Indra received news that Nala had regained consciousness; he rushed to the infirmary to meet him.

The physicians had just finished tending to the warrior when Indra arrived. Dhanavantri looked towards Indra and shook his head. Indra looked at the ashen face of his commander. Nala was in agony but he was trying to keep a brave face as he tried to sit up to greet his king. Indra pushed him back gently on to the bed.

'You look well, old friend. In much better shape than you were last night.'

Nala looked down at the gaping wound in his belly and smiled.

'Last night, I was dead if you had not got there so quickly. You moved faster than I have ever seen any man move. It is true what the men say about you then. You have bathed in the Divine Light, you are now a god.'

Indra did not know what to say. He tried to make light of the situation.

'No, I am just a king who is not doing a very good job of looking after his men.'

Nala winced in pain as he laughed; the wound in his belly began to bleed again.

'That may be true. But it has been an honour to serve under you, my lord. Please, help me up.'

Indra helped him up to an upright position. Nala gasped as he tried to shut out the pain.

'Do it now, my king.'

Indra put one arm around his shoulder and held him in a tight embrace.

'You honour me, old friend. I will miss the trueness of your aim in the battlefield.'

He placed his forehead against Nala's and plunged the dagger he held in his other hand into the heart of the dying warrior. He then laid the body gently back on the bed and walked away.

Indra fought back his tears with difficulty. Although it was common practice among the northern tribes for a mortally wounded warrior to ask a trusted friend to end his life, Indra had never had to do it before and he prayed he would never have to do it again.

Outside the infirmary, an anxious Riktim waited to meet him.

'I have news from Aranya. I'm afraid it is not good. Sargon's son Naraka has arrived at the head of a huge army. He blames the Adityas for your escape. He has vowed to chop down every tree in the forest till he finds Aranyapura and destroys it.'

'We must go back and save them. Ask your man to leave word with Aryaman to wait for me under the giant oak tree where we met the first time. You organise a fast boat that can carry about twenty men to leave now. The rest of them can follow later.'

Riktim rushed off to do his bidding. Soma, who had just arrived, turned to his friend in disbelief.

'Twenty men! Naraka has over seven thousand men under his command. I hope you have a plan.'

'No, but I'll think up one along the way. Pick the men and meet me at the wharf.'

By noon Riktim had procured the boat and they were off. The smaller boat meant that they could use the narrow channels in the delta, which made the return to Aranya much quicker. When Indra arrived at the rendezvous, Aryaman was already there. From the north, they could hear the crashing sound of trees being felled. Indra quickly outlined their plan of action and the part that the Adityas would have to play in it.

Naraka, son of Sargon, stood on a small hillock and watched the destruction of Aranya with a smug smile. Below him, seven thousand Asuras armed with axes were clearing the forest at a rapid rate. Like all sons who lived under the shadow of a famous father, Naraka was constantly in search of ways to prove himself a worthy son. He had forced his father to send him on this mission. He had hoped to kill Indra, the demon whose victories against them had granted him the status of a folk hero in Sumer; he had in fact just received news of the defeat and death of Hiranya. What better way to prove to the people that he was the worthy son of a great father? Unfortunately, the Deva king had slipped out of his reach.

Naraka decided then that the Adityas would bear the brunt of his wrath. He would wipe out the men. Their beautiful women would be forced to bear the Asura seed. The Adityas as a tribe would no longer exist. Even as his mind was occupied with the horrors he planned to inflict on Aranyapura, his commander informed him that one of the river pirates had arrived with the most heartening piece of news. Indra had returned to the forests of Aranya to help the Adityas. The man told a delighted Naraka that Indra was on the river in a small boat with twenty warriors and he could lead them to him. All he wanted as reward for delivering the Deva king to them was the return of his captured boats and amnesty for his clan.

Naraka readily agreed to his terms. He asked the man how many boats he had at his disposal. The river pirate informed him that he had three medium-sized boats that could accommodate about a hundred Asuras. Naraka smiled triumphantly. A hundred warriors would be more than enough. He hoped he would be able to take Indra alive. He wanted to personally cut his body into several parts and nail it to the walls of every city in Sumer as a lesson to those who would dare rebel against the Asuras.

The Asura boats took to the water and set off in search of the elusive demon. As they rounded a bend in the river, they saw a boat docked on the far bank. The captain of the boat saw the Asuras arrive and panicked. He screamed at the Deva soldiers who were boarding her to hurry. Naraka's eyes lit up as he saw the handsome man with golden hair at the bow of the boat. It was Indra. He egged his rowers on, promising to cover them with gold if they caught their elusive quarry today.

A chase ensued through the waterways and wetlands of Aranya. The Asura boats were faster and soon started to narrow the gap between them. Riktim, who knew these waters like no other, steered the boat between the trees of the submerged forest. The Asura arrows and javelins began to land uncomfortably close to the boat. Naraka heard the anxious cries of the Devas and urged the boats to go faster. As the

Asuras pushed forward, Riktim glanced back anxiously. Two of the boats in pursuit swept out in a wide arc—Naraka planned to surround them and take them down.

At the bow, Indra spotted a narrow channel and shouted to Riktim to steer towards it. The Asuras were forced back into single file again as they manoeuvred their bigger boats carefully into the narrow channel. Soon Naraka's boat started to close in again. The Devas watched in alarm as the Asura archers notched arrows to bows.

Before Naraka could give the order, a dead branch dropped from the trees into the water in front of them. The captain of Naraka's boat was quick to spot the danger and steered the vessel to one side, narrowly avoiding the log. The boats that came up behind him did not stand a chance: the second one crashed into the log and capsized. The third struck the second and deposited its occupants in the water. The Asuras with their heavy armour and weapons struggled to stay afloat. Then things got a lot worse for them. Even as they struggled out of their armour, arrows began to rain down on them from the trees.

Aryaman and his archers were deadly accurate, perched high on the trees as they picked off the enemy. The river pirate guiding the Asuras, his role in Indra's plan complete, leapt into the water and swam to Riktim's boat. In a matter of moments, Naraka was the only one left on his boat. The blood and the thrashing about of bodies in the water brought the big crocodiles in to feast. The Asura crown prince watched in horror as the giant reptiles played tug-of-war with the bodies of his warriors. He shut his eyes and clamped his ears shut with his hands, but he could not drown out the screams of his men as their limbs were torn from their bodies.

From the safety of his boat, Indra watched the crocodiles bring the final curtain down on the bloody drama. It had been a perfect trap. Naraka had fallen into their hands and not one of them had got hurt in the bargain.

The magnificent Throne Room of Assur wore a dark and desolate look. The court had long been dismissed. On his ornate gold and ivory throne, Sargon the Grey Wolf sat and stared up at his brightly frescoed ceiling. He did not wish for anyone to see his helplessness. A few barbarians and pirates had brought his great empire to its knees. News of their recent victories had spread to the distant corners of the land. This demon Indra was being lauded as a hero, and alarmingly, more and more men were flocking to his banner.

Now they had his only son, his heir, and he had just received the terms for his return. The forests of Aranya and the river delta should be freed from Asura dominion and safe passage be granted to Indra and his army through his lands. The second demand intrigued Sargon. If he demanded safe passage, did that mean Indra and his army would leave his lands forever? The thought brought him some relief as he agreed to all the terms unconditionally.

The sound of heavy footsteps brought his attention back. It was Mahisha, his brother and second-in-command. The warrior kept his gaze down as he made his report.

'The troops have begun their withdrawal from Aranya, Excellency.'

Sargon nodded and asked him to call it a night. The Grey Wolf watched him go with a sigh. He had seen the naked rage that Mahisha had tried hard to control. Sargon could empathise with his brother; he felt exactly the same. But Naraka . . . he could not forsake Naraka. He was the only fruit that had sprung from his old loins.

The Asura king was a pragmatic man. Although he was still able to keep the young wives of his harem happy, he did not think he would be able to father another child. The boy was a little spoilt and impulsive, always looking to make his father proud. But no one could take away from Naraka the fact that, in spite of his tender age, he was already a great warrior and he would make a great emperor one day.

Indra watched the celebrations unfurl at Aranyapura. Most of the Asura troops had left the forest, with only a small number remaining to escort Naraka back. King Savitra announced a grand sacrifice in gratitude to the gods and a feast to celebrate the victory. With the ceremony over, as it was with his people, wine had taken over the gathering.

Savitra called to the guards to bring Naraka to the hall. Aryaman tried to dissuade his father, but the old king would have none of it. Soon the Asura prince was brought into the assembly, his hands bound behind his back. Savitra and his cronies, who were now thoroughly intoxicated, began to heap insults on the young man and his father. They pelted him with food and doused him with wine.

Naraka bore it all in silence. He looked his tormentors in the face and did not flinch when they threw hot broth on him. As a guest, Indra could not intervene, but he admired how well the young man handled the humiliation. Now some of the king's cronies got bolder. One of them rushed up and knocked Naraka down. As the Asura prince struggled back to his feet, another arrived and slashed him across the chest with a knife. The wound, though superficial, started to bleed.

Brihaspati could not bear it any longer. He shouted at the

men to stop, calling them cowards. He asked the guards to take the prisoner away. Savitra tried to stand up and take control, but the priest silenced him with a withering look. The king slouched back in his seat, sulking.

As he was being led away, the Asura prince shook off the grip of the guards and turned to address the gathering.

'People of Aranyapura, you have bound my father's hands with this treaty just as you have bound mine. But know this, one day I will be emperor and my hands will be free. That day, I will burn down this forest and scorch these wetlands. I will hunt each and every one of you across the far corners of this earth. Your names will be struck from the annals of history. It will be like none of this ever existed at all. I, Naraka, son of the Grey Wolf, swear this.'

There was silence in the gathering as Naraka was blindfolded and taken away from Aranyapura. Although the celebrations continued, there was a muted ring to it. Before long, Indra and Brihaspati left the hall, followed by Aryaman.

The three of them walked along one of the ethereally beautiful avenues of Aranyapura. After the way things had gone down in the hall, it was a relief to get out into the fresh air. Indra looked around at his surroundings. The full moon filtered through the leaves and bathed the city in its silvery light. It was like he had been transported to another world. Brihaspati's voice broke the surreal silence.

'Why do you wish to leave the land of your ancestors? Your father and his father before him have shed blood here.'

'That is one of the reasons why I leave. This land seems to have an endless thirst for the blood of my people.'

'Where will you go?'

'I plan to head southeast to the city of Harappa. With the gold from that city, I will build an empire to rival that of the

Grey Wolf. But before that, I'm going to need horses. The Asuras do not have any—they seem more keen on eating them than taming them.'

Aryaman spat on the ground in disgust.

'We know that better than anybody else. Our herds and our horses all went into Sargon's cooking pot. But I will be honoured if you will permit me to ride alongside you.'

Indra was pleased. He had come to grow rather fond of Mitra's nephew.

'The honour will be mine, Prince.'

Brihaspati was thoughtful.

'Perhaps I can be of some assistance in getting your horses back.'

Indra could not believe his ears.

'Get our horses back? They scattered across the distant corners of Sumer more than a year ago. How do you propose to get them back?'

'From the men who took them.'

'Men! Was that truly the work of men? I suspected it to be Asura sorcery!'

'It was the work of our cousins, many times removed, of course. The world knows them as the Ashvani twins, masters of the Ashva, the horse. They are sons of Vivasvat the wise, chief of the Ikshvaaku tribe.'

'But why would they help us? They serve the Grey Wolf.'

'The Ikshvaaku are their own masters. They honoured an old treaty with Sargon when their princes helped him against you; now their obligation to the Asuras is over. But like the Yavanas and us, they will serve the warrior who will unite the northern clans. I shall send word at once to Vivasvat.'

The next day, Aryaman informed a shocked Savitra that he and a select group of five hundred warriors would accompany

Indra. All the king's threats and pleas were to no avail. To further add to the king's dismay, Brihaspati announced his decision to accompany Prince Aryaman.

Aryaman was touched and surprised by the farewell he received from the citizens of Aranyapura. In an unprecedented move, the entire city showed up at the docks to bid them farewell. King Savitra was conspicuous by his absence.

From his position on the boat, Indra turned to look upon the forests of Aranya one last time. Somewhere within its green depths, the spirit of Valli, the warrior princess, roamed free. A part of him would always remain there with her.

13

It was dusk on the endless expanse of the Sumerian plains. One by one the campfires were being lit. On a little rise, from a tent no less ostentatious than the other ones around, Indra emerged to greet his commanders and new high priest, Brihaspati. His position in the camp offered Indra a panoramic view of the surrounding plains that were now slowly being covered by darkness. He looked towards Soma, who had his ear close to the ground.

'Tell me you hear something.'

Soma nodded, not taking his ear off the ground. Indra heaved a sigh of relief. Around them stood their chariots, all assembled, awaiting the arrival of their horses. It had been a week since they had been there, at the very spot where their horses had been taken. Indra, who had only put faith in those words because they had come from Brihaspati, had almost lost hope that their horses would be returned to them. Now they all began to hear it in the distance, the thunder of thousands of hooves across the hard earth.

Slowly they began to appear, like phantoms in the firelight. There was a buzz of excitement in the camp at the sight of the animals. Indra's jaw nearly dropped in amazement; their numbers had grown considerably. His keen eye for horseflesh had already spotted quite a few new foals among them. At the head of what looked like a perfect cavalry formation, two men mounted on his war chargers rode bareback and without any reins. Indra himself had never attempted that.

A sharp whistle was heard and the enthralled audience saw the horses move perfectly into a narrow two-line formation. The Ashvanis tugged gently on the flowing manes of their stallions and slowed them down as they entered the empty corral. Within a few minutes, the astounded grooms shut the gates of their corral with it once again bustling with horses.

Indra turned to his high priest in delight.

'If I had not seen it with my own eyes, I would never have thought it possible. You were right wise one, these two alone are worth an army.'

The Ashvanis arrived at Indra's campfire amidst curious glances. The twins were identical, tall and very slender in build. Their faces were handsome, with fine features and devoid of any facial hair. They bowed formally to Indra and announced their willingness to serve under him. The Deva king welcomed them to his fold.

Brihaspati smiled to himself as he saw Yadu, Aryaman and the Ashvanis standing together with the Deva king. Indra had fulfilled the first part of the prophecy; he felt certain that the key to the fulfilment of the second part lay in Harappa.

With the onset of winter in the mountains, the passes that led to Harappa were snowed in. Indra had no option but to wait for spring and find a guide to take them across. He used the time to strengthen his depleted arsenal and rebuild his chariot divisions. The Devas, who were only too glad to get back behind the wheels of the chariot, did not complain through the long days and endless drills.

The Adityas, many of whom had not been born when the clan had to leave the plains and take to the forests, took to their training with gusto. Aryaman and his men longed to emulate their forefathers and get back behind the reins of a good horse. The blood of the pastoral nomads that flowed through their veins and the help of the Ashvanis ensured that they were soon as comfortable as any of the Devas on horseback.

Yadu and his men had no desire whatsoever to get on the back of a horse. Indra watched them as they practised their infantry drills and was glad that he would not have to lead a charge into that formidable-looking line of shields.

Soon it was spring, and Indra sent his scouts on patrols along the various routes to the south. One day one of them reported to him the arrival of a caravan that was headed southwest towards Harappa. With a small division of chariots, Indra set out to meet it.

The caravan did not stand a chance as the division of chariots surrounded it. The armed guards threw down their weapons and fell to their knees in surrender. Indra suddenly noticed a portly figure clad in fine robes running towards them. As the figure approached, Indra recognised him as the merchant who had been escorting Valli when he first found her.

The merchant rued his ill luck at falling into the hands of the Devas for a second time. He fell to his knees and begged for mercy. Indra informed him that he did not wish to loot him, but he would like to discuss a business proposition. The relieved merchant requested Indra to dine with him.

Later that night, after a scrumptious feast in the merchant's lavish tent, Indra laid down his proposition. The merchant listened to him carefully before he made his reply.

'My lord, it would be my honour to be of service to you. But before you embark on this quest, there is something you should know. Unlike the cities of Sumer, Harappa has no walls or great defences to speak of, yet no hostile army has ever got within a day's march of it. Tribes that have grown fat on Harappa gold control the mountain passes. Only trade caravans are allowed to pass through. Any sign of an armed force and they will start a rockslide or an avalanche and knock them off the mountain like fleas off a camel's back. I know this because Sargon has already lost an army in those mountains. I cannot allow this to happen to you and your fine men, my lord.'

What the portly man did not tell Indra was that the merchant who had guided Sargon's army had been skinned alive in the city square of Harappa. His carcass had been thrown to stray dogs, while his skin had been cured and sent to his family in Assur.

Indra was bitterly disappointed.

'Is there no other way?'

The merchant nodded.

'There is another way, my lord, though I do not know anyone who has successfully taken it. If you head south to the oasis of Ashkavan, with a little luck and a lot of gold you may be able to find guides to escort you east to Harappa.'

Soma, who had been keeping their host under close observation, now spoke.

'If it is easy to find guides in Ashkavan, how is it you do not know of anyone who has successfully taken that route? If you have kept something from us, be sure I will be back to find you to carve your tongue out.'

The merchant squealed in terror.

'I did not say it was easy, my lords! The desert nomads of Ashkavan are godless bastards who will betray their own mother if there was profit in it. They call the land to the east Um Bakher; in their tongue it means "the long thirst". It is an endless expanse of parched earth where nothing grows. In my humble opinion, you are better off taking your chances on the mountain. At least death will be quicker and more merciful.'

Just then one of his slaves, her eyes and mind focused on Indra, spilt some wine on his clothes. The merchant screamed abuse and threw his wine goblet at her. The metal cup hit her on the forehead, causing a deep gash. The servants quickly removed her from the hall. The merchant apologised for the behaviour of his slave, citing the excuse that she was new and untrained. He promised to give her a good thrashing and set her right. The incident ended the evening on a sour note. Indra and his entourage thanked the merchant and took their leave.

Early the next morning, unnoticed by anyone in the caravan, a little pigeon flew out of one of the tents and winged its way out in a south-westerly direction.

It was well into spring when Indra and his men began the gruelling first leg of the journey to the oasis of Ashkavan. The decision to take that route had been a unanimous one. They were a few days' march from the great river Mittani when a scout rode up to inform Indra that they were being followed. He had been on a rise ahead and spotted the dust cloud raised by a small bunch of horses a half day's march from the rear of their column.

Indra asked Atreya to take charge and keep the column moving while he and Soma saddled up a couple of mares and went off to investigate. It was dark by the time they spotted the light of the campfire made by the strangers. They dismounted and made their way ahead cautiously. In the light of the fire, they saw the outline of three horses against the stark landscape. Three men, bundled up in blankets, were lying around the fire, fast asleep.

Indra and Soma drew their swords and approached the men cautiously; the bodies did not stir. Soma used his sword and moved the blanket aside. Saddlebags had been arranged to look like men asleep.

Suddenly they heard a voice; it was reproachful in its tone.

'Indra and Soma! Brash and impulsive, as always! Do you'll not remember anything that Master Mitra taught you?'

Indra shouted out in joy as he recognised the voice.

'Varuna! I'm so happy to hear your voice. It's about time you three lazy louts showed up.'

Three arrows flew out of the darkness at them, and Indra and Soma easily knocked them aside with their swords. Three men walked into the firelight. Agni gave one of his guffaws.

'I'm glad their reflexes have not dulled like their wits.'

The men ran to each other and warmly embraced. Agni playfully wrestled Soma to the ground. Vayu grabbed Indra in a bear hug while Varuna ruffled his hair. For a moment, all five of them were transported back to their happy and carefree childhood in Gandhar.

The five of them spent the next few days exchanging stories of their adventures. They finally arrived at the crossing of the river Mittani where it cut through the arid plains before it emptied itself in the western gulf. As they took a dip in the familiar waters, Indra was reminded of Aryavarta. He asked his three friends of news of his queen Sachi and his people. He was surprised to note that they were unusually evasive. He prodded further, and was shocked at their revelations.

At first he was overjoyed to learn that he was the father of a beautiful baby boy, Jayantha. His first impulse was to postpone the siege of Harappa and follow the course of the river upstream all the way back to Aryavarta. He could not wait to see his wife and child. With the birth of their son, surely Sachi would have forgiven him, he thought. But he learnt to his dismay that he could not have been further from the truth.

Varuna, Vayu and Agni took turns to relate the events that had occurred in Aryavarta since his departure. The three of them had finished their training with Bhrigu and returned to an Aryavarta that they barely recognised. Makara, the new high priest, informed them that Indra had perished at the hands of Sargon the Asura. They were also told that the citizens now preferred to call themselves Vasus, instead of Devas.

To his further dismay, Indra heard that his friend and regent Paras had died in a riding accident under mysterious circumstances. The Sabha had appointed Sachi as the new regent to the crown prince Jayantha. General Kanak, who refused to be called anything but a Deva and had opposed the new regent's plan to change the name of the clan, had been struck by a strange malady. His body had wasted away before he'd finally died.

Sachi, on her part, had invited the three of them for a meal but denied them access to the young prince Jayantha. Mahisi had advised them not to touch the wine and they had used the revelry as a distraction to swap goblets with the people next to them. The next day, sure enough, three of Sachi's cronies had taken violently ill.

Mahisi informed them that there had never been any substantiation to the rumours about Indra's death. She had arranged horses to get them out of town quickly and they had ridden to Susa, where stories of Indra's exploits in Sumer were being sung on the streets. From then on it had been easy to pick up their trail.

Indra was appalled at the intensity of Sachi's hatred towards him. Time and his absence had done nothing to diminish it. It was clear that she had set out to erase all traces of his memory from Aryavarta. According to Mahisi, she had told Jayantha that his father was a god who watched over him from heaven. His son had no idea his father was still alive. It was with a heavy heart that the Deva king continued the journey across the desert.

Ugra, commander-in-chief of the city of Harappa, stood on the balcony of a rather modest house on a hill and surveyed the city that lay spread out in front of him. It was the early hours of morning, just before sunrise, and the city was beginning to awaken. He had been unable to sleep; the news that he had heard would ensure that this would be the case for many nights to come. He had just returned from the temple where he had learnt about Indra and his plans for Harappa.

Ugra's body was beginning to show the first signs of age, his waist had started to thicken and his thick, curly hair showed the first signs of grey. He thought back over the years he had spent serving this great city. Ugra's rise in the Harappa social hierarchy had been meteoric and unprecedented. From his humble origins as a slave, he was now one of the most powerful and influential men in the city.

Harappa had changed much in all these years. The prosperity and wealth had brought a sense of complacency and security amongst its citizens. It had been years since the Harappans had been to war or even had an army of their own. They relied on loyal slaves and mercenaries to do the job.

Now, the task of protecting Harappa from this latest threat

lay squarely on Ugra's shoulders. He had no great army or high walls to defend the city. Although from what he had heard of the siege on Susa, walls did not present a problem for this barbarian and his horde.

The sun came up and Ugra decided that he could not wait any longer. He called out to his aide and asked the man to send word to convene the Supreme Council.

Later that morning, Ugra stood before the ruling body of Harappa and delivered his report. The council, which comprised of five oligarchs chosen from the richest and most powerful families of Harappa, now huddled together to confer. Ugra looked up at a small window that overlooked the assembly hall. There behind a veiled curtain sat Anga, high priestess of the temple of Raksha, the source of his information. He had never felt the need to question her sources; her information was always reliable and accurate.

Anga was a statuesque, beautiful woman. As with all the women of her priesthood, she did not wear any jewellery and only adorned herself with jasmine flowers. Raksha was a goddess who demanded austerity from her worshippers.

The old men were still talking in hushed whispers and Anga noticed how Ugra was trying to control his impatience. She recalled with a smile how he had been such an impatient lover; it had taken all her skill to teach him the benefits of patience, and now he was an expert. He did not make her feel the need to take on another lover anymore. As she watched the proceedings unfold below her, a frown appeared on her perfect brow.

This one they called Indra worried her. She had heard about how the skies had rained fire on Susa and destroyed its mighty gates. Either this man was a god, or he had the sky gods on his side. No ordinary man could think of crossing the Um Bakher with an army. He had to be either very courageous or completely insane. From what she had heard of Indra, he seemed to have both these traits.

Anga knew she could not rely on the oligarchs to defend the city. She'd already made plans to make this extremely difficult journey an impossible one for Indra and his Devas.

The oligarchs appeared finally to have arrived at some consensus. Their spokesman, Marat, the most pompous of them all, now cleared his throat as he addressed Ugra.

'You say this Indra is trying to cross the desert with over two thousand men. I say he is a fool. The desert will finish them long before they see our borders.'

Ugra tried to hide the irritation that crept up in his voice. These were the very men who had prevented him from maintaining an army or building any defences.

'My lord, this man has sacked Susa. He killed the Asura Bhadra in single combat. He is the only man to inflict a defeat on Sargon's army. He leads an army of determined warriors such as our world has not seen. It is said that they will follow him to hell and back. I'd say there is plenty of reason to worry. We must call on the Alliance to get every man they can muster.'

The Alliance was a motley crew that comprised the chieftains of all the neighbouring tribes. It had been formed to protect the land against outside invasion. But it was Harappan gold more than any patriotism that kept it together.

The oligarchs huddled together once again to confer.

It was sunset on the desert as Indra gave the order to march. In the fading light, on the horizon, they could see the glow of the lamps of Ashkavan. The first part of their journey through the desert had largely been uneventful; their water reserves had seen them through. Now they would reach the oasis by sunrise.

The oasis of Ashkavan was a refuge for a veritable rogues' gallery of the ancient world. Thieves, bandits, political criminals and all manner of fugitives from justice found safety in its remoteness. It was a lawless, dog-eat-dog kind of a world that existed within its streets. Murders and robberies were rife; justice was often cruel and meted out instantly with the help of a club or blade.

Indra was cautious in his approach to the settlement. He made camp a fair distance away and sent in a few men to replenish their water and supplies. Later in the evening, he and the Falcons went into Ashkavan to visit the local taverns. Their objective was to make discreet enquiries for a guide to take them across the Um Bakher.

As they made their way through the streets, they were amazed at the life they saw around them. It was one big carnival: there were musicians, dancers and acrobats. The street corners were filled with hawkers selling all kinds of exotic wares. As they weaved through the crowd, they saw a disagreement occur in front of them. Within minutes the two principals had cleared out an area in the throng and a knife fight ensued. Meanwhile, an enterprising onlooker began to accept wagers. Indra had to drag a very tempted Agni and Soma away from the action.

They soon found a tavern that they thought would best suit their needs and entered. There was a lull in conversation as the regular patrons surveyed the strangers. The Devas walked up to the bar where Indra ordered some wine. Slowly the crowd lost interest in them and went back to whatever it was they were doing before the interruption. The tavern keeper was a surly-looking old man. He served them the wine and immediately put out his hand to collect the money. Indra decided this would be a good place to start their enquiry.

'We are looking for the relatives of Timon of Ashkavan.'

The man studied them carefully. Although they were unarmed and dressed as peasants, their build and the way they carried themselves told him these were fighting men of the highest order.

'I do not recollect the name.'

Indra decided to allay his fears a bit.

'We are friends and have ridden many miles with Timon.'

The man's eyes flashed to a corner for a brief moment. Indra turned and saw a group of men at a table there; they were engrossed in their supper.

'Stay and have a drink. Perhaps I might remember something.'

Indra's friends had already knocked back their first drinks and were ready for another round. Indra sipped his drink slowly and kept his eyes on the tavern keeper. He noticed the man walk across to the corner table and whisper something. There were a few curious glances in their direction, and then one of the men got up and left the tavern.

The evening went on and a lot of wine was consumed. Soon the mistress of the house, a buxom woman with a temperament as surly as her husband's, came to them and asked them to drink up and leave. Indra noticed that they were one of the last ones left at the establishment. The owner was nowhere to be seen. Agni and Vayu protested loudly and had to be dragged out by the others.

They staggered through the lonely streets, loudly singing bawdy songs. Even the roughnecks of Ashkavan steered well clear of them and they soon found themselves on the outskirts of the settlement. Their camp was just beyond a grove of acacia trees. As they made their way through the vegetation, a voice came out of the trees.

'Are you the friends of Timon of Ashkavan?'

Indra answered in the affirmative. A man stepped out of the

trees, his face concealed by the shadows. He seemed to be nervous as he scanned the darkness behind them for any signs of movement.

'I am Aghar. Timon was my brother. Come! We will go somewhere we can talk.'

Aghar led them to a little tent that had been pitched in a clearing a little way away. He offered them some wine and lit up a hookah and passed it around. Indra introduced himself and informed him about the death of Timon. Aghar bowed his head and said a prayer in his native tongue for the soul of his dead brother. Although there was no real resemblance between the two, they both had that lean yet tough-as-nails appearance characteristic of the desert nomad.

'Now tell me what I can do for my brother's friends.'

'We are looking for a guide to take us across the desert.'

Aghar had a big smile on his face as he stood up and took a bow.

'Let me offer you my services then. My favourite wife belongs to a tribe that lives across the Um Bakher. Love has made me cross that hell many times. I will be glad to take you across.'

Then he cleared his throat and said, 'For a price, of course.'

'Name your price. You will find us more than generous.'

Aghar asked for twenty horses and a substantial amount of gold. It was a small fortune, especially in these parts. He also insisted that he be paid in full before the trip. He said the journey was fraught with danger, and he could not let his wives and children starve if he did not make it back. With no real choice in the matter, Indra accepted his offer and asked him to meet them at the camp the next morning. As they left, Aghar had one last word of caution for them.

'My lord, it is not my business to ask why you intend to take an army across the desert. But there is great interest in your movements from the people back east. As your faithful servant, it is my duty to tell you that every move of yours is being watched and reported. I suggest you limit your movements through the settlement and keep a watchful eye on your food and drink. If there is anything you require, I will be glad to get it for you.

Aghar was as good as his word, ensuring that they were well stocked and prepared for the perilous journey ahead. Soon Indra and his army were off across the desert towards Harappa. They marched through the night and spent the hottest parts of the day resting their horses and getting some much-needed sleep. The days went by quickly, and slowly the little scrub vegetation gave way to hard salt flats that extended for miles across the horizon. Their water supplies began to rapidly diminish. Aghar reassured them that water was close at hand, but soon every man was down to half rations and there were still no signs of water.

Finally Aghar took a couple of scouts and set out to look for water. For three days Indra and his men awaited his return, till their water rations were down to a couple of mouthfuls during the day. Indra realised that to turn back towards Ashkavan would be suicidal. Their only chance was to press forward and hope they find water. He turned to Varuna, who regretfully informed him that he could only control the element, not create it. Just then the Ashvanis arrived, leading a few horses.

'These horses were born and bred in the desert. We've kept them without water for a few days. If there is water around, they will surely find it.'

One of the twins went to the dominant member of the herd,

a young male stallion. He placed his forehead against that of the horse and whispered to it before he let it go. The stallion led them out of the camp. The men watched as the animal sniffed the air and then took off in a south-easterly direction. Indra and Varuna joined the Ashvanis on fresh horses and followed the herd. Periodically the stallion stopped to smell the air before he took off again. The men followed at a safe distance.

A short while later, the horses disappeared from sight right before their eyes. As the astonished men reached the spot, they saw a gaping hole in the ground, as if someone had split open the earth with a giant axe. Unless one knew about the place, it was impossible to find against the stark landscape of the salt flats. The horse tracks lead straight into it. The Ashvanis spoke gently to their mounts and coaxed them down the steep incline.

As they reached the bottom, they realised they were at the entrance of a massive subterranean cave complex. Within, they saw the deep blue waters of a giant pool. As the horses drank, Indra noticed fresh tracks there—he wondered if Aghar and the scouts had made it to the cave.

The water was cool and refreshing, sheltered from the heat of the desert sun by the overhang. Their thirst quenched, they returned to fetch the others. It was then that they noticed the circling vultures. The birds led them straight to a spot where Indra found his scouts lying dead. The Ashvanis swept the area for tracks and soon found a place where they could tell that five men had lain in wait. Aghar had led the scouts straight into an ambush; they had not stood a chance. The twins informed Indra that Aghar and his men had proceeded eastwards after the attack, which meant they were ahead of them. Indra hoped that he could catch up with him and repay him for his treachery.

The army, now refreshed, pushed on east through the murderous saltpans. They stopped for rest only for a few hours during the hottest part of the day. The heat was so oppressive that the men had to tie strips of cloth over their eyes to prevent their pupils from being scorched by the sun reflecting off the blazing sands.

At long last they came across more hospitable terrain comprising sparse patches of grass and bushes. They also saw, much to their delight, herds of ibex dotting the landscape. Excited at the prospect of fresh meat, Indra and Aryaman led a team of hunters and brought down many of the beasts. The men had a great feast and rested that night under the brilliantly-lit desert sky. They tended to the horses and, for the first time during the journey, their songs could be heard for miles across the sands.

Days went by, their water resources dipped, and they were soon confronted with the same situation again. To find a watering hole this time was not a problem though; they had to just follow the animal tracks that led them directly to it. However, many of their horses, especially the old ones from the original northern stock, could not handle the searing heat and dehydration. They collapsed one by one in the hard unforgiving sands.

Soon, in the distance, they saw the tops of many palm trees. Some of the men let out a whoop of joy and urged their tired mounts to move faster. The horses smelt water and began to pick up the pace.

When Indra made his way through the palm trees, he was surprised at the grim silence near the watering hole. As he approached the water, the reek of rotting flesh made him step back in disgust. In the middle of the pool there floated several carcasses of ibex and antelope. The water had a thick, dirty layer of sediment floating over it. He let out a roar of anger: he could not believe anyone would do this in the middle of the desert.

They had rendered the only water available for miles impossible to drink. He saw the arrows that stuck out of the bodies of the slain creatures and recognised it as the work of Aghar and his men. These men were born of the desert; they should have known better.

Indra promised himself that they would pay a terrible price when he caught up with them. Then he realised that there was a likelihood that he might not live long enough to fulfil the promise. He suddenly felt a hand on his shoulder; it was Varuna.

'Ready your bow.'

Indra did not hesitate; he quickly strung his bow and notched an arrow to it. Varuna asked everybody to step back and away from the pool. He closed his eyes and mentally chanted a mantra. Then he slowly raised his hands up and away from each other. Indra watched in fascination as the waters of the pool began to whirl faster and faster like a vortex with a gaping hole in the centre. Without opening his eyes, Varuna asked Indra to shoot an arrow into the centre. Indra drew back his bow and let fly the shaft. The arrow went deep into the earth and from its bowels a spring of water leapt out like a fountain. The force of it flushed away the carrion and foul waters of the pool into the dry sands of the desert. Then, as Varuna lowered his hands, the fountain settled down and filled the pool with fresh, crystal-clear water.

Varuna's feat did wonders for the men's morale. Over several months, rumours had abounded in the camp about Indra and Soma's divinity. Now after witnessing Varuna's powers, the men were convinced that they were in the presence of gods.

Over the next few days, with their bellies and water-skins filled with the water, the men braved the scorching sands and dry, hot winds and marched merrily on. Soon, the first signs that they would leave the desert behind began to emerge. They could smell flowers in the easterly breeze. They saw shapes of aquatic birds and sure enough, in the distance, they could see the silvery blue ribbon of a river beyond which was the dry, brown foliage of a jungle that awaited the rains.

Full of hope, the men marched on. And then, as they neared the river, they saw lined up on the opposite bank two thousand men armed with short, heavy stabbing spears and rawhide shields. They had long, curly hair and dark faces painted with ochre stripes that gave them a fearsome appearance. Their ebony bodies were thick and heavily muscled. They shuffled from side to side and made whooping noises that seemed to come from their throats. They beat their spears against their shields as they eagerly waited for action.

Ugra stood at his vantage point on the hill and surveyed the scene that was unfolding in the distance. He saw Indra's army across the river, but there was something wrong. This did not seem to be an army dying of thirst. They did not make a beeline for the river as he had expected. Instead they lined up in orderly fashion well out of range of his frontline archers. The Malavas, a warrior tribe from the south of Harappa, had volunteered to be the first line of defence. Ugra noted with a smile that the Malava Crocodile was in position and no army had ever escaped its jaws.

The Crocodile was a battle formation that had been perfected by the Malavas. Six thousand of their spearmen were hidden in the jungle in a V-like formation. A smaller force would engage the enemy and slowly give ground during the battle. The enemy would gradually but surely be drawn into the jungle, into the jaws of the crocodile. Once they were in the kill zone, the two lines of spearmen would quickly close in, snapping the jaws shut. The enemy forces would be surrounded and crushed. It was a manoeuvre that Ugra had never seen fail. Now the trap was ready, but the enemy had not yet taken the bait.

Yadu went to Indra and requested permission to cross the river and engage the enemy. Indra saw the restlessness in the enemy ranks; this was exactly what they expected him to do. He was not ready to oblige them.

'Patience, Prince Yadu. I will make them come to you.'

He turned to Agni and Vayu and spoke briefly with them. Soma came with the chalice and handed it to the two warriors in turn. Their pupils dilated as the drug began to take effect. Deep in concentration, Agni and Vayu stepped forward. In his hand, Agni held some dry wood shavings. Vayu used a couple of flint stones and created a spark in them.

Agni cradled the little fire in his palm, chanted a mantra and began to move his arms in circles around the fire that now started to burn in midair. He opened his arms and continued to move them in a circular motion working the ball of fire. It started to get bigger and bigger until it hung in front of them like a fiery orange globe. Agni used his powers to contain the heat within the cloud so it would not harm any of his men. Then Vayu chanted a mantra and took a deep breath. He slowly exhaled and the globe of fire started to roll through the air towards the enemy.

The Malava chief, clearly distinguished by the bright red plumes on his headdress, watched open-mouthed as the cloud of fire swept towards them, growing bigger as it approached. The chief screamed to his men to take evasive action and barely had time to throw himself to the ground when the fire swept over him and singed the plumes of his fine headdress.

Like a wave the fire swept over the dry jungle and scorched everything in its wake. The six thousand Malava warriors did not stand a chance. As the fire raged, the screams of dying men and animals rent the air. The heat from the flaming forest forced the Malava vanguard that had survived the flames to cross the river. The unfortunate men ran straight into the merciless bronze shields and spears of the Yavana infantry.

Ugra watched in horror as the Yavanas made short work of the Malava survivors. A few ran out of the blaze towards them, their bodies and hair on fire. Ugra ordered his archers to shoot them down before their screams demoralised his own ranks.

As the fire died, only a few gnarled stumps remained of what once had been a thriving forest. Aryaman and his men arrived with a prisoner. Indra was pleased to see that it was Aghar. The traitor and his men had hidden near the river and hoped to get away in the heat of the battle. Just as Aghar thought he had slipped past Indra's lines, Aryaman and his men had intercepted them. Aghar had watched his men fall like flies to the Aditya arrows. He now threw himself at Indra's feet and begged for mercy.

But there was no compassion in the Deva king's eyes for the desert nomad. Just as the army prepared to march, he was stripped of all his clothing and tied spread-eagled on the riverbank next to the destroyed forest. Soma then poured a jar of honey over his naked body. Aghar begged and pleaded, but his cries fell on deaf ears.

The nomad watched the ash and dust raised by the departing army slowly settle back on the forest floor. Just then he noticed the burnt ground in front of him change colour from ash to black. Slowly the dark floor started to move towards him. Aghar paled when as he realised what it was. Millions of ants, the only creatures to survive the flames, were emerging from colonies under the ground. The swarm climbed over him and soon all that could be seen was a mound of excited black ants.

Ugra watched Indra and his army march out of the smoky remains of the forest. In spite of the distance, Aghar's screams carried to his ears. The man called to his gods to give him a quick death, but the end was long and excruciatingly painful. Ugra tried to put the man's cries out of his mind. He could see the effect it was having on the men around him. But he had more important things to worry about. Eight thousand of his men had been lost with barely a scratch on the enemy. It had happened in front of his eyes yet he could scarcely believe it. The gods not only showed this barbarian favour, they seemed to ride beside him in battle.

The Harappan commander had one trump card, one he had planned to use later in the battle, but he was now forced to rethink all his carefully laid-out plans. He turned to one of his men and spoke grimly.

'Summon the Mahavats.'

The man raised a black and gold banner and waved it high in the air.

As Indra marched on to the wide plain, he saw to his left the hillock on which Ugra stood. He realised that it was the Harappan command post. Up ahead he saw what looked like a moving grey wall, and it was headed straight at them. As it got closer, Indra and his men watched wide-eyed in astonishment as five hundred war elephants charged towards them. Indra had never seen an elephant before; now the horizon seemed to be filled with the terrifying beasts.

In spite of their great bulk, the beasts moved with alarming speed. As they neared, Indra saw that the animals wore leather armour inlaid with bronze over their broad foreheads, and their tusks were tipped with bronze cones that had been honed till they were needle sharp. The dominant males each carried a Mahavat rider on his back. They were the only tribe in the world to have mastered these beasts. At the behest of their riders, the elephants raised their trunks and trumpeted in unison, startling the horses.

Indra called to Atreya and led two chariot divisions to intercept them. He hoped they would be able to buy the rest of his men enough time to spread out across the relative safety of the broad plain. He began to pour arrows into the animals as Soma drove the chariot straight towards them. The arrows posed no threat to the beasts and only served to infuriate them further. One of them raised his trunk, trumpeted a challenge and charged towards the Deva king. Indra shot five arrows in quick succession into the open mouth of the elephant, and one of them found the creature's brain. It fell like a small hill right in the path of Indra's chariot.

Soma let out a roar of triumph that was rapidly cut short as another bull charged right into them. Its massive tusk took one of the horses right in the chest and lifted it bodily off the ground. With a shake of the giant head, it threw the hapless animal into the path of the others. Indra swung the black sword and lopped off its trunk. The creature roared in pain and slammed its head into the chariot, showering the two men with blood from its mutilated trunk. The two occupants of the vehicle were thrown clear right into the middle of the charge.

Indra and Soma weaved, rolled and twisted out of the path of the charging beasts. Around them the Deva chariots were being taken apart. They heard the screams of men being gored or crushed under those giant legs.

The Mahavat chief—realising that the enemy had scattered—now called off the charge. He did not want to exhaust his mounts in a futile chase. Indra and Soma found themselves surrounded by elephants. Mace and sword in hand, they prepared for the inevitable.

Suddenly a piercing whistle rent the air. Indra turned in the direction of the sound. It was the Ashvanis on horseback. They had somehow found a way through the forbidding grey wall. They reached the two warriors who hoisted themselves onto the backs of their steeds, and with some sublime horsemanship rode literally between the enormous feet of the infuriated beasts back to their own lines.

Indra was soon back at the helm of his army in a new chariot. He issued orders to Aryaman and his cavalry archers to take down the riders of the elephants. Aryaman and his men rode up and concentrated their arrows on the Mahavats. Under their accurate assault, many of the elephants were soon left without riders. The Mahavat leader crouched low on his mount and continued to direct the charge. The Ashvanis pointed him out to Indra and informed him that the only way to stop the assault would be to kill that man and beast.

Indra directed Soma to drive the chariot towards the lead bull. As he neared the gargantuan beast, Indra leapt off the chariot. In his hand he carried Kadaag, the black sword. The Mahavat leader saw Indra come and turned the great beast towards him. Indra roared out a challenge and sprinted towards the charging animal. The elephant hesitated, unused to such behaviour. One brief second was all Indra needed: he leapt towards the beast and, stepping on its tusk, launched himself upwards. The rider let out a startled yell as Indra suddenly appeared in front of him. He raised the elephant goad to strike Indra, but he was too late, Kadaag took his head clean off his shoulders.

Indra stood on the elephant's head and kicked the lifeless torso off its back. The elephant roared and tried to turn its head to dislodge the intruder. Indra drove his sword into the thick neck of the beast right where it met the skull. The elephant screamed in agony, turned tail and ran. Indra twisted the sword viciously and severed its spinal cord. The great beast stopped, swayed for a moment, and then dropped down dead on the battlefield. Indra leapt off its back and ran back to his lines. The other elephants had followed the lead bull and turned their backs on the enemy.

Aryaman and his archers now attacked their unprotected rear with a volley of arrows and sent them on their way. The leaderless elephants needed no further encouragement as they charged back towards their own lines.

Bheda, chief of the Vrisni clan, looked out at the dust cloud in the distance. He could hear the bellowing of the giant beasts. He hoped they had left him some of the enemy to deal with. He had six thousand spears thirsting for blood. His men were packed together in a tight line as they waited for the signal from Ugra.

The Vrisni were the greatest warriors in the land. For generations they had been hired as mercenaries to protect the borders of Harappa from invasion. They were supremely confident and scoffed at the thought of wearing any armour. With their speed and skill they did not feel the need for any extra protection.

Clad only in loincloths of tiger skin, their beautifully sculpted dark bodies were marked with white clay. It gave them a fearful appearance. They now sang and shuffled their feet in a rhythmic dance as they waited to rain death and destruction on the enemy.

Suddenly, through the cloud of dust, he saw that the elephants were out of control and running straight for the Vrisni line. Bheda realised what had happened and screamed for his men to break ranks and scatter. His timely action saved a lot of his men from being trampled underfoot by the giant beasts. But even before he could close ranks again, Indra's chariots and cavalry had hit the broken line. Bheda watched in horror as the Devas scythed through his army and emerged behind them. Before he could order his men to turn and face the threat of another cavalry charge, Yadu and his Yavanas attacked.

The Vrisni, in all their years of fighting, had never encountered such a disciplined and cohesive unit as Indra's army. Now they were caught between the proverbial rock and a hard place. Indra, Soma, Varuna, Vayu and Agni consumed huge quantities of soma and waded into the throng of Vrisni.

Sandwiched between Yadu and Indra's army, what followed was a massacre unlike any the Harappans had ever seen before. Although outnumbered, Indra and his army unleashed a furious attack against which the hapless Bheda and his men had no answer. Before sunset, all of the mighty Vrisni had fallen on the blood-soaked earth.

Ugra and his handful of Harappan soldiers bowed their head in subjugation to the Deva king and escaped with their lives.

14

As the victorious army marched into the city of Harappa, Indra remembered Valli and her eloquent descriptions of her city. He realised now as he marvelled at Harappa's order and beauty that her words had not been exaggerations prompted by the love of her native land. Even Susa, with all its beauty, paled in comparison to this magnificent city.

As they marched through its broad central avenue, the citizens gathered by the sides to catch a glimpse of their new rulers. They were all dressed in white flowing robes, and both men and women adorned themselves with heavy gold jewellery. Their faces betrayed no emotion sans a mild curiosity as they watched the parade. They did not behave or appear like a conquered people.

Indra was surprised to discover the complete lack of fear in their eyes. They seemed almost haughty as they met his gaze. He looked around at his own men who appeared strangely subdued, as if awestruck by the beauty of the city.

Brihaspati realised that there was more to this scene than met the eye. There was something about this city. He felt a strange power here. A dark, sinister, all-encompassing power. He turned to Ugra who marched next to him and spoke to him in a whisper.

'Tell me the truth for I will know if you do not. There is something wrong. My men are strangely subdued while your people show no fear for their future. What is this strange power I sense here?'

Ugra did not turn to him but spoke in a soft whisper so the others would not hear.

'What you sense is true, Master. Raksha, the patron goddess of Harappa, protects this city. It is she who controls the minds of your people. We will speak more about this later.'

Indra tried to shake off the ominous feeling that had crept into his mind as he stared at the local populace. He curled his nose in disgust and whispered to Soma.

'Look at them! With all that jewellery, it's impossible to tell the men from the women. Pompous little peacocks. I wonder if they'd maintain those stoic faces with my sword up their arse.'

Soma looked distinctly uncomfortable under their scrutiny.

'I do not trust these dark ones. They are like snakes waiting for a chance to turn on us.'

The road took them past a huge reservoir. Ugra informed them that this was the only water source left in the city. The river Sindhu that had once been the lifeline of this great city was now a muddy swamp. This tank fed by underground springs was the only thing that kept the city alive. Indra laughed unsympathetically.

'Do not worry. When your water runs out you can melt down all that gold you'll wear on your bodies and drink it.'

They were led to one of the oligarchs' palaces that had been hurriedly vacated to accommodate Indra and his commanders. Indra called for soma and after downing a few cups felt distinctly better. After the long trek through the desert, he settled down to enjoy the luxuries the palace had to offer.

Later his commanders arrived along with Brihaspati. Indra

asked Soma to bring out more of his brew. Soma was reluctant; they were not going into battle and Indra had already drunk more of it than he could handle. Besides, they were in the company of Yadu, Aryaman and Brihaspati. He looked towards the other Falcons who shook their heads. Soma decided to ignore Indra.

The Deva king would have none of it; he went to his friend and grabbed him violently by the throat.

'When I give an order, I like to see it obeyed, old friend!'

Soma looked deep into the eyes of his king. He did not recognise the person he saw lurking there. A shudder went through his body as he nodded his acquiescence. Indra let go of his throat and Soma rushed off to do his bidding. When he returned Indra snatched the chalice from him and, to Soma's horror, offered it to Brihaspati, Aryaman and Yadu.

'Drink, my brave friends. Today you will know what it feels like to be gods.'

Yadu and Aryaman stepped forward, but Brihaspati declined the offer. He took Ugra and left the room. Indra was not finished, he asked Soma to make sure that every man in the army got one measure of soma along with his dinner rations that evening. Agni, Varuna and Vayu joined Soma in trying to make Indra see reason, but to no avail.

Soon the dancing girls arrived and the entertainment for the evening began. Yadu and Aryaman were pleased to discover that the drink greatly enhanced their performance with the ladies. Indra and the others drank more and more soma and convinced the dancing girls of Harappa that they were now lying with the gods.

Brihaspati, who had stayed away from the celebrations, stood on a balcony and looked out into the city. It was deathly quiet—most of the citizens were indoors. He could not sleep. Something was bothering him, a premonition of some terrible event. The moon was full and from somewhere in the distance he could hear wolves howl. Then he heard a commotion in the dark deserted streets and long shadows began to appear.

As he watched silently from his vantage point, he saw that it was their own soldiers who were on the move. The soma seemed to have broken the spell Raksha had woven on them. They now moved through the streets like predators out on a hunt.

Had Indra been in his senses, he would have realised why Mitra had warned him about giving soma to ordinary men. But he was being transported into the higher realms of pleasure in the expert arms of the dancing girls.

That night, high on soma, the Devas, Yavanas and Adityas ran amok in the streets of Harappa, unleashing a holocaust of murder, rape and plunder. Like rutting animals, they barged into houses and dragged the women out into the streets. Children, rudely awakened from sleep, watched their fathers being murdered and their mothers brutalised. Their cries pierced the ears of Brihaspati like barbs. He prayed to the heavens and asked the sky gods to show mercy. They had flouted one of their fundamental rules of war, to honour the terms of surrender. He knew for certain that the consequences would be severe.

As the sun came up, the soldiers awakened as if from a trance. Some of them awoke covered in blood, others in the middle of some heinous act. They backed away from the ravaged city and sheepishly made their way back to camp. The looks of bewilderment on their faces said it all—they had no idea what had occurred the previous night.

The next morning an irate Ugra informed Indra of the violations of the surrender treaty and of the cruel excesses committed by his soldiers on the streets. Indra's drug-addled brain struggled to come up with a reply. When it did, it stunned the dark warrior.

'It is all right, my friend. War makes monsters even of gods, and these are mortal men after all.'

Then he laughed as he thought of something.

'Perhaps they will put some brave sons in these cowardly bellies. Who will grow up and be able to defend this land properly.'

Ugra looked up at the man whose courage during the battle he had begun to admire. This was not the hero who had proudly stood tall against everything the Harappans threw at him. This man who stood in front of him was like a petulant child who did not want to admit to his mistakes. Ugra bowed mockingly.

'Unfortunately the people were deprived of even that privilege, my lord. Your men thought it would be fun to disembowel these women with their swords after they raped them.'

Indra did not know what to say. In his current state of mind, he was above petty things like morality. He asked his guards to take the man away and screamed out to the others to fetch him more soma. More of the brew was consumed. Soon the women began to bore Indra and he shouted out to one of the Harappan attendants.

'Get rid of these cows and bring me some real women. Where is the high priestess Anga? She seems to keep the best girls, bring them to us.'

The man bowed and left to do his bidding. Brihaspati tried to reason with Indra, explaining to him that he should treat the Harappans with respect. These were a great people and there was much the Devas could learn from them. But his words fell on deaf ears. Soon the man returned with a message from Anga. He informed Indra that the high priestess had expressed her inability to fulfil Indra's wishes. In turn she asked for Indra to come to the temple and beg the goddess for forgiveness for the actions of his men.

The hall went quiet as everyone looked towards Indra for his reaction. He laughed out loud and called to his companions to accompany him to the temple. Brihaspati went along in the hope that he could prevent things from getting ugly.

The temple of Raksha, patron goddess of Harappa, stood on a little rise of land in the middle of the city. As they climbed to the top of the hill, Indra and his companions were surprised to see there was no structure. There was only a huge tree unlike any they had seen before. Its trunk was massive in girth and bone-white in colour. Its branches spread wide, and its broad leaves were of a green so dark, it almost looked black. In its dense foliage lived a variety of birds and small animals that, like the tree, looked alien to the land. A square mud-brick platform had been constructed around its base, on which the priestesses performed their rituals.

In front of the tree stood Anga, the high priestess, along with her retinue of beautiful young women. Indra looked around arrogantly and asked her where her temple was. She explained to him that Raksha was a spirit of the forest and that she chose to live in that tree. So the tree was both the temple and the deity. It was the bringer of prosperity to their great city.

Indra was amused that the luxury-loving people of Harappa worshipped a tree. He and his companions had a hearty laugh. Anga looked at these men and realised there would be no repentance for their actions. She and the other priestesses bowed their heads and joined their hands in prayer.

Indra rudely interrupted and asked her to summon the goddess in her true form. He expressed his inability to bow to a tree. More laughter followed his statement. Anga was remarkably calm through all this provocation. She ignored him and continued with her prayers. It angered Indra that he was unable to get a rise out of her. He walked up to her and grabbed her by the shoulder.

'Tell your goddess that Indra, king of the Devas, has done her the honour of coming to her door to meet her. Ask her to reveal herself to me.'

Anga laughed in his face, her beautiful dark eyes filled with contempt. Even the animals and birds that lived in the tree began to screech and call out in alarm.

'Be careful what you ask for, barbarian. Leave now and perhaps you may still save yourself.'

She shrugged off his grip, turned her back to him and went on with her prayers. Livid, Indra shoved her rudely towards his men. His voice was low and menacing now.

'Amuse yourself, my boys. Perhaps the mother goddess will come to beg for her beloved daughter's honour.'

Brihaspati watched in horror as Indra's commanders tore the clothes off the high priestess and spread-eagled her on the platform under the tree. The other women shut their eyes and began to chant in a low voice that seemed to emanate from deep within their throats. As the men took turns on her, Anga did not struggle, scream or even protest. She lay there, her face turned towards Indra, staring defiantly at him through her ordeal. Brihaspati averted his eyes in shame, distressed that there was nothing he could do. Anga had wounded the king's pride and Indra would not be stopped till she was humiliated.

But if the Aditya priest thought that Indra was finished with his vengeance, he could not have been more wrong. He called to Agni who picked up a torch and, like a fire-eater in a carnival, blew the flames towards the tree. A wail of anguish went up among the women as the giant tree caught fire. Soma and the others dragged them away to safety. The Devas were amazed to see that the residents of the tree did not flee, and the dying screams of the birds and animals rung in the ears of the gathering long after the temple of Raksha had burned down to the ground.

Indra and his men left with their pick of the women. Anga sat there long after they were gone. All that was left of the majestic living temple was a gnarled, burnt stump. As the smoke melted away, Anga heard a voice. It was young and sweet and in a language that was from Anga's long forgotten childhood.

'I am cold, big sister.'

Anga looked up and saw a beautiful young girl squatting on the floor in front of the burnt stump. Her arms were wrapped around her knees and she looked up at Anga with wide, dark eyes. The high priestess was suddenly conscious of her own nudity. She asked the remaining acolytes to fetch some robes. The girl stood up and pushed her long, dark hair away from her face. On the inside of her left wrist, Anga saw a mark that caused her to step back in alarm. It was the tattoo of a coiled serpent.

Anga cautioned one of the priestesses as she handed the girl a robe.

'Do not touch her. She bears the mark of the serpent.'

The girl accepted the robe with a smile and used it to cover her perfectly-shaped body.

Indra lay in the darkness, unable to sleep. His mind raced under the influence of the drug. Although his body craved sleep, his mind showed no signs of calming down. He thought about the events of the night and felt no guilt for the needless slaughter. He was above such petty morals. He was a god, a warrior god with an unquenchable thirst for blood and sex. He had lost count of the women that had come to his bed. He had felt no desire for them, only a sense of triumph as he made them commit the most depraved of sexual acts.

His thoughts then went to Valli and he smiled. How different it had been with her: she had not been in awe of him like these women were. For her, it had been desire, raw and primal, that had slowly transformed to love over the short time they had spent together. She had challenged him to please her, and how he had responded. His eyes welled up; he shut them and let the tears flow down the sides of his face.

Just then a light footfall alerted him of someone's presence in the chamber. He looked up and saw her standing at the door. It was Valli. Indra could not believe his eyes as he saw her walk towards him, her eyes drinking in his naked beauty. He sat up in bed, eager to be taken into her embrace. She opened her arms as she neared him and he noticed the serpent tattoo on the inside of her wrist.

'That's strange,' he thought to himself. Every detail of her beautiful, bronzed body was imprinted in his mind, yet he could not recall that particular mark on her. She took him in her arms in a gentle embrace and placed her lips softly against his.

Indra parted his lips as she eased her tongue between them. He felt no desire, only a strange sense of calm as his eyelids began to grow heavy and he sank down onto the bed with her on top of him. For the first time in days, Indra, king of the Devas, drifted off into a deep sleep.

Brihaspati was troubled by what had happened at the temple. What he had sensed on his arrival in the city was but a fraction of the true power that was Raksha. They had awakened an ancient force, a power beyond anything he could fathom. He had felt it under his feet at the temple, deep within the bowels of the earth, like a giant serpent raising its head. He could not shake off the feeling that there would be some sort of retribution. He hoped Indra and the others still had the presence of mind to see it coming.

Just then, a man interrupted his thoughts with the message that Ugra had something very important to discuss with him. The messenger escorted him through the dark, deserted streets of the city to a majestic building.

Inside the great hall, Brihaspati saw many men furiously inscribing on tablets of wet clay. After they were done, the slaves took the tablets to a giant kiln to be fired. Ugra was in frantic discussion with a few of the scribes. He looked up as Brihaspati entered. He seemed greatly troubled and was terse in his greeting.

'Salutations, wise one. Welcome to our library. I apologise for calling you here at this late hour, but this is the only place in the city where you can still get reliable information. All major events in our history since the founding of this city have been recorded here.'

Brihaspati saw the rows and rows of shelves lined with clay tablets. These were an ancient people with a long history. 'We still sing songs to maintain our records and yet we call *them* savages,' he thought to himself. In his view Indra had committed a great blunder in dismissing the Harappans as a greedy and ignorant lot. There was so much to be learned from these people and their mysterious ways.

Ugra led him into an antechamber where they could have

some privacy. Once he had ensured they were alone, he came straight to the point.

'You'll are no longer safe here, you must leave Harappa at once.'

Brihaspati was sceptical: why was the man ready to help them after all the atrocities they had committed against his people?

'We have slain your men, raped your women and yet you try to protect us. Why, Ugra?'

'What you have done is no more than what the Harappans have done to any of the people they defeated. They took this land from somebody and now somebody will take it from them. That's the way it has been and always will be. There is a saying amongst my tribe: men will come and go but the land will always endure.'

His voice choked as it caught in his throat.

'But now that land is dying, my lord. The seven great rivers that gave life to it now run dry. The great plains of the Terai, where my people once roamed, now resembles an endless desert.'

Ugra was overcome by emotion and took a moment to compose himself before he continued.

'You scoff at the love Harappa has for gold, but it is that gold that keeps the city alive. There are no more farms here to produce grain; it is bought at extravagant prices from the merchants of Tyre and Sidon. To the outside world the Harappans lead grand, hedonistic lives, but the sands of time are running out for this great city.'

'You are not from Harappa?' Brihaspati asked.

Ugra gave him a look like he had been insulted.

'I am Gond. My forefathers were the first to set foot on this land when the one we call the Supreme Being led us out of the Dandaka forest. He taught us how to farm the land and grow our own food. Our people ruled over these lands all the way to the eastern sea. Then one day the rainclouds disappeared and the rivers went dry. Drought and famine hit the land. The Gonds ceased to exist as a people and roamed the parched lands like packs of wild beast. Some of us were hunted and killed. The rest were captured and condemned to a life of servitude. Today the spirit of my people only lives on in the hearts and souls of a few survivors who are scattered across these lands.'

Ugra led Brihaspati up a flight of stairs to the roof of the building. He looked out towards the east, onto the brown, stark landscape.

'It was foretold by my people that a great king would come from the west to free the waters and the clouds. He would bring in the thunder and the rain and the land would live once more.'

He turned to Brihaspati, gripped his shoulders and looked deep into his eyes.

'I believe your king Indra is the one from the prophecy. So it is in my interest as well as yours that I tell you this. Today your king tangled with a power that is far beyond anything your people can imagine. Raksha is one of the great spirits of the Dandaka forest. Her kind has ruled that ancient forest from a time way before the arrival of the first man on this earth. Your king is in grave danger here. I implore you, we must bring him back to his senses and leave Harappa at once.'

Brihaspati looked for any signs of insanity in the man's eyes, but he found only a deadly earnestness there. He scanned the man's aura for any trace of lies or deceit; he did not wish to be led on some wild goose chase by a stranger who he had more than enough reason to distrust.

'Where is this land where the clouds and waters are trapped? How will you find it?'

Ugra parted the rawhide strips of his short leather skirt. Tattooed on the inside of his right thigh was a strange design. As Brihaspati examined it closely, he realised that it was a detailed map that was cleverly disguised as an abstract symbol. It depicted a high mountain range, rivers and other geographic landmarks with amazing detail.

'Every Gond of the royal bloodline had to bear this mark when he became a man. It is my father who tattooed this map on my thigh, just as his father had done for him. This mission is as much a part of my destiny as it is Indra's.'

Brihaspati's doubts were far from dispelled. He still wondered how Ugra's tribe had such intricate knowledge of the mountains when they were clearly people of the forests and plains. His thoughts were interrupted by the arrival of a messenger with news that the Ashvanis had requested Brihaspati's presence. The two of them decided to continue their conversation later.

To the south of the city of Harappa, under the shadow of the Vindhya Mountains, stretched a great forest. Its northern boundary was marked by the mighty river Narmada and to the south it stretched all the way up to the ocean. In a huge clearing in the middle of this forest, surrounded on all sides by impenetrable vegetation, stood the dry, shrivelled stump of what had once been a giant tree.

Now the stump started to grow, branching out and pushing its way up towards the forest canopy. Dark green leaves began to appear on its branches as they spread out across the clearing. Soon a magnificent tree stood in place of the stump. Its massive white trunk and branches shone like ivory.

A group of women emerged from the surrounding forest and

stood around the tree, gaping at it in awe. Their dark naked bodies were marked with red clay. They were fully armed and their faces were flushed with excitement. Their leader, a woman with grey matted hair and the body of a warrior, raised her spear high in the air and spoke. Her voice was loud and clear and rang through the dense forest.

'The great Mother has returned. Now the songs of the Vahini will once again resound through the Dandaka.'

Ugra and Brihaspati stood in a makeshift hospital where the Ashvanis and Dhanavantri were treating the wounded. They stood around the body of one of the men who had been assigned to guard Indra's palace. The corpse had turned a dark blue. Their faces wore a puzzled expression, something Brihaspati was not used to seeing.

'We cannot understand this. He shows all the signs of a victim of snakebite, but we cannot find the mark of any fangs on his body. Also the venom is a strange cocktail of both plant and animal toxins, far deadlier than that of any serpent we know.'

Ugra looked worried. He asked if any of the other guards on duty were around. One of them, a Harappan, stepped forward. Ugra asked him if any stranger had entered the palace. The man told him that a beautiful young woman had entered the palace late in the night. She looked like she belonged to one of the tribes from the southern forest. She had informed him that she was a gift for the Deva king. The soldier, used to the arrival of such gifts, had not thought anything of it and let her in. Ugra's eyes widened in fear and anxiety; he ran for the palace, asking the others to follow. He hoped he was not too late.

As they entered Indra's chamber, they saw the king lying in his bed, staring at the ceiling. When he saw them, he began to scream in fear and begged them not to harm him. Brihaspati was shocked. He had been in many tough situations with Indra—fear was not an emotion he had ever seen in the Deva king. He immediately sent everyone away, keeping only Ugra and the Ashvanis with him. He and the Gond held Indra down and allowed the twins to examine him thoroughly.

When the twins had finished, one of them removed a flask from his robe and poured its contents gently down Indra's throat. The other turned to Brihaspati and Ugra.

'The strength of his prana has helped his body fight off the effects of the poison, but it continues to ravage his mind. We have given him an opiate; it will help him sleep. In the meantime, we must find a way to remove the toxin from his mind. There is no telling what it could do to him'

Brihaspati had no idea what to do. The Ashvanis were the best healers he knew; if they could not come up with a solution, he did not know anybody who could. He turned to Ugra. The warrior was staring at the sleeping Indra with an expression of terror on his face.

'You know something. Tell us Ugra, what caused this?'

Ugra snapped out of his trance and turned to Brihaspati. The dark warrior had not seemed so dejected even after his defeat.

'It is over, don't you see? He has been touched by a Vishkanya. There is nothing more you can do for him except pray that his passage into the other world is easy.'

Brihaspati grabbed his shoulder and shook Ugra.

'What are you talking about? What on earth is a Vishkanya?'

Ugra took a few deep breaths and calmed himself down before he spoke.

'The Vishkanya belong to an ancient order of serpent worshippers that once roamed the Dandaka forest. Rich and powerful tribal chiefs used them as assassins in the old days. The most beautiful girls from all the forest tribes were picked to join the order. It is said that these girls were brought up on a diet of plant toxins and snake venom from a very tender age. It made even their mere touch lethal to other beings. To my knowledge, no one has ever survived an encounter with a Vishkanya. What I cannot understand is the appearance of a Vishkanya here. The order was disbanded a long time ago during the time of my great-grandfather by the Tribal Council of the Dandaka forest. No one has ever seen or heard of them ever since.'

Ugra lowered his voice to a hoarse whisper.

'This is Raksha's revenge. We must leave this city and make for the mountains in the north. She has no power there; perhaps, away from her malevolent influence, you king will be able to fight off the poison.'

Indra stirred in his sleep and began to call out to his friends to save him from the serpent. Brihaspati looked at his king helplessly and agreed to Ugra's suggestion.

The next day Indra's army marched out of the city. Among the crowd that had gathered to watch the procession leave was Anga. She had her face covered and was dressed like a slave. At the head of the army, Aryaman wore Indra's armour and rode in his chariot with Soma. He wore the Yavana helmet with a visor that covered his face; he easily passed off as the king even to the discerning eye. Somewhere in the middle of the column, in a covered wagon, gravely ill and heavily sedated, rode the king of the Devas.

The deception did not escape Anga. She looked at the covered wagon and allowed herself a smile. The barbarian's nightmares had been brought to her attention. At first she was dismayed that he had survived the lethal embrace of the Vishkanya, but now she knew that Raksha did not want to give this man a quick death. She wanted to make him suffer.

She watched Ugra as he said his last goodbyes to the people of his adopted city. The only man she had ever loved was riding off with the men who had raped and violated her. She admired his unshakeable faith in the old prophecy, however misguided it seemed to her. How could a barbarian like Indra save this land when he could not save himself?

Ugra led the army east across the Sindhu that had now been reduced to a few stagnant pools in the dry riverbed. As they made their way up north and began their ascent into the mountains, Brihaspati looked down at the vast plains of the Terai. All the way across the horizon the land of the seven rivers now resembled a dry, arid desert.

Agni, Vayu, Varuna and Soma were subdued during the journey, and this began to have its effect on the other men. In spite of their best efforts, Brihaspati and the Ashvanis had not been entirely successful in hiding the king's illness. Rumours were beginning to fly thick and fast about Indra's health and the circumstances that had led to his plight.

Most of the men viewed Ugra with suspicion: they were sure he was leading them into a trap. They wouldn't let him share their food or campfire during the cold nights. The Gond warrior, to his credit, did not let their behaviour get to him. He kept to himself and went about his business in a quiet, efficient manner. The more time Brihaspati spent with him, the more he liked Ugra.

The expedition made their way through inhospitable but

breathtakingly beautiful terrain. Days went by and at long last they stood amongst the Trikuta Mountains and looked down into paradise. Spread out below them was a valley of stunning beauty. It impressed even the Devas who had grown up in the scenic plateau of Gandhar. The floor of the valley was filled with meadows of wild flowers that created a splash of colours, interspersed with fresh water lakes fed from the constant snowmelt by numerous streams. This was the valley of Kash. That evening they made camp on the shores of one of the great lakes at the foot of the valley.

The next morning Indra emerged from his tent at sunrise, took a dip in the tranquil waters of the lake and calmly asked one of his squires to fetch him breakfast. Brihaspati and the Ashvanis were amazed at his recovery; there was no trace of the madness left in his eyes. He greeted them and asked them to join him for breakfast.

Brihaspati told Indra what had transpired since his near fatal encounter with the Vishkanya. Indra listened quietly as the priest narrated the prophecy of Ugra's tribe and the circumstances that had led them to this beautiful valley. Indra voice was calm, but there was no mistaking the menace in his tone.

'If that is our destiny, then let us prepare to embrace it. However, I do not share your trust of the dark one. Tell him to lead us to the place where the waters and clouds are trapped and then stay out of our way. If I get even the slightest hint of treachery, I will tear his body to pieces and feed them to his pagan god.'

He then called to Soma and asked him to mix up some of his brew. Brihaspati smiled. He was glad to see that Indra had fully recovered. He took the king's leave and rushed off to find Ugra.

The priest found the Gond warrior on the shore of the lake,

sitting cross-legged, hands joined in prayer. In front of him, fashioned out of the wet mud, was an idol that looked suspiciously like a human phallus to Brihaspati. As an Aditya priest who worshipped the elements in their purest form, the idea of worshipping the male organ repulsed him. He waited for Ugra to finish before he allowed his curiosity to get the better of him.

'Why do you worship your god in so base a form?'

Ugra turned to him with a quizzical look on his face; he did not understand why the form of his deity was repulsive to his friend.

'The Supreme One led us out of the forest where we barely carved out an existence into the great plains of the Terai. He gave us seeds for crops and taught us how to farm the land. Our tribe grew and prospered. We worship him in this form to always remember him as the giver of life.'

The gods that Brihaspati was accustomed to were angry beings that had to be appeased with sacrifices so they wouldn't unleash their fury on his people. He had never heard of a god that took the hand of his people, taught them how to live and led them to prosperity. This god did not seem to want anything in return for his service. He instilled unwavering faith in his devotees even when they were going through their worst times. As he looked at Ugra's little mud idol, his path ahead became very clear to him. Before he discovered the answers to all the questions that ran through his head, he must first discover himself.

That evening Brihaspati informed Indra and his commanders that he would not be accompanying them any further on this journey. There were furious protests from Aryaman and some of the other Adityas at this announcement. Indra looked into the eyes of the Aditya priest and saw something there that took him back to his childhood. It was the same look Mitra had whenever he was about to set off on one of his mysterious trips. Brihaspati, like Mitra, had become a seeker of the Light.

Ugra had mixed feelings when he heard of Brihaspati's decision. The priest was his only friend in this expedition. He would miss him, yet he knew that each of them had to follow the path Fate had ordained for them. The dark warrior looked up into the night sky. Around them the peaks of the mighty Himalayas gleamed in the moonlight. This was the domain of the Parama Purusha, or Supreme One. Brihaspati, like many great men from around the world, had fallen under His spell. Now, no worldly duties or attachments would hold him back.

From the entrance of a cave high on the Trikuta Mountain, Brihaspati watched Indra and his army as they left the valley of Kash and made their way east. From that height the formidable army looked like a column of ants on the march. Brihaspati sighed to himself; all his worldly attachments seemed to be leaving with that departing force.

He had been taken aback to see that his decision had not surprised Indra one bit. It was almost as if the king had expected it. He regretted that he had been unable to explain the situation satisfactorily to Aryaman. Through the years, he had come to love the Aditya prince like one of his own brothers, and he was pained to see the sadness and confusion in the eyes of the young warrior. But he had no explanation to give him; Brihaspati barely understood why he was doing this himself. He just felt in his heart that it was the right thing to do.

Ugra was at the head of the column. A fair distance separated him and the rest of the men. The dark warrior stopped and looked up in his direction. In spite of the vast distance between them, Brihaspati could feel the strength of his gaze. Ugra raised his hand in farewell, and Brihaspati reciprocated the Gond warrior's gesture.

Ugra tore his gaze away from the mountain and concentrated on the trail ahead. They made their ascent out of the valley of Kash and set out in the direction of the rising sun. It had taken a lot of persuasion on his part to convince Indra to leave the horses behind. It was only the Ashvanis' decision to stay behind and care for the animals that had finally made Indra agree. The Devas' and the Adityas' distrust of the Gond warrior increased greatly after this decision. The hostilities were so open now that Ugra made sure he slept away from the main encampment when they stopped to rest at night.

Their journey took them through hills and dales of exceptional beauty. Although the rivers of the region all ran dry, there was plenty of water to be had from the many glacial lakes that dotted the landscape. But the terrain became increasingly difficult: they encountered sheer rock faces and treacherous glaciers that tested the limits of their strength and endurance.

They soon arrived, exhausted, on the shores of a beautiful lake in the shape of a crescent moon. Ugra announced that the final leg of their expedition would begin from there. He advised them to stock up on water as there was none to be had for the rest of the journey. The men refreshed themselves in the waters of the lake and made camp for a couple of days while Ugra went ahead to scout the uncharted terrain.

When the Gond warrior returned, he was immediately summoned to Indra's war council. Atreya was the first to address the assembly. He was frank and forthright with his views. He expressed the apprehensions of the majority of his men. He posed the question that was on everybody's mind, including Indra's. How did a warrior, who had never left the plains of the Terai, know his way through this terrain? What if they were being led into a trap?

Ugra looked around at the gathering of men. Of one thing he was certain: these northerners did not fear an honourable death in battle. What they feared was an inglorious end to their lives through altitude sickness or a fatal drop into the deep ravines and crevasses that dotted this landscape. They did not want to put their lives in the hands of someone they distrusted immensely.

Ugra addressed Indra as he spoke.

'My lord, the fears of your men are justified for no one truly knows for sure what awaits us at the end of this journey. Many years ago my tribe, just like the many others in this land, sent an army to these mountains to investigate the cause behind the death of our rivers. Only one man returned: he was terrified and half-crazed with fear and did not make any sense. But he had this map tattooed on his thigh.'

He parted his skirt and revealed the tattoo on his leg.

'This map is inscribed not only on my body but in my mind as well. Every prince of the royal house of the Gonds bore this mark and considered it his foremost duty to serve the liberator of these waters. I am the last of my kind. Once I am gone, this secret will die with me.'

Yadu laughed sarcastically.

'So we embark on this quest based on the testimony of one crazy man. What was it that caused him to go mad with fear?'

'He spoke of an army of monsters that descended on them from the clouds. They tore the men from limb to limb and devoured them alive.'

Ugra now had their undivided attention. He knew now that all he had to do was wound their warrior pride a little and they would fall in line with his plans.

'I understand your fears. It is possible that an enemy unlike any you have ever faced before awaits you. So do not worry, my lords, history will not think any less of you if you wish to turn back and abandon this perilous mission.'

'Silence, you impudent dog!' Indra roared as he got to his feet. 'I would rip that tongue out of your mouth if I did not need you to fulfil my destiny. We are Devas. We fear nothing. You saw what we did to the monsters you dispatched against us; the same fate awaits this enemy of yours. Now hold your insolent tongue and lead us to this place.'

Ugra hid his triumphant smile and bowed low to the king. He knew he would have no more trouble with these foreigners.

15

Days after they left the beautiful crescent lake, they encountered a frozen desert. Thanks to Ugra's warning, they had stocked up on their food and water and were now able to admire the stark beauty of the landscape ahead rather than be intimidated by it. They saw a few herds of mountain goats, but no sign of any human presence in the vast lands. They soon came upon another dry riverbed; the smoothened rocks and pebbles that littered the ground were the only signs left of the great river that had once flowed through there.

Ugra informed Indra that this dry river would lead them to their destination. They followed its course up into the great mountains. Ugra had wisely divided them into groups of twenty men who were then roped together. Thus, when they encountered snowdrifts and avalanches, casualties were minimised.

In spite of these precautions many fell to their death into the treacherous crevasses and ravines they encountered. At long last they came upon a green plateau hemmed in by magnificent snow-capped peaks. The lack of any shrubs and trees gave them a clear view all across it.

'The people that once lived here called this place the roof of the world,' Ugra told Indra when he was summoned by the Deva king.

'What happened to them?'

Indra's question was answered soon enough when they saw the grass ahead littered with human bones bleached white in the sun. Ugra stopped to examine them; they bore marks caused by razor-sharp teeth. There were no remains of the creatures that had done this. It had not been a battle. It looked more like a feeding frenzy. These men had been slaughtered and eaten, their bones picked clean.

As they continued their march through this graveyard of bones, the mood became sombre. The Devas now realised that whatever they were up against was clearly not human. As they moved on, the piles of bones only started to get bigger and there were quite a few nervous faces among the men now.

A thick gathering of clouds lay between the two great peaks ahead, in the otherwise clear evening sky. They decided to make camp for the night. There was an uneasy silence around the encampment as fires were lit and the men settled down for some well-deserved rest.

That night, Indra, Soma, Varuna, Vayu and Agni gathered around a fire. None of them slept, but spent the night drinking copious amounts of soma as they readied themselves for battle. Ugra watched them in the darkness; he hoped these warriors would be the answer to the troubles that ailed his land.

As day broke, the members of the last watch woke the rest of the men. Indra and his men watched spellbound as winged creatures emerged from the clouds. They floated high above them on leathery wings and their numbers seemed to blot out the rising sun as they started to swoop down on them. They were unlike anything the men had seen before. They looked like giant winged lizards. They had thick heavy-set hind legs on which they walked and their forelegs were smaller but covered with lean cords of muscle and talons at their business end. They also had formidable jaws filled with razor-sharp teeth.

The archers began to unleash volley after volley of arrows into them, but they merely bounced off the thick armour-like scales that covered their bodies. Indra was quick to spot that their wings were the only parts vulnerable to injury. Even as the first creatures began to swoop down on the men to carry them off, Indra screamed to his archers to aim for their wings.

The men responded to his call and directed their volleys into the creatures' wings, tearing them to shreds. The great beasts fell to the ground but picked themselves up and charged at the archers. Yadu and his Yavanas closed ranks around the unprotected bowmen and prepared to face the threat from the ground.

More and more creatures burst through the clouds and began to fill the sky. They learnt quickly from their first attack and this time swooped down upon the Devas with the sun behind them. With the sun's glare in their eyes, the archers were severely disadvantaged and unable to get a bead on their targets. Indra watched in dismay as they picked up his men and soared high in the air before they dropped them to their death.

Ugra worked his way through the throng of warriors and reached the king. The survivor of the last expedition here had been dismissed as crazy by Ugra's grandfather and lived on the largesse of the other members of the tribe. Ugra had taken food to him on several occasions and the old man had told him about these flying lizards. He had told him that one beast, their leader, controlled the creatures telepathically. Ugra had not repeated the story lest he be dismissed as insane. He had scarcely believed it himself until now.

'My lord, we must kill their leader, that is the only way to stop these creatures.'

'Lead me to him,' Indra screamed over the din of battle.

Varuna and the other Falcons formed a protective ring around their king as they hacked and cleaved their way through the creatures and made their way forward as they followed the Gond warrior.

Ugra thrust his spear into the neck of one of the beasts that accosted him; its armour was weak around that area. The spear bit deep into its flesh. Ugra twisted it viciously and wrenched it free, and the creature fell to the ground. Drenched in its warm blood, Ugra smashed its head with an axe that he carried in his left hand. He roared in triumph, and the Devas, Adityas and Yavanas now took his cue and began attacking the vulnerable necks and bellies of the creatures.

Now the battle was more or less evenly matched. Indra and his small band made their way towards the valley under the clouds. A high wall that had several ridges running horizontally across it blocked the gorge formed between the two mountains like a huge dam. Ugra called out to him frantically.

'The waters lie trapped beyond this wall. We must break it.'

The creatures had by now noticed Indra and his men and turned their attention on them. Varuna and the others were now hard-pressed by the attack as they put themselves between Indra and the beasts. Indra, Kadaag in hand, made his way towards the wall and struck it with a mighty blow. The wall twitched and then began to move along its horizontal ridges. Indra realised to his amazement that the wall was made up of the coils of a giant serpent. Then the head of the reptile appeared—it was bigger than an elephant. Indra ran to the mountain on his right and began to frantically scale it.

The soma that coursed through his body gave him tremendous

strength and agility as he leapt from rock to rock up the steep slope. In a few minutes he found himself at the top. The giant snake turned its head towards him. Indra held the black sword in a two-handed grip and leapt at it. He swung the blade with all his might and struck the creature on the side of its head. The snake did not even flinch and the black blade shattered like glass on impact. Indra fell back, staring at the hilt of his broken sword in disbelief.

As he got to his feet the serpent opened its mouth and bared its great fangs at him. They were more than the length of his body. Two drops of venom fell from their needle-sharp tips to the earth around him. It scorched the snow off the mountaintop, turning the grey rock below dark as coal.

Suddenly Indra felt a strange sensation in the pit of his stomach. It was unlike anything he had felt before. When the serpent struck, it was only his superb reflexes that saved the Deva king. Indra threw himself to the side, barely avoiding the lethal blow. The mountain shook from the impact of it and caused him to lose his footing and topple over the far side. He rolled down the steep incline away from his men and the battle.

On the plateau, the battle raged on. The men, oblivious to the fate of their king, continued to fight gamely on amidst the carnage being inflicted around them. Slowly the shadows began to lengthen on the roof of the world. As darkness fell, the creatures disengaged themselves from battle and melted into the landscape.

Exhausted, Varuna leant on his sword and looked around him. All his comrades, except for Indra, were accounted for. A little further away, Ugra stood, his left arm a bloody stump. One of the creatures had chewed it off at the elbow and eaten it. The dark warrior had bound the injured limb with his loincloth and continued to fight naked.

In spite of all his misgivings, Varuna could not but admire the man's bravery and fortitude. He asked Ugra if he had seen any sign of Indra, but the Gond shook his head dismally.

When Indra came to his senses, he was in a clearing surrounded by pine trees. He sat up and found himself staring at the hood of a king cobra. He screamed in terror. The snake crawled away to a little rock on which sat a man. His matted dreadlocks were piled high on top of his head; his ash-covered body, lean with sinewy muscle, looked like it had been carved out of black granite. He wore a loincloth of tiger skin and held a trident in his hand. The snake went to him and hissed.

The man smiled.

'Raksha's poison has scarred his mind. She has left him with an intense phobia of serpents.'

He stood up and went to Indra.

'You have finally known fear, oh brave warrior. Perhaps you are now ready to be a god.'

Indra was still shaking with fright and barely heard the man's words. The man took the Deva king by the shoulder in a firm grip and raised him to his feet. He then took Indra's face in his hands and drew it near. Indra felt an intense beam of heat emerge from the man's forehead and enter his. Then it was gone. The man gently rubbed Indra's temples and let go.

Indra felt all his fearfulness leave him. He looked at the man in front of him, confused. The man led him to the rock and made him sit beside him. His tone was comforting as he addressed Indra.

'Do not judge yourself too harshly. No man or god has ever faced Vrtra and lived to tell the tale.'

358 | RAJIV G MENON

'Who is this Vrtra? And how did a lowly being such as a serpent accumulate so much power as to trap the waters and the clouds?'

There was a hiss of annoyance from the king cobra at his words. The man playfully admonished the snake.

'Don't take it personally, Vasuki.'

He turned back and looked into Indra's eyes as he spoke.

'Vrtra is much more than just a serpent. He is the king of the Danavas, or Dragons, an ancient race of beings that ruled the earth before the time of man. Their greed for power was such that they slaughtered and devoured everything and almost ended all other forms of life on earth. It was then that the sky gods decided to punish them. They rained down fiery missiles that scorched the land, made the waters of the oceans rise and destroyed the Danavas. Only a small number survived and found shelter in the mighty Himalayas. Amongst them was their queen Danu. She was farsighted enough to realise that in order for her race to regain their former glory, physical strength alone would not be enough. She assumed the form of a beautiful woman and seduced a powerful being. Vrtra was born of this union. He inherited great wisdom and intellect from his father and the physical prowess of his mother's race. In his mountain stronghold Vrtra waited, steadily increasing the Danava numbers while he weakened the humans by taking away their most vital resource, water. If he is not stopped now, he and the Danavas will sweep down from the Himalayas and take over the earth once more.'

Indra listened in shocked silence as he realised the enormity of the task at hand.

'How can I slay such a being?'

'Do not worry, help is at hand.'

Indra heard footsteps behind him and turned to see the man

he knew as Travistr. He gave Indra a curt nod and bowed solemnly to the other man. His expression was grave.

'I am ready, Master.'

Indra looked at the two men in front of him. He did not understand what was happening.

'I know this man. Without his help I would never have gotten this far. How does he fit in with all this?'

The Master got to his feet and picked up his trident.

'Travistr is the cause of the problem that is Vrtra. You, Indra, are its solution. He has guided you before and he will guide you from here on. Farewell. May good fortune smile upon you.'

Indra looked at Travistr confusedly. Although the weapons master was doing a good job of concealing his emotions, Indra could sense that he was going through some kind of turmoil. Travistr turned to him and read the question in his eyes.

'I am Vrtra's father.'

Indra was stunned at this revelation. He turned to where the ash-covered man had stood a moment before, but he was gone.

'Come, we must hurry. Your forces will not last another day against the Danavas,' Travistr said as he led Indra down the mountainside. It was dark and the two men used the moonlight filtering through the pines to guide them. They soon came upon a clearing similar to the one they had just left. In the far corner of it, Indra saw a man sitting in a deep meditative trance. Travistr went to him, folded his hands in greeting and bowed low.

'Greetings, sage Dadichi.'

The seer opened his eyes and looked at the duo. His body had been ravaged by time and the severity of his penance. Indra wondered how such a man could be of service to them. Dadichi studied Indra carefully.

'Is this the one who will slay Vrtra?'

Travistr nodded gravely. It was clear he took no pleasure in this task. Dadichi looked at Indra with a smile that the Deva king could not quite fathom. He then shut his eyes and from his throat a deep chant began to resonate. Travistr took a few paces back and made a sign to Indra to do the same. Even as Indra complied, he saw Dadichi's soul leave his body in a blaze of blue light and speed away towards the heavens. As Indra looked on, stunned, Dadichi's earthly body burst into flames till all that was left of his mortal remains were his vertebra and a few bones.

With great reverence and care, Travistr gathered the remains of the sage and began fashioning a weapon from them. He worked tirelessly through the night, and as the first rays of the sun lit up the clearing, he stood up and handed Indra a weapon fashioned from the adamantine vertebrae of the sage Dadichi. It was unlike any the king had seen before. The weapon was pointed at both ends and shaped like a lightning bolt. Its double-edge, fashioned from the joints of the backbone, was jagged and razor sharp. It was smoothened along the centre to create a grip.

As the lord of the Devas held the weapon, he felt all his strength and resolve return to him. He held it up high, and a clap of thunder sounded from the skies. Travistr watched him solemnly.

'That, my lord, is the Vajra. It is a weapon befitting a god. This will be the source and symbol of your power. The nations of the world will tremble and your enemies will flee at its very sight.'

'Will it be enough to kill Vrtra?'

Travistr nodded solemnly and handed him a quiver full of arrows, the arrowheads of which had been fashioned from the bones of the sage.

'It is the only weapon that can stop Vrtra. These arrows will take care of his army. Now go, for time is of essence.'

Travistr turned and made his way down the hillside; his shoulders were slumped and his gait resembled that of an old man. Indra's heart went out to him who Fate had ordained to device the weapon to kill his only son.

The sun was well up in the sky by the time Indra made his way to the top of the hill to confront the great serpent. As he looked down at the plateau, he was dismayed to see that the dragons of Vrtra had decimated his army. Yadu and his Yavanas, who had been in the frontline of their assault, had been annihilated. The Yavana lord lay dead on the battleground, his body ripped to pieces by the monstrous beasts. The Devas and Adityas had fared only marginally better. A small band of survivors led by Varuna were bunched together, fighting for their lives against the furious Danava assault that continued unabated from the ground and sky.

An enraged Indra roared out his challenge to Vrtra and the great snake responded. Indra saw the giant head emerge out of the water and the lidless black eyes focused on him. In his head he heard the deep sonorous voice of the Danava king.

'You cheated death once—that will not happen a second time. The bones of you and your men will lie bleached on this plateau, your names forgotten by time.'

Indra raised the Vajra and held it aloft in his right hand. The clouds above them began to move and swirl about as they gathered together directly above him. Suddenly a gigantic clap of thunder resounded through the mountains. Below them, the battle stopped as Deva and Danava looked up to witness the epic duel. Vrtra looked up in alarm. Something was wrong: he had no control over the clouds anymore.

From amidst the thick mass of clouds, a bolt of lightning emerged and headed directly towards Indra. As the bolt approached, it forked into two and struck the two points of the Vajra. Indra screamed as he felt a surge of elemental energy course through his body. He bent his back and hurled the weapon at Vrtra.

The Vajra struck the gargantuan head of the serpent and split its skull into two. A cry of anguish went up among the Danavas as the great sinuous body of their king fell to the ground, lifeless. As the coils of the great snake loosened, the waters threatened to burst forth and sweep the Devas to destruction. Varuna used his power and held back the waters. He asked his men to form a tight line behind him. As he gently let go, the waters gushed down to the plains in seven great streams.

Indra used his new arrows to pick off the remaining dragons from the sky. As they crashed to the earth they were mercilessly hacked to pieces by the Devas and Adityas. It wasn't long before the last of the mighty Danavas fell to the ground, dead. The race that aspired to rule the world was now confined to be a minuscule part of its history.

Manu, the Lawgiver, stood on the mountaintop and watched the seven great rivers flow down into the parched plains of the Terai. The swift-flowing torrents of water gathered momentum as it came down the Himalayas and swept through the cities of the Harappan empire, including its capital. It destroyed everything in its wake till only a few mud brick walls and broken pottery remained as a mute testament to a once great civilisation. His dark eyes shone with feverish excitement as he turned to his three companions. Though he did not look very much older than the others, it was clear that he was the unquestionable leader.

'It is as it was foretold. The Danavas are now extinct, the waters are free and the cities of the dark ones have been destroyed. Our time has come, Vashishta. Go, bring those warriors back to our land with honour.'

One of his companions bowed low and went to do his bidding. The Lawgiver turned to the other two.

'Come! We must prepare for the arrival of these heroes and welcome them with warmth.'

One of them looked at his master incredulously.

'They are barbarians, my lord. They know little else other than the way of war. They might do to us exactly what they have done to the Danavas. I implore you, Master, please reconsider your decision and call back Vashishta.'

Manu turned to the other young man, the quiet one.

'What about you, Agastya? Do you share your friend's misgivings about these warriors?'

Agastya took his time to answer.

'It is too early for me to entertain any misgivings, my lord. I would prefer to trust your judgment in this case.'

Manu smiled as he addressed the first boy.

'Would you be willing to trust my judgment, Pulastya? Because I believe that these barbarians could be the answer to our problems.'

Pulastya bowed low in reverence and nodded his assent.

Manu was pleased as he led the two young men down the mountain. He was the fourteenth of his line, and if his illustrious predecessors were to be believed, the last. Like Kasyapa all those years ago, Manu's ancestor and namesake too had come to this land when a flood had destroyed Jambu, an island in the middle of the southern ocean. But unlike his northern predecessor, the first Manu had been better prepared when disaster struck his land. With him he had brought the future of his people. Hundred of the brightest and most beautiful young men and women had escaped with him on a ship. After sailing for many days they had found themselves on the estuary of a river he named Saraswati.

Manu named the land Bharata. Here he would establish the nation of the Aryas, or noble ones. But like Kasyapa, he had his task cut out for him. The land was filled with wild animals and fierce tribes who were not welcoming to strangers. Manu and his followers talked, fled and bartered their way through the hostile territory of the dark tribes. When he reached the great city of Harappa, he was given a grand welcome befitting his status as one of the most learned of men. He in turn gave the Harappans their script and the knowledge to work metal in exchange for the safe passage of his people to the mountains of the Himalayas, their present home.

There they had built a small settlement in one of the beautiful hidden valleys of Mount Meru and bided their time. When his body aged, Manu had used his powers gained from a lifetime of penance to reincarnate into another body of his own choosing. He had also attained the power to retain all that he had learned through his previous incarnations. So the present Manu shared the same soul and possessed all the knowledge from across seven generations of his predecessors.

Under his strict tutelage, the young men spent all their time in the pursuit of knowledge and academic excellence. He called them Brahmanas, the seekers of Brahman, the supreme consciousness. The women were encouraged to take up music and dance, along with perfecting skills like weaving, cooking and farming.

Like Kasyapa before him, Manu had been sent by his doomed people to re-establish their culture and way of life in a new, foreign land. In order to do that, he first had to find a way to subdue the hostile dark people who would never bend to him. For that he needed to breed a race of warriors such as the world had never seen. These warriors would be the cornerstone of a civilisation that would last till the end of time. It was for precisely this reason that he needed Indra and his Devas.

Indra stood on the hill, Vajra raised in triumph. The weapon had returned to his hand after beheading Vrtra. As the thick clouds swirled restlessly above him, Indra used the Vajra like a wand and directed the clouds south onto the parched plains of the Terai. The heavens opened up and the clouds burst, sending down a flood of rain. Thunder and lightning rent the sky. Indra's battle-weary soldiers looked to the heavens in apprehension. They had just about exhausted their last ounce of strength in combating the dragons; they hoped no fresh threat loomed there.

As he returned to the plateau, the torrents of water had slowed down to gentle streams. Indra's triumphant manner changed as he set foot on the plateau again. Amidst the fallen dragons lay scores of his warriors, limbs ripped from their bodies. The Yavanas had been slaughtered to the last man. Indra saw the mangled body of their commander, Yadu, as he lay across the back of a dead Danava. His arms were outspread and torn from his body. Yet they still gripped his spear and shield, signalling his defiance till the very end.

The Deva king saw the small band of victors huddled behind Varuna, Vayu and Agni. Atreya and Aryaman were tending to the wounded. He cast his eyes around for Soma, and to his relief found his friend and charioteer alive and well. He was mixing up another batch of his mysterious brew. Their grim faces told the story. Although the bards would record it as another one of Indra's glorious victories, every soldier still alive on that plateau knew they had not won. They had merely survived.

As night fell, the funeral pyres of the fallen warriors lit up the roof of the world. The exhausted soldiers, glad to be alive, slept soundly that night. Not so their king. Indra lay awake and mourned the loss of his once great army. He felt for the Vajra by his side. He could still feel the divine energy course through the weapon, but what use would it be to him without his troops. How would he replace such brave warriors? His ambition to conquer this great land all the way to the southern ocean would now only remain a dream.

He shut his eyes; the stench of the burning bodies enveloped his senses. He did not feel very godlike now; only like an extremely tired man. He prayed for sleep to come. Maybe sunrise would show him a way out of this predicament.

Vashishta came upon the dead Danavas as the first rays of the sun hit the plateau. He saw scores of bodies strewn like giant boulders amidst the flat grassland. His heart was filled with enormous relief. Few men knew how much the fate of humanity had depended on the outcome of this battle. Had the Danavas won, it would not have been long before Vrtra got his horde to sweep down from these mountains and take back the world from the race of men. He saw the mutilated bodies of Indra's soldiers and said a prayer for their departed souls. This would have been the fate of every human on the planet had Indra lost this battle.

The Deva king had already sensed the arrival of Vashishta; his aura had revealed him to be a great man of knowledge. Indra stood outside his tent as Vashishta approached. He was amazed to see how young the sage was, but he had no doubts of the man's great wisdom.

Vashishta beheld the great king. He could sense Indra's divine strength and great power, yet oddly his soul seemed to be in turmoil. While this was normal in humans, it was quite unbecoming in a god. However, Manu had great hopes from Indra, and Vashishta was not one to question his master's instincts. He bowed low as he addressed the king.

'Greetings, Lord Indra, wielder of thunder, master of the clouds and the rain. I am called Vashishta. I come to you with an invitation from my master Manu, the Lawgiver. He requests your presence at his Sabha. He has planned a yajna in honour of your great victory.'

Indra smiled; perhaps the young sage's master would have some answers for him.

'I accept your master's invitation, oh wise one. Lead us to him.'

As Manu stood before his Sabha of Brahmanas, his heart swelled with pride. He was sure that the collective wisdom present there was more than any other place in the world. The front row had seven seats and was set a little away from the rest. Six of these seats were occupied by the brightest men in the gathering. These young men, through severe penance and austerities, had gained the right to be called Rishis. They were Atri, Angiras, Agastya, Bharadwaja, Gautama and Pulastya. The seventh, Vashishta, was escorting Indra there.

He addressed the gathering with great joy in his voice.

'Rishis and Brahmanas, it gives me great pleasure to inform you that Vrtra has been slain. The age of the Danavas is over and mankind will not have to fear the dragon anymore.'

Manu was a great orator. He raised his staff high as the audience burst into cheers. He raised his other hand and the applause died down.

'It is time for us to breed the race of the Arya. Noble men who will go forth and conquer the world and fill it with the light of knowledge.'

The Rishis did not participate in the thunderous applause that followed the Lawgiver's words. They conferred amongst themselves before Gautama spoke.

'How do you propose to breed men for conquest from amongst us, Master? We are seekers of the Light. We can create men of knowledge, of wisdom, men who will teach the others your laws. But we cannot spring warriors from our loins.'

The audience was quiet; Gautama had made a fair point. Manu smiled, he had been expecting this question.

'On my invitation, Indra, king of the Devas and destroyer of Vrtra and his Danavas, makes his way to our land with his victorious army. No greater warriors exist on earth than these men. They will provide the solution to our problem.'

Atri and Angiras stood up indignantly.

'How can you treat our women like harlots and let them lie with these barbarians? They will defile the pure blood of our women.'

Manu tried to hide his irritation. It was he, after all, who had taught them not to accept any idea without a healthy debate.

'Why do you insult my intelligence? After all I have done to preserve the purity of our race, do you think I would do anything to defile it? These barbarians, as you call them, carry the bloodline of Kasyapa, the first Arya.'

A hush fell over the audience as they digested this piece of information. Atri and Angiras hurriedly sat down.

Pulastya now stood up to address the Lawgiver.

'Is that enough, my lord? Their history tells us that the blood of Kasyapa did nothing to tame their brutality. Brother slaughtered brother overcome by lust. What is to prevent them from unleashing the same savagery on us? They might rule us by force, make us abandon your laws and resort to their barbaric ways.'

Manu smiled affectionately at Pulastya.

'They will not have to use force. I will invite Indra to rule us.'

Voices of protest and dismay erupted from the gathering; the Rishis looked at their master in shock. Manu raised his hand and made a sign for silence, his audience was quick to oblige.

'I will invite the Devas to rule us not as men, but as gods. Gods, whose benevolence people will crave and whose wrath they will fear. We will be their priests, the conduit between them and the people. It is our laws that we will implement, but in their name.'

The protests died quickly and the audience was stunned into silence by the astuteness of their master. Manu addressed only the Rishis now, in a low voice.

'I need your assistance. We do not have much time and I do not want to keep Indra and his Devas in our land any longer than necessary.'

The Master walked through the deserted plateau surveying the aftermath of the battle. The smouldering funeral pyres of the Devas, Yavanas and Adityas cast a smoky pall of gloom over the battlefield. He grabbed a handful of ash and smeared it all over his body. He walked through scores of Danava dead till he came upon the fallen body of Vrtra. The Danava king lay in a pool of blood. The Master shut his eyes and prayed for the departed soul.

Vrtra, like many other accomplished beings of the time, had been his disciple. Travistr had hoped to alter his son's doomed destiny and had sent him to the Master as a child. The Danava had been a brilliant pupil till his hunger for power and his obsession to restore his race to their former glory corrupted his bright mind. He had turned away from his Master and transformed into this reptilian monster that now lay dead at his feet.

Some distance away lay the naked body of Ugra, the Gond. His belly had been ripped open by a Danava claw. Ugra had used the bloody stump of his left hand to hold his entrails in and continued to fight till he had finally collapsed from loss of blood and exhaustion. In spite of his agony, the warrior still clung to life; it was almost as if his soul did not want to leave his body.

The Devas had taken care of their dead and wounded, but none among them had deemed it fit to release the dark warrior from his agonising existence. Ugra bore them no malice; he had been privileged to fight shoulder to shoulder with such brave warriors. Unlike him they were not driven by any sense of duty or attachment towards this land; they had fought and died for their king and for glory.

Through his hazy vision, Ugra saw the figure of a man approach. Ugra's sight began to clear and he saw the man's face. His dark eyes shone as he smiled at him and Ugra felt all the pain and exhaustion in his ravaged body vanish. Although he had never seen him before, the dark warrior knew he was looking into the eyes of his god, the Parama Purusha. The

Master knelt beside him and cradled the dark warrior in his arms. Ugra smiled and tears ran down his cheeks as his soul finally left his body.

The Master picked up the dead warrior like one would a sleeping child and started to walk away. He stopped for a moment and looked down to where the blood of Ugra and Vrtra had formed a puddle at his feet. The Master allowed himself a sigh; the blood of two great warriors, the last of their respective kind, had merged to stain the earth red.

In a cave on the southern slopes of Mount Kailash, the Master worked tirelessly as he prepared Ugra for his final rest. He cleaned the body and removed the viscera. He then filled the cavity with a mixture of herbs and rock salt. Every care was taken to ensure that the funeral was befitting that of a Gond chief. He then placed the body in a squatting position with its head facing south. After a prayer, the Master sealed the entrance of the cave.

As he left the tomb of Ugra, the Master had a smile on his face. He looked out to the south and saw the Gond warrior's soul make its way across the plains of Terai where Ugra's forefathers had roamed, over the vast expanse of the dark forests of the Dandaka, past the Vaitarnya, the river of the dead, till it finally came to rest on a giant tree that stood alone on a knoll. This was the tree of souls. This was where it would lie in wait until the land was in need of another great warrior.

Manu watched as the six Rishis began preparations for the yajna. Each of them had gone separately into the forest and gathered wood that they energised with their mantras. The six then proceeded to arrange the wood in a pre-determined symmetrical order, all the while continuing to chant their mantras. Once the wood had been arranged in the fire pit, Manu lit the fire. The chanting continued as the Rishis took turns to pour ghee into the fire, causing it to burn brightly and emit a thick white smoke.

Meanwhile, Vashishta led the Devas into the valley that housed the settlement of Manu and his Brahmanas. They reached a stream and Vashishta was dismayed to see that Brahmana women had gathered on the other side to bathe. The Devas began to gawk at the beautiful women, their eyes filled with desire.

Indra saw a woman emerge out of the water. Her amber skin shone through wet white robes that left no part of her stunning body to the imagination. Her face was lovely, with perfect features framed by a thick mane of raven hair, and big dark eyes that were now firmly fixed on Indra. His throat went dry as he drank in her beauty; he tried to speak but could only manage a hoarse whisper to Vashishta.

'Who is she?'

The young Rishi made no attempt to hide his displeasure at the Deva king's behaviour.

'Look away, my lord. That is Ahalya; she is betrothed to the Rishi Gautama.'

Indra had no desire to antagonise Vashishta. He held Ahalya's gaze for a moment longer and then turned away. The Rishi pointed to a thick plume of white smoke in the clear blue sky.

'That is where we must go.'

Manu was pleased as he watched Vashishta arrive with Indra and his Devas. As always the Rishi's timing was perfect. The smoke from the yajna had created a halo in the sky above them. Manu scooped up some ghee and threw it into the flames as he began the final rites of the ritual. He began to chant the last of the mantras in a deep voice. The other six voices accompanied him. Every face was turned to the sky in rapt attention.

In the middle of the halo of smoke, the skies seemed to part, creating a portal into another dimension. A beam of light that threatened to dwarf the sun with its brilliance emerged from it. The beam started to make its way towards Vashishta and the group of Devas who stood still, hypnotised by the spectacle. The intonation of the mantras made the air around them vibrate like a drum.

Manu and his Brahmanas watched with bated breath. As the beam fell on the Devas and Vashishta, they were lifted up into the sky through the halo of smoke and then disappeared from view.

The watching men were astounded; they could not believe what they had just witnessed. A young boy who had assisted Manu with the ritual voiced the thought that was going through every member of the audience.

'Where did they go?'

Manu spoke without taking his eyes off the sky.

'They are in Swarga. It is from there that Indra will rule the world of men.'

The Rishis, who had never attempted a yajna of this magnitude before, were amazed with its results. They sang Manu's praises, admiring their Master's wisdom and resourcefulness. Only Pulastya still remained sceptical. He bowed to Manu and requested that he be permitted to leave the settlement to continue his tapas.

It was with mixed feelings that Manu gave the young Rishi permission. Pulastya had been his favourite pupil. Unlike some of his colleagues, he had shown no interest in marriage and children after becoming a Rishi. He was single-minded in his devotion to the pursuit of knowledge. But lately, it had come to the Master's notice that his pupil had been voicing some radical thoughts. Vashishta had informed him that Pulastya, during his penance, had come under the influence of a dark sorcerer who roamed these mountains. This being was worshipped as a god by some of the tribes of the Dandaka and some of his teachings were in direct conflict with the Laws of Manu.

The Lawgiver was sad to see him go, but he was in the process of building the greatest civilisation in the world. The Rishis and the Devas were an integral part of that plan, and he would tolerate no dissent from either.

He glanced up and saw that the sky was clear again; the portal that they had opened to Swarga had now shut. His thoughts went to Vashishta. The Rishi had an important part to play in his plans. He said a quick prayer for his success and dismissed the rest of the gathering.

As the Devas emerged from the bright tunnel of light through which they seemed to have journeyed, they looked at each other in awe. Their weapons had disappeared. Their bodies had healed completely, scars vanished and severed limbs regenerated. In their minds, they felt nothing but complete bliss.

Indra looked at the land around them. It was not at all unlike the valley they had just left behind. Yet he felt so completely different. He felt no hunger or thirst. Not even the yearning for soma, something that had been his constant companion ever since he had tasted the brew for the first time.

'What have they done to us?' He looked around at his men, reading their thoughts.

'Embrace the change in yourselves, for you'll are men no more. This is Swarga, the land of the gods. Your land now, oh Devas.'

It was Vashishta's voice they heard in their heads.

'You will find that it is not necessary to speak here. You can communicate with thought. Now come, let me escort you to your palace.'

The Devas set off behind Vashishta. As they moved forward, the Devas realised that their feet did not touch the ground— they seemed to glide through the air a few inches above it. They passed groups of people running across the grasslands of green and gold, indulging in playful banter and childhood games. They paid no attention to the passersby. Vashishta explained.

'These are the righteous souls who have completed their karmic obligations and attained moksha.'

They moved on and reached a city unlike any they had ever seen before. There were no high walls or gates for protection. Even the exquisitely built homes did not have any doors on them, only open entrances and windows. Beautiful music could be heard everywhere.

They passed all manner of strange creatures: the Yakshas, short, stocky beings who wore hooded robes that covered them from head to toe. They were the builders and craftsmen of Swarga. There were also Gandharvas, musicians and artistes who were half-men half-goat; and the Kinnaras, warriors who were half-men half-horse. They all acknowledged the Devas by raising their tools, harps and weapons in salute.

Vashishta continued with his narration.

'This is Amravathi, the most beautiful city in all the worlds, and these are demi-gods, the inhabitants of this land and now your loyal subjects. They are the only beings other than Rishis that can travel between earth and Swarga at will.'

As Indra studied them carefully, he noticed something.

'Their weapons—their swords have no edge to them, their arrows are blunt.'

'Their weapons are ceremonial, my king. There is no place here for emotions like anger, jealousy and hatred, hence no need for weapons or wars.'

Indra was stunned when he heard Vashishta's words.

'No wars! Then what are we doing here? We are warriors; the way of the sword is the only way we know. All these powers I and my companions acquired—how will they serve us here?'

Vashishta tried to pacify the king.

'You will have little use for them here, I'm afraid.'

Indra could not believe what he was hearing.

'My men are the greatest warriors to walk the face of this earth. Are you telling me that they must while away the rest of their lives in idle pursuits of pleasure?'

Vashishta looked towards Indra's companions. Enthralled by Amravathi's ethereal beauty, they were paying no attention to the conversation.

'No, my lord! In time your services as warriors will be called upon to aid the Arya kings in battle, but for now we need you and your Devas for a delicate and far more important task.'

The Rishi paused for a moment and chose his words carefully.

'You and your men will be called upon to lie with the brightest and most beautiful Brahmana women to breed the Arya nobility. You will be the progenitors of the Kshatriyas, the absolute warriors. It is with the help of these Kshatriyas that we will spread the Aryan civilisation across the far reaches of the earth.'

Indra voice was lowered to a gasp at the outrageousness of Manu's plans.

'Are you trying to tell me that Manu will decide when Indra and his Devas will walk on earth again?'

Vashishta tactfully evaded the question.

'Once you have tasted the pleasures of Swarga, it is unlikely any of you will ever want to visit earth again. Look, my lord, we have arrived at our destination, your palace.'

Indra and his companions found themselves in front of the most magnificent building they had ever seen. It was made of white marble with domes of glittering gold; its walls were inlaid with precious gemstones of various sizes and hues unlike any they had ever seen before. The temples and palaces of Susa and Harappa paled in comparison to this marvellous edifice.

At the entrance to the great palace of Amravathi, a gigantic white elephant greeted the Devas. It was twice the size of the biggest war elephant they had encountered in their battle against the Harappans. Its tusks were bigger than the length of a man. The creature got down on its front knees and raised its trunk high in the air in a gesture of submission. Vashishta made the introduction.

'This, my lord, is Airavat, the guardian of Amravathi, and your personal vehicle.'

The mammoth beast stepped aside and let them pass. As they made their way through the grand doors of the palace, Indra was glad to see a familiar face greet them.

'Travistr! It is good to see you again, old friend.'

Travistr bowed, his manner was stiff and a bit formal.

'I no longer use that name, my lord. I gave it up along with my earlier profession.'

Indra was not sure he understood. The man he knew as Travistr explained.

'The Vajra was the last weapon I ever made. I no longer manufacture any instruments of war. I am now called Vishwakarma. I am an architect and a builder and this palace is my gift to you. Now come, let me introduce you to your court.'

As Indra and his Devas followed Vishwakarma into the magnificent courtroom of the palace, Vashishta deliberately hung back and allowed the master builder to take the lead. Music began to echo through the hall as they entered. At the far end was a magnificent gold and jade throne. But before they could get there, they had to walk the gauntlet through a throng of dancing Apsaras.

Although the Devas had grown up on ballads about these celestial nymphs, they realised now that the words of the bards had failed to capture the true essence of their beauty. The Apsaras were now dancing suggestively around them. The magnificent contours of their bodies were draped in sheer silk, leaving very little to the imagination. With eyes that were filled with promises of forbidden pleasures, they took the Devas by the hand and led them into the dance. Vashishta watched these rough warriors abandon all reserve and prance about with the nymphs to the divine music.

As the song reached a crescendo, Indra watched the nymphs lead some of his men into little antechambers located on the sides of the great hall. Just then he heard a husky voice in his ear.

'Come, my lord, let me remove the weariness of travel from your body.'

He turned to look into the eyes of Urvashi, the queen of the Apsaras. She was draped in white silk, which drew attention to her marvellous body that was the colour of burnished gold. Her dark hair and soft brown eyes were fixed on him. Her full lips, coloured a bright red, were twisted in an enigmatic smile. She was impossibly beautiful, and for one brief moment Indra lost all reason and like a child allowed her to lead him into one of the antechambers.

When they were alone, she fell into his arms, her mouth

hungrily reaching for his. As Indra tasted her sweet lips, he felt light-headed. He wanted to lose himself in her arms forever. However, he used every ounce of self-control in his possession to push her away. Her eyes hardened and one of her perfect eyebrows went up in surprise. This was not something she was used to. Then she smiled and bowed slightly.

'I am at your service, my lord. I will be right here if you need me.'

Indra threw himself on the comfortable bed and closed his eyes, enjoying the few brief moments of solitude. His mind was racing as he processed all the information he had got from Vashishta. He could not believe how he had handed the reins of his destiny into the hands of Manu and his Rishis. He and the Devas were now in a prison, albeit a gilded one.

He racked his brains for a way out of this predicament, but there was none forthcoming. He had led his men into a honey trap from which there did not seem to be a way out. There is always a way, he told himself determinedly. Manu had weaved a masterful plan, but he had made one elementary error in his judgment of Indra. He had assumed the Deva king was a savage barbarian filled with lust, and hoped that the pleasures of this magic land would dull his senses and make him toe the line. The Lawgiver had insulted the Deva king's intelligence and thrown him a challenge.

There was only one way Indra knew how to respond to a challenge: to stand up and fight. If the Rishis had found a way to move in and out of Swarga undeterred, so would he. Manu was going to be in for a surprise. He heard the sound of soft footfalls as Urvashi entered with two other nymphs.

'Your presence is required in court, Your Majesty.'

She and her companions led Indra to a warm bath filled with rose petals. They washed his body and gently massaged his limbs. Then, decked in a robe of purple silk, his body adorned with jewels, they led him back into the hall to the throne. Standing by were Manu and six Rishis. Pulastya had stayed away.

As he walked to the throne, Indra noticed Manu's gaze on him. He realised that the Lawgiver was trying to read his mind. Indra used a technique that Mitra had taught him to empty his mind of all thought. It was something that Mitra had impressed upon him to master. Indra had never felt any use for it until now. He walked up to the throne and took his seat. Cheers went up in the hall.

Manu waited for the applause to subside before he approached. In his hands he bore a glittering golden crown studded with gems, befitting the king of the gods. As he scanned Indra's mind, he found himself hitting a blank wall. A furrow appeared on his brow. This level of mind control was an art that took even an adept like him several years to master. It was not something he'd expected from Indra. Was there more to this barbarian than met the eye? Manu dispensed the thought from his mind as he placed the crown on the Deva king's head. The Rishis took up the chant.

'Hail Indra! God of Thunder! Sovereign lord of Amravathi! Liberator of the clouds and waters! Bringer of rain! Slayer of Vrtra! King of all gods and men!'

The chant began to echo through the hall. Indra was calm as he watched the glee on the faces of his companions. It had been a long while since he had seen them this happy. Manu made a sign for the dancing and revelry to continue.

Indra did not participate in the festivities. He sat on his throne and watched his jailors, an inscrutable expression on his face, as Manu and his Rishis bowed low to him and walked out of the hall. He would wait, bide his time and gather his strength.

If the Lawgiver thought that he would be able to hold the Deva king in this gilded cage and use him like one of his breeding bulls, he was in for a surprise. Indra would not rest till he washed his bloodied weapons in the waters of the southern ocean and completed his conquest of the land. The world of men had not seen the last of the one they would know and fear as the Thundergod.

Epilogue

As the blizzard abated, the frozen Himalayan plateau had an eerie stillness to it. The storm had raged on for months and now as far as the eye could see, a thick blanket of snow covered the ground. In the middle of the plateau stood a mound of ice, breaking the monotony of the bleak, flat landscape. Although the storm had subsided, thick clouds still hung over the sky like a pall of gloom.

The wind began to pick up. It brushed the fresh powdery snow off the mound revealing the top of a block of ice in the shape of a pyramid. Within the confines of the icy block stood a man, his arms raised and hands joined in prayer. His face was tilted up to the heavens as he stood on one leg in the yogic tree pose.

It was the man once known as Mitra, unrecognisable, however, in his current state of existence. The rigours of his penance had caused his body to completely waste away. His silver hair and beard were matted and hung in thick clumps around what was once a serene, handsome visage. It now resembled a grotesque mask, like the face of a badly preserved mummy. The skin was grey and crinkled like thin parchment. It had split in several places revealing dried up tissue and bits of his skull. Only his eyes were alive. Deep within their sockets they blazed with a manic intensity as he stared up at a fixed point in space.

Suddenly his body started to shiver and twitch uncontrollably. The icy confines of his prison began to crack and slowly break off and fall to the snow. The man dropped his foot to the ground and brought his arms down as he tried to make sense of what was happening to him. Then he felt an intense heat, deep within his lower abdomen in the region where his inner thighs met. His body began to convulse violently and his eyes rolled back up into their sockets. He felt the heat now move upwards into the area between the base of his spine and his loins.

The man began to see visions of beautiful women, scantily garbed, their eyes filled with longing, enticing him with lewd gestures. He found himself transported into the middle of an orgy with hedonistic music and dancing. He felt the arousal in his loins and was ashamed at his own inability to control it. His body continued to shake and he felt himself ejaculate violently. Now the visions began to change, the beautiful faces started to turn demonic. They abused and taunted him, increasing his sense of shame and revulsion. He opened his mouth to scream but no sound came out. The visions disappeared and he now found himself looking down into a narrow, dark tunnel. He suddenly realised that he was looking into his own body from the head down to his abdomen along the spinal column. From the bottom of this tunnel he saw a fiery serpent begin to rise up till it reached the area around his navel. The brightness of its flames now forced him to look away into darkness.

He now felt an intense hunger and thirst. He stuck his tongue out, lapping up the air, craving to taste something. Strange sounds began to emanate from his mouth. He felt a sense of foreboding that turned to fear and slowly transformed into pure terror. He began to sob uncontrollably. A myriad negative emotions like jealousy, anger and hatred rushed through his mind. As the heat began to course upward through his chest and throat, the agitation in his physical body began to subside. He felt a deep connection with all other life forms. A great sense of love and compassion for the Universe engulfed him and he began to revel in it.

Then the force began to push itself up into his head. The man's eyeballs returned to their normal position and he found himself floating in an infinite white void. He felt nothing but a supreme sense of calm. As he opened his eyes, he saw an intense beam of light like a golden spear burst through the top of his head, pierce through the thick clouds and make its way into the heavens. As he looked down at his body he realised he was no longer flesh and blood, but a creature made up of pure light. As he looked up again, the clouds seemed to explode soundlessly, turning the sky into a vibrant gold that shone with the brightness of a million suns.

That was the last vision of Raja Mitra, the warrior sage and ruler of the Adityas, before he fell to the ground, lifeless. How long he lay there he did not know, then from somewhere within the dark recesses of his mind he heard the voice of his Master, clear and strong.

'You, Mitra, have been destroyed and resurrected. You are no longer a seeker of the Light but a part of the Light itself. Rise, Rishi Vishwamitra! Go forth and illuminate the world.'

Vishwamitra opened his eyes and found himself lying in the snow, curled in the foetal position. He picked himself up and made his way across the frozen landscape; naked as the day he was born. His body had returned to its prime physical condition and it cast a warm glow that could be seen for miles across the endless plateau.